THE MURMANSK VENTURE

THE AUTHOR WITH HIS CHIEF OF STAFF, COLONEL E. O. LEWIN.

[*Frontispiece*

THE
MURMANSK VENTURE

BY
MAJOR-GENERAL SIR C. MAYNARD

The Naval & Military Press Ltd

❖

Reproduced by kind permission of the Central Library,
Royal Military Academy, Sandhurst

Published by
The Naval & Military Press Ltd
Unit 10, Ridgewood Industrial Park,
Uckfield, East Sussex,
TN22 5QE England
Tel: +44 (0) 1825 749494
Fax: +44 (0) 1825 765701
www.naval-military-press.com
www.military-genealogy.com

© The Naval & Military Press Ltd 2010

The Naval & Military Press ...

...offer specialist books for the serious student of conflict. The range of titles stocked covers the whole spectrum of military history with titles on uniforms, battles, official histories, specialist works containing Medal Rolls and Casualties Lists, and numismatic titles for medal collectors and researchers.

The innovative approach they have to military bookselling and their commitment to publishing have made them Britain's leading independent military bookseller.

In reprinting in facsimile from the original, any imperfections are inevitably reproduced and the quality may fall short of modern type and cartographic standards.

PREFACE

Since my return from North Russia in the autumn of 1919, friends have urged me on many occasions to compile and publish a record of the doings of the Murmansk Force.

They argued that no account of its activities had been or appeared likely to be written, and that, of all our military undertakings, there was none regarding which greater misconception existed in the mind of the general public. Moreover, the campaign, even if of minor importance in its purely military aspect, was in many ways unique; seeing that it was carried out by one of the most motley of forces ever created for the purpose of military operations, and under climatic conditions never experienced previously by British troops. Further, those responsible for its conduct had found themselves enmeshed by a skein of political intrigue so complex and tangled that many of its threads remained yet unravelled. Could there be a doubt, therefore, that its history would prove of interest to the many thousands who, wondering at the time why we had gone to North Russia and what we had hoped to accomplish there, were left wondering still?

Whilst admitting the general truth of my friends' arguments, I have nevertheless been averse hitherto from undertaking the task they suggested: for there were reasons which, to my mind, rendered it inadvisable that any early account of the enterprise should be published.

There might, for instance, be a danger, however slight, of incriminating further in the eyes of Moscow those Russians still living who, having thrown in their lot with the Allies, had declined to accept the opportunity offered them of seeking an asylum outside their own country.

Moreover, feelings in England in connection with our attitude towards Russia ran exceedingly high for a considerable period after the termination of hostilities, and it appeared inopportune for a serving soldier to publish an account of the operations of a force the employment of which was still causing much bitter political controversy.

Nearly nine years, however, have now elapsed since our withdrawal from the Murman Area, and it cannot be doubted that the question of the safety or otherwise of those Russians who took part in our joint effort to reconstitute their country, and who remained to face the consequences, has been answered long ere this.

Political disputations as to our relations with Russia are still, it is true, of frequent occurrence. But these deal with the future rather than with the past; and our action in 1918–19, though not forgotten, is now employed but rarely on the political platform as a cudgel wherewith to belabour an opponent.

I feel justified therefore in concluding that such objections as existed in my mind originally may now be disregarded—and of this conclusion the present volume is the outcome. As will be evident, it lays no claim to anything in the nature of a detailed report : nor has any effort been made to draw strategic or tactical deductions, with a view to their consideration by the military student. My aim has been merely to tell a tale of a boldly conceived venture, wherein we, as a nation, played a part of which we have no cause to feel ashamed.

C. M. M.

CONTENTS

CHAPTER I
WHY WE INTERVENED IN RUSSIA 1

CHAPTER II
INCEPTION OF THE MURMANSK FORCE 10

CHAPTER III
EARLY IMPRESSIONS 22

CHAPTER IV
LENIN SHOWS HIS HAND 35

CHAPTER V
SOME BUSY WEEKS 54

CHAPTER VI
ADMINISTRATIVE TROUBLES 72

CHAPTER VII
DEFENCE SCHEME FOR MURMANSK PORT . . . 82

CHAPTER VIII
OPERATIONS IN KARELIA 88

CHAPTER IX
STILL AT WAR WITH GERMANY 100

CHAPTER X
A PERIOD OF TRANSITION 113

CONTENTS

CHAPTER XI
AFTER THE ARMISTICE 134

CHAPTER XII
PREPARING FOR WINTER OPERATIONS 152

CHAPTER XIII
SEGEJA 167

CHAPTER XIV
THE IDES OF MARCH 193

CHAPTER XV
WE REACH LAKE ONEGA 216

CHAPTER XVI
RELIEF FORCES FOR ARCHANGEL 236

CHAPTER XVII
FINLAND COMPLICATES OUR TASK 251

CHAPTER XVIII
KAPASELGA AND AFTER 267

CHAPTER XIX
LORD RAWLINSON ARRIVES 288

CHAPTER XX
WITHDRAWAL 301

APPENDIX
PRÉCIS OF AN ADDRESS TO BRITISH OFFICERS GIVEN AT MURMANSK ON MARCH 21ST, 1919 . . . 312

ILLUSTRATIONS

THE AUTHOR WITH HIS CHIEF OF STAFF	*Frontispiece*
	PAGE
KEM CATHEDRAL	48
GENERAL HEADQUARTERS AT MURMANSK	80
ALEXANDROVSK AND THE KOLA INLET	86
ADMIRAL GREEN WITH THE AUTHOR	132
SOME BRITISH AND FOREIGN OFFICERS	148
INFANTRY OF A MOBILE COLUMN TRAINING	162
A REINDEER SLEDGE CONVOY	170
DOG TEAMS EMPLOYED WITH MOBILE COLUMNS	174
CROSS-COUNTRY TRANSPORT	194
DEMONSTRATION PARADE AT MURMANSK	202
A TEMPORARY HINDRANCE TO OUR ADVANCE	230
INSPECTION OF THE R.A.F. AT MEDVYEJYA GORA	234
SABOTAGE	264
A CORNER OF LAKE ONEGA	268
SEAPLANE BASE AT MEDVYEJYA GORA	286

MAPS

SKETCH MAP OF NORTH RUSSIA . *At end of volume*

PAGE

ROUGH SKETCH ILLUSTRATING DEFENCES OF MURMANSK PORT 82

SKETCH MAP ILLUSTRATING FINAL OPERATIONS . 304

AUTHOR'S NOTE

I am indebted to Flying Officer J. Sewell for the loan of the photographs from which six of the above illustrations are reproduced. The photographs used for the remaining illustrations were given me at various times by officers of the Murmansk Force, and I am unable now to recollect the respective donors. I cannot, therefore, make individual acknowledgements, and must confine myself to expressing my thanks to all collectively.

C. M. M.

CHAPTER I

WHY WE INTERVENED IN RUSSIA

WHAT were the reasons for our intervention in Russia in the spring of 1918?

If this question were put to a hundred average Britishers picked at random from various walks of life, it would, in all probability, elicit from no single one of them a really intelligent and accurate reply. A few there might be whose answers would show a partial appreciation of our aims; but, of the remainder, some perhaps would assert that we had no valid reason at all, and that the whole undertaking was mad and motiveless; whilst others, constituting in all likelihood the majority, would hold that we had intervened solely for the purpose of overthrowing the Bolshevik régime.

Even should the above be regarded as an overstatement, it is beyond dispute that widespread ignorance exists with regard to the objects we had in view when first we decided to despatch troops to Russia; and until this is replaced by an understanding of the motives by which we were actuated, no clear idea can be formed either of the task originally entrusted to the Murmansk Force, or of its activities under the altered conditions with which it was afterwards confronted.

Our motives, however, cannot be grasped fully without a study of the military situation as it existed at the opening of 1918.

At this time both France and England had tapped their respective resources in man-power almost to their limits, and the armies of both nations were not only dispirited, but nearing a state of exhaustion. Italy was in even worse plight. For Caporetto had brought her nearly to her knees, and, pending her recovery, it was found necessary to lend her substantial aid, and thus weaken still further the strength of the Entente forces in France.

Germany, on the other hand, profiting by the disintegration of the Russian armies, was making a rapid transference of troops from east to west, and at the commencement of the year had withdrawn already twenty-three divisions from the Russian front.

The position of the Allies therefore was not reassuring; for the armed forces of America could not make their influence felt in France for many months to come, and before then Germany would be in a position to mass for offensive action on the Western front an ever-increasing proportion of her troops liberated from the Russian area.[1]

It was thus imperative to consider what steps could be taken to prevent, or reduce to a minimum, the flow of German divisions from Russia to the west. Unless this could be achieved it was certain that, within a very short period, our exhausted troops would be subjected to so fierce an onset that its issue must in any case be regarded with misgiving, and might even result in our overthrow before the practical support of American backing could be forthcoming.

The most effective method of preventing Germany from transferring troops to the Western front would be the launching of a vigorous offensive elsewhere. But, unfortunately, there was no hope of being able to undertake in any theatre an offensive on the scale demanded.

There was, however, one possible means of bringing about the desired end, namely, the building up in

[1] Between September 1917 and May 1918 no fewer than 75 enemy infantry divisions (54 of them German), together with 9 cavalry divisions, were withdrawn from Russia. The German infantry divisions, almost without exception, were destined for the Western front, and some 40 of them arrived thither in time to take an active part in the great offensive of March 1918.

Russia itself of a new Eastern front. Should this plan prove feasible, not only might it put a stop to the transfer from that front of further German forces, but it might also produce other results almost equally far-reaching.

Chief of these would be the denial to Germany of access to the vast material resources of Russia,[1] the exploitation of which would enable her to regard almost with equanimity our naval blockade, at that time commencing to make its pressure a very real factor in the struggle.

There was, too, another danger which the constitution of the new front might well hope to avert.

It was known that Germany was pressing northwards through Finland towards the ports of Murmansk and Petchenga, with a view to establishing new submarine bases.

Murmansk was ice-free throughout the year, was connected by rail with Petrograd, and possessed already many of the conveniences required for a submarine base.

Petchenga, though difficult of access on the land side, and partially ice-bound during the winter months, could nevertheless be utilized for submarines during a portion of the year. Both were so situated that submarines operating therefrom would find our North Sea mine-fields no bar to their activities in the Atlantic —and that just at a time when the transportation of American troops to France would be in its full tide.

Such were the advantages which it was calculated would accrue to us in the January of 1918 by a reconstruction of the Russian front.

But it is easier to make calculations of this nature than to take action upon them—especially so in the case of Allied Powers, each one of which has its own especial viewpoint and, with its eye to the future, is

[1] Including the masses of stores and supplies accumulated at Archangel, all of which had been despatched by us for Russia's use, when she was still our Ally.

maybe suspicious of ulterior motives on the part of others.

France made a small but abortive effort in the Ukraine, and our Admiralty prepared to despatch some 400 Royal Marines as a reinforcement for Rear-Admiral Kemp commanding the North Russian Station. But beyond these, and the encouragement lent to a Cossack movement by subsidizing its leader, no active steps had been taken when the hurricane of the Germany offensive burst on the Western front in the month of March.

By the grace of God and the dogged pluck of our troops the storm was weathered, but the situation remained for all that full of the gravest anxiety.

German divisions fresh from the Russian front were still arriving in the Western theatre; the Allied Armies had reached almost the limit of their endurance; whilst the number of American troops in France fit to take the field was as yet negligible.

It cannot be said therefore that the calculations made at the commencement of the year in respect of the value of establishing a new Russian front were in any way upset by our success in bringing to a standstill the great March onslaught.

There was still the danger of Germany risking all in yet another endeavour to crush us, before American troops should arrive in sufficient numbers to enable us to assume the offensive; and, apart from this, even the most confirmed of optimists could scarcely have entertained hope in the early spring of 1918 that the following autumn would see the collapse of the Central Powers.

For what was to prevent Germany from waging a long-protracted war of defence, even after our numerical superiority had been established by the advent in the field of America's armies? The Allies were as yet far from the Rhine, and it must be many months before the grim realities of the battlefield could be brought home to her people in all their force. Her submarines were still taking heavy toll of our merchant shipping, and could look for even more substantial results if bases were established on the North Russian sea-board. She need have no fear, either, of her national existence being imperilled by our blockade, were the resources of Russia at her disposal.

Thus, on our side, the arguments in favour of an endeavour to reconstruct an Eastern front were as conclusive in April as in January.

It remained therefore to obtain the agreement in principle of all the Allies, and then to take stock of the material on which we could draw.

In Russia itself there was a strong undercurrent of anti-German feeling. The educated classes, and especially the corps of officers, had been justly indignant when Russia failed in her obligations to the Allies by concluding an independent peace, and were smarting still under the stigma thus cast upon their country. They were unwilling, too, to submit tamely to the usurpation of power by the alien Lenin and his associates, whose policy was dictated so clearly by Berlin. To the peasants, ignorant, stolid, and easy-going as they have always been, the nature of their Government was indeed a matter of little moment, provided they were left undisturbed to seek a scanty livelihood on their homesteads; but in the hearts of many was rooted a deep hatred of Germany, whose ambitious projects had brought about those long months of indescribable agony when they were starved, were led to slaughter, and starved again. Certainly they had no wish for a German penetration of their homeland, and, war-weary though they were, thousands were prepared to play their part in preventing it by force.

It was thus clear that Russia could furnish very considerable numbers ready to oppose Germany's further advance eastward. Whether they would receive the countenance of Moscow was problematical; but Lenin's position at that time was none too secure, and it was open to doubt whether he could afford to permit Germany to overrun western Russia against the openly expressed wish of so large a section of the Russian people. Further than this, as the anti-German elements would receive the united backing of the Allies, his opposition to an endeavour to build up the new front would entail his Government breaking off diplomatic relations with all the Allied and Associated Powers. Would a persistence in his pro-German policy be worth the candle in face of an eventuality such as this?

In considering the resources available for the contemplated enterprise, it seemed therefore that, to a limited extent at least, reliance could be placed on the anti-German elements in Russia herself.

But these alone could not achieve the desired result, even if the acquiescence of Moscow were assured, and moral and financial support from the Allies were forthcoming.

Germany had already driven before her in rout the ponderous but ill-equipped armies of the Czar, and knew that she had little to fear from any new and hastily raised Russian force, unless its organization were taken in hand by one of the Entente Powers, and unless it were stiffened by a backing of Allied troops.

It was certainly possible for the Allies to assist in the work of organization; but, in view of the needs in France and elsewhere, the provision of sufficient fighting troops was a matter of extreme and almost insuperable difficulty. Both France and England proclaimed their willingness to take a share in shouldering this new burden; but their contingents must necessarily be small, as on them lay the responsibility for holding in check the German armies in France and Flanders. Italy might now be able to do more, and America could do much—were she so inclined. Also the opening of this new front might give an opportunity for the employment of the land forces of Japan, a vast reserve of Allied power hitherto untouched.

Allied backing in men and material could thus be

relied upon. It might be of less weight than could be considered safely as adequate for its purpose, but it was hoped it would prove sufficient to afford a reasonable prospect of success.

It must, however, be a matter of weeks and perhaps months before even such small Allied detachments as it was possible to spare could reach Russia, and there was a danger of the northern ports falling into Germany's hands before their arrival. For the preliminary protection of these ports, it was therefore essential to make the fullest use of any military forces then in Russia on which reliance could be placed. Foremost of these was a body of some 50,000 Czecho-Slovak troops which had been collected in the Ukraine and, under French influence, was being withdrawn from Russia by way of Vladivostock for service elsewhere, the Bolshevik Government having granted the necessary railway facilities. It was of excellent fighting material, and all ranks were imbued with the strongest pro-Ally sentiments.

With the tacit approval of Moscow it was decided to divert to Archangel and Murmansk all such as had not reached already too easterly a point in their journey. The number of these was estimated at 25,000, and it was hoped that they, together with a Serbian battalion which was working its way northwards from Odessa, the artillery of a small French Mission lent originally to Rumania, and our own naval force at Murmansk might serve to frustrate Germany's endeavour to reach the coast pending the arrival of Allied reinforcements.[1]

It cannot be contended that our scheme of intervention was devoid of elements of uncertainty; but such is ever the case in the great gamble of war.

---

[1] As a matter of history, no single man of the 25,000 Czecho-Slovaks arrived at the northern ports; for they were attacked by Bolshevik troops in the neighbourhood of Ekaterinburg, and all hope of their transport northward was at an end. The Serbians and French Mission succeeded, however, in reaching Murmansk.

The essential consideration was that it held out a not unreasonable prospect of re-establishing the Russian front against Germany, and thus of reducing enemy pressure on the main battlefield of France. It was a strategic measure demanded by the military situation, and was directed solely against the Central Powers. In no way could it be interpreted as an endeavour to interfere in Russia's internal affairs, except in so far as it was part of our programme to gather once again under the Allied standard those Russians whose express wish it was to oppose further German penetration into their country.

The question of why we intervened in Russia has received its answer. But, for the sake of additional clearness, the following recapitulation is given. It shows categorically the eventualities with which, in all probability, we should have had to reckon, and the advantages which we should have had to forgo had we remained quiescent and taken no steps towards intervention in Russia during those fateful summer months of 1918:

(*a*) Many more German divisions would have been withdrawn from Russia and employed against the Allies in France—possibly with decisive results.

(*b*) Germany, being free to draw on the immense resources of Russia and Siberia, would have been enabled to establish her national industries once again on a prosperous footing, and to supply the pressing needs of her civil population. The effect of our maritime blockade would thus be annulled.

(*c*) North Russian ports would have been converted into enemy naval bases, submarines operating from which would have circumvented our North Sea minefields, and found our Atlantic commerce open to their attack. This, too, when the safe transport to Europe of America's armies was of all-importance.

(*d*) The chance would be lost of employing to any useful purpose either the army of Japan or the equivalent of several divisions of Czecho-Slovak troops of high fighting value, and full of enthusiasm for our cause.

(*e*) The anti-German movement at that time beginning to gain a hold in Russia would, if unsupported by the Allies, be quite unlikely to achieve any tangible result.

Is it possible that any man endowed with honesty and intelligence, having given consideration to the above, can deny that our intervention was justified as a measure of sound strategy ?

Those who claim that no useful purpose was served by our action in Russia appear, either from ignorance or bias, incapable of regarding in focus the undertaking as a whole. Their astigmatic gaze is directed solely on its final phases, and even of these they see but a distorted image. Of its original aim to assist in the overthrow of an enemy with whom we were waging a life-and-death struggle they take no note, nor are they aware that this aim was fulfilled with a measure of success out of all proportion to the slender means employed.

CHAPTER II

INCEPTION OF THE MURMANSK FORCE

THE month of May 1918 found me in England invalided home from the Salonika front. I had reached a stage of comparative convalescence, and was awaiting anxiously the time when a medical board should pass me as fit once again for service in the field.

On Empire Day I chanced to be lunching at my club, where I ran across Colonel Richard Steel, an old friend then employed at the War Office.

Steel greeted me by informing me that I was the very man he wanted to meet, and asked me to accompany him to the War Office, as he had been authorized to lay before me a proposition for my employment which he believed would be after my own heart.

Of this I felt some doubt, since I knew that his work was in connexion with the eastern theatres of war, whilst my ambition was a divisional command in France. Naturally therefore I enquired what sort of a job he had in contemplation for me. But Steel declined to give me any details, saying that he could make no further reference to it till he got behind the closed doors of his own room. Having discovered that he really meant this, and was not aiming at a " leg-pull," there was nothing for it but to repair with him to the War Office and hear what he had to say. At any rate, it looked like a chance of work once more, and that was the main thing ; also, to all appearance, it was something out of the ordinary run, and this perhaps might prove a compensation for my non-employment in France. Thus, a few minutes later, I was seated with him in his office, waiting for him to

INCEPTION OF THE MURMANSK FORCE 11

throw additional light on his somewhat cryptic utterance at the club.

" Ever heard of a place called Murmansk ? " he asked.

I replied that I was far from certain of being able to put my finger upon it on the map, but that I had a hazy idea it was some forsaken spot in the Arctic, to which the Russians had run a railway a year or so back for the transport inland of the war stores we had been lending them.

" You're right, so far as you go," said he ; " but it's probable you'll make its closer acquaintance in a few weeks' time."

I had learnt, then, my intended destination, and the attractions it had to offer did not appear to me outstanding. But I had yet to discover how a trip to the polar regions was to furnish me with a job " after my own heart."

For over an hour Steel talked, with frequent references to a large-scale map fastened to his wall, and handicapped by constant interrogations on my part.

He commenced with a general review of the military situation ; led up to the decision of the Supreme War Council that every effort should be made to re-establish a Russian front ; and gave me finally an outline of the plans to be adopted in order to give effect to this decision.

Both the military situation and the factors influencing the Supreme War Council are set out in Chapter I. It is therefore needless to cover this ground again, and I pass direct to our contemplated action as explained to me on that afternoon of May 24th.

The main difficulty confronting the Allies was the provision of fighting troops. It was certain that no appreciable number could be withdrawn from France ; and, so far as we were concerned, the situation demanded that every man in England who was trained and fit and could be spared from home defence duties should be sent across the Channel. Italy had consented to provide a contingent; but America was less than lukewarm, and though it would be immeasurably easier for her to spare troops than for any other Western Power, it was unlikely that assistance from her would be forthcoming on anything approaching the scale we might have hoped for. Japan had agreed to co-operate in Siberia, but in view of the susceptibilities of America it was improbable she would take any great part, or would penetrate sufficiently far westward to exert a marked influence on the course of the undertaking. It was evident, therefore, that we must look to Russia to furnish the bulk of the fighting forces. Initial steps had been taken to lend encouragement to such Russian elements as were opposed to further German penetration, and promising movements had already been set on foot in various parts of the country, notably in Siberia and the Northern Caucasus.

The main sphere of British intervention was to be Northern Russia, and the immediate steps we proposed taking were as follows :

We were to despatch to North Russia :

(*a*) A strong military Mission of some 560 all ranks.

(*b*) A small expeditionary force.

The Mission was to consist mainly of officers and non-commissioned officers selected as instructors from combatant and administrative branches, and thus could not be regarded primarily as a fighting unit. It was to proceed to Archangel as soon as the White Sea was ice-free, in order to equip and train such Czecho-Slovaks as should find their way to that port (see p. 7), and also to take in hand the organization, equipment, and training of a local Russian contingent, which it was anticipated confidently would reach a strength of at least 30,000.

When ready to take the field, the whole force was to endeavour to join hands with the pro-Ally forces in Siberia, and then to assist in opening up a new front against Germany.

INCEPTION OF THE MURMANSK FORCE 13

The equipment required for the newly raised troops could be obtained at Archangel, where there were vast accumulations of warlike stores provided originally by us for the use of the Russian army.

Up to the present, no objection to the enterprise had been raised by the Soviet Government.

The expeditionary force was destined for Murmansk, where small British naval detachments had been landed already, on the invitation of Moscow, for the protection of the port. Its immediate task was to prevent the occupation of Murmansk and Petchenga by the Germans, or by the Finnish troops co-operating with them.

The strength of the German army in Finland was about 55,000, in addition to some 50,000 " White Finns," who were acting under the orders of General von der Goltz, the German commander.

Strong detachments from these forces were pushing northwards, and there could be but little doubt that the German aim was to seize one or both of the ports mentioned, with a view to securing a submarine base. Finnish troops had, in fact, attacked Petchenga already, but had been beaten off by a naval landing party. No attempt had been made so far on Murmansk, but the Petrograd—Murmansk railway had been raided at various points, and enemy concentrations were reported along the Finnish frontier.

A further task of the Murmansk force was to pin down the German army in Finland for as long a period as possible, and thus prevent reinforcements being sent from it to the Western front. Little success could be hoped for, however, in this respect, without the raising of local forces. It was therefore part of the duty of the commander at Murmansk to organize and train local troops to supplement the expeditionary force.

The whole of the operations in North Russia were to be under British control, Major-General F. C. Poole (who had arrived at Murmansk that very day) having been nominated as commander-in-chief.

The proposal was that I should command the

expeditionary force, and all Allied troops that might be collected eventually in the Murman Area.

The expeditionary force was to consist of a meagre 600 men, almost all of whom would be of a physical category so low as to render them unfit for duty in France; whilst 400 Royal Marines, a few Royal Engineers, a battalion of Serbian infantry, and some French artillery would come under my command on arrival.

In view of the inadequate means at our disposal, the enterprise must perforce be regarded as somewhat in the nature of a gamble, and it was realized that I might find myself unable to maintain my footing. The crisis in France, however, precluded all possibility of our despatching a stronger force.

Steel's narrative was concluded. He paused, and then added, " Well, old chap, I've given you the hang of the thing, and there's no need to go into further details now. Are you for it ? "

Now, there was a spirit of adventure about the whole enterprise that made a strong appeal to me. I was to be given what must seemingly amount to a practically independent command, and was to be entrusted with certain definite tasks. In everything else about the undertaking, including the possibility of accomplishing these tasks, there was an alluring uncertainty. The scheme as a whole, however, was undoubtedly sound, and the probabilities were that my diminutive force (unemployable as it was elsewhere) would achieve more for the common good than a force many times its strength thrown direct into the conflict in France. Thus I had little hesitation in giving my reply.

A difficulty, however, then arose. I was still on the list of the unfit, and my medical board was not due for several weeks. The first thing to be done therefore was to get the decision of a board that my period of inactivity need last no longer ; and it was arranged accordingly that I should be medically examined at once.

INCEPTION OF THE MURMANSK FORCE 15

But I was destined to receive a rude shock, for my board reached the unanimous conclusion that I was still unfit for general service. Protests proved vain ; and I was informed that I should be boarded again in a couple of months' time, when there was hope of my being permitted to return to duty.

Here was a blow demanding immediate countermeasures, and I hastened to the War Office to see what backing I could get to bring about a reversal of this untoward decision.

Unconstitutional action seemed called for, and was taken. A distinguished officer holding a high position informed the board (and heaven forgive him !) that the appointment contemplated for me, though it could not be divulged, was of a purely sedentary nature, and that it was of great importance that I should take it up forthwith.

This led to further parley, with the final result that the medical board washed its hands of me, and I was confirmed in my appointment.

During the ensuing weeks, beyond visiting Colchester to inspect the units of my small force,[1] there was little I could do except keep in touch with the situation in Russia, which appeared to me to become more nebulous as each day passed. This was perhaps to be expected ; for it did not suit the Soviet Government to be overcommunicative, and our accredited representatives, though still at their posts, and strongly suspicious of increased anti-Allied leanings amongst the higher officials, were not in a position to form any reliable opinion regarding the attitude likely to be adopted ultimately by Moscow.

Lenin and company were, in fact, sitting on the fence. They were not yet prepared for an open rupture with the Allies, though it was possible that this step might prove of benefit to them subsequently as Germany's vassals. For it was necessary first to rid the neighbour-

[1] 1 company 29th London Regiment, 253rd Machine-gun Company, 2 sections 584th Field Company R.E.

hood of Moscow of the 50,000 Czecho-Slovaks, imbued as these were with the strongest of anti-Bolshevik sentiments, and also to procure some semblance of order amongst the chaotic remnants of their military organizations. They would free themselves of the menace of the Czechs by acquiescing in the Allied request for their transport to Vladivostock and Archangel, and this was all to the good; whilst our war stores at Archangel, if only the time necessary for their removal could be secured, would go far towards re-equipping their freshly constituted units.

On the other side of the scale was the insistent pressure exercised by Germany, and all that continued resistance to this pressure might entail.

Thus, despite assurances already given, it seemed that the prospect of maintaining amicable relations with the Soviet Government was becoming daily more problematical. Weight was added to this view by information received shortly before I sailed to the effect that Bolshevik troops had attacked the Czechs, who were scheduled to move northwards, and that severe fighting had taken place.

This was serious news. Not only was it the surest indication yet afforded of the changing attitude of the Soviet authorities, but it banished the hope of the Czechs reaching the northern ports, and thus rendered impossible of achievement one of the main objects of the Archangel Mission.

In the meantime the personnel for the Mission was selected, and my own small staff nominated. The latter, comprising my A.D.C., a brigade major, and a staff-captain, was considered ample for the force expected to come under my command on arrival. In ordinary circumstances this should have proved the case; but events were to show that, even from the very outset, it was wholly inadequate to cope with the administrative difficulties, and the mass of political and military problems with which I was to find myself confronted.

INCEPTION OF THE MURMANSK FORCE 17

One incident occurred during this period of preparation which was not without its touch of humour.

Certain officials of the Treasury had been admitted necessarily into the secret of the enterprise, and I went to one of these to ascertain the extent of the financial assistance likely to be afforded me. I was going to a country with a currency of roubles of doubtful stability and, in the remote region I was to occupy, the supply of even these roubles would certainly be very limited, and its replenishment from the south might (as it eventually did) prove impracticable.

Probably I should have to make local purchases of timber and other building material, and it was evident I should have to rely on local labour. It seemed to me therefore that my position would be strengthened, and my chances of retaining the goodwill of the inhabitants improved, if I were furnished with even a modest sum in honest English currency. I put this before the Treasury official, but was told I could be provided with no cash. He placed before me, however, another alternative.

It appeared that there was stored at Vardo, in Norway, an immense number of barrels of salted herrings, purchased by us some time back, but not yet shipped from the port. His suggestion was that these would make an excellent substitute for cash. The Russians, he said, would certainly be short of food; so why should I not feed them with herrings, instead of giving them any money payment for services rendered?

He could give me no inkling as to how I was to get these tons of salted delicacies transported to Murmansk, nor any guarantee of their condition. Moreover, I had some doubt whether a long-continued diet of salted herring would appeal to the Russian workman, and greater doubts still whether he would regard it as a welcome substitute for a money wage. Besides this, I had a strong objection to adding the running of a glorified fish-shop to my other duties. I was unable therefore to regard the suggestion as a satisfactory alternative.

By dint of much insistence I obtained at length the promise of an insignificant sum, which could at least be regarded as better than nothing. But I was to find in a few months that a lack of ready money very nearly resulted in a breakdown of the whole undertaking, and certainly endangered needlessly many lives.

On the day of my first initiation into the secret of our contemplated action in North Russia, the importance had been impressed upon me of uttering no word that could give a clue to our intentions, and I was therefore prohibited from informing even my own family of our destination.

Both the Mission and the expeditionary force were designated by code names; and all that any member of either formation could tell his friends and relatives was that letters addressed to him care of the G.P.O. and giving the appropriate code name would be likely to reach him after an interval of unknown duration.

On June 18th the two contingents sailed from Newcastle on board the *City of Marseilles*. Her captain was under sealed orders and, with the exception of Brigadier-General Finlayson, who was in charge of the Mission, and of myself, it is unlikely that any man on board could have given more than a shrewd guess at the port for which we were bound, until we were clear of the Tyne and chunking our way northward through the cheerless waters of a grey North Sea.

Though our voyage could not perhaps be described as thrilling, it was not without its moments of excitement and even of anxiety.

Our course lay athwart that followed by German U-boats making for the Atlantic, and during the first few days there came to our ears frequently the sullen boom of an exploding depth charge, a sure indication that some enemy submarine was in the vicinity, and had not escaped the notice of our fast-moving craft based on Scapa Flow. On such occasions our two

INCEPTION OF THE MURMANSK FORCE

escorting destroyers would show redoubled vigilance, one or other, and sometimes both, dashing outwards and scouring the waste of waters, lurching and rolling as they plunged at full speed through the tumbling seas, half hidden in a smother of wave and spray.

The confidence inspired by the navy in the lay heart of the soldier is stupendous. In that submarine-infested area, the presence of our escort was for us an almost certain guarantee of safety. Without it, we should have felt as helpless and insecure as would some unwieldy convoy which, in an Indian frontier campaign, had been forced to halt at fall of night in a wild ravine, far from the entrenched camp that was its goal.

There was little we could do to help towards our own safeguarding; but officers with glasses were posted for look-out duties day and night in regular relief, and the guns of my machine-gun company were mounted and manned at various points of vantage. The experience I had gone through previously in the Mediterranean of being shelled by a submarine at a range of several miles did not, however, encourage me to place over-great reliance on the efficacy of a machine-gun defence.

On nearing the limit of the waters which enemy submarines might be expected to traverse, we were attacked by another and even more subtle foe, against whose onset neither escort nor machine gun could avail —namely, the germ of Spanish influenza in all its 1918 virulence. One after the other, officers and men were stricken; but most serious of all was the violence of the epidemic among the Indian stokers. Within twenty-four hours of its outbreak, the captain informed me that so many stokers were sick that his speed was reduced already to a little more than half the number of knots prescribed him—a disquieting statement, seeing that we were due to meet our escort into Murmansk at a given spot at a given hour. I suggested, therefore, that we should ask our attendant destroyers (then about to leave us) whether they could transfer to us some of their stokers. The request was made and complied with cheerfully, despite the fact that it must have entailed a sacrifice of sleep and rest for the reduced crews on their homeward run. Our gain, however, hardly proved commensurate with the sacrifice. For the destroyers burnt oil fuel, and thus the men so ungrudgingly provided could furnish little more than unskilled labour. Volunteers were therefore called for from amongst the troops, and with this combined assistance the engine-room staff contrived to accelerate our pace almost to the normal.

Further delay was, however, in store. On rounding the North Cape we ran into a thick belt of fog, and this continued for so long that there arose a considerable risk of failing to sight our new escort, for we were nearing our appointed rendezvous and were already overdue.

When the fog lifted at length, we saw in the distance two vessels of strange appearance, thickset and ungainly; and it was some time before we realized that they were armed trawlers sent out from Murmansk to act as our guides and escort for the closing stage of our journey.

Very different-looking craft were they from the slim and speedy destroyers with which we had parted company recently; but nevertheless the service which trawlers of this type rendered our navy during the course of the war can well fill with pride the heart of a seafaring nation.

As passenger-carrying vessels I am unable to belaud them. In the months to come I was destined to make numerous trawler trips both in the North and White Seas, often in weather of more than average inclemency; and the memory of the turbulent discomfort then experienced is with me still.

Thus shepherded we crawled slowly on; turned south into the Kola Inlet; and viewed for the first time that barren and inhospitable region, the denial of which to Germany might contribute so much to

INCEPTION OF THE MURMANSK FORCE

the safety of the crowded transports hastening from America's Atlantic ports to the shores of England and France.

It was early morning; and most of us thronged the deck gazing, some with feelings of anxiety and all with curiosity, on the desolate landscape.

Had it been night, it would have made but little difference as regards visibility; for during the past forty-eight hours there had been no apparent dividing line between day and night. At midnight the Arctic sun still showed well above the horizon, and shone with all the brightness requisite for a snapshot photograph.

From the open sea to Murmansk is a distance of some 30 miles. The estuary is narrow—so narrow, indeed, that rifle fire could have been brought to bear on us from either shore throughout nearly its entire length.

Both banks are steep and rugged, and for the most part fir-clad. Save at the small village of Alexandrovsk (where the cable from Peterhead is landed) there was no sign of habitation, till we rounded a bluff headland, and found ourselves with startling suddenness in full view of our destination.

CHAPTER III

EARLY IMPRESSIONS

AT first sight Murmansk belied my preconceived notions. I expected desolation, but was apparently entering a port well filled with shipping and having extensive quayside accommodation.

In mid-stream lay H.M.S. *Glory*, the flag-ship of Rear-Admiral Kemp; and near by was his yacht.

Beyond rose the funnels of two Russian men-of-war; whilst numerous smaller craft were anchored in the fairway or moored alongside the quay.

But I was soon to find that my initial conception was in reality correct.

Of the Russian ships, one [1] was firmly aground, leaking badly, and worthless as a fighting unit; and the other [2] could not have put to sea without an extensive overhaul and a largely increased complement.

The small craft, other than those flying the British flag, were for the most part deserted, and sadly in need of repairs; and the quays were not only in a state of dilapidation, but lacked cranes and nearly every facility looked for as a matter of course at any ordinary commercial port.

The town, which lay entirely on the eastern bank, was a mere collection of log-built houses, and boasted no single building of brick or stone. A few dwellings of fair size could be counted on the rising ground of its outskirts, but the majority bore the appearance of workmen's huts or store-sheds.

With its backing of fir slopes merging into the wilder

---

[1] The *Chesma*.
[2] The four-funnelled *Askold*.

and more rugged heights beyond, the place, as we first viewed it, could claim a certain picturesqueness. Any pleasing impression then formed was, however, obliterated at once by a closer contact with the sordidness of the town itself. Litter and rubbish were heaped on the foreshore and alongside the unkept tracks that served as roads. Piles of fir logs, some partially shaped for building, but for the most part yet unfashioned, lay scattered about in seemingly hopeless confusion, suggesting that the land must be peopled by a giant race whose national game was spilikins. Outside many of the huts was such a conglomeration of unsavoury refuse that one shrank from the very thought of ever being compelled to enter them.

Except for some small scrub near the fringe of firs there was no vegetation. Nor indeed could such be hoped for, since the whole Murman Area is devoid of soil in which even the homely radish could flourish. It is a region of tundra, akin to coarse peat; and for mile after mile, from Murmansk almost to the shores of Lake Onega, there is no sign of cultivation—nothing but tundra and the eternal forests of pine and fir.

Adding to the general look of squalidness was the appearance of the inhabitants themselves.

Prior to the war, Murmansk was non-existent, and Kola, a fishing-village six miles distant at the head of the inlet, was the only inhabited centre in the neighbourhood. When, however, the railway was pushed hurriedly up, workers of numerous nationalities were employed for its construction, and many of these remained at Murmansk after its so-called completion. Thus, in addition to Russians, the population included Poles, Koreans, Letts, Chinese, and other foreigners—a motley and unprepossessing crowd.

Much of the above, however, relates to knowledge gleaned at a later date, and I must return to June 23rd, and the *City of Marseilles* as she bumped gently against the timber quay and made fast her hawsers.

Our welcome was not enthusiastic. A few loafers were visible in the distance, but the quay itself was deserted save for a couple of Marine sentries, who took but a languid interest in our arrival. Leaning over the rails, one of my men addressed the nearest with a friendly " What cheer, mate ! How goes it ? " The Jolly looked up, and after allowing himself sufficient time to collect his thoughts replied, " There's cheer enough to make yer dream of ' 'ome, sweet 'ome,' and *we 'opes* as there ain't more than 'alf a million —— Boches just round the corner." With this lucid and not too encouraging summary of the situation we had to rest content, until I could get ashore and obtain a more authentic account from General Poole.

I found him on board the *Glory* with Admiral Kemp. The Admiral was pacing briskly to and fro, pulling his beard vigorously—characteristic actions, when his feelings were aroused, which have always clung to my memory of him.

Poole's broad face, as he held out a hand to me, wore a cheery grin, very symbolical of the man himself. For he was one of the most confirmed optimists it has ever been my fortune to meet, and his optimism served to inspire with his own confidence all who came in contact with him. This alone was an asset of immense value in the position in which he was placed. But, in addition to this optimistic temperament, he was endowed with many splendid qualities. By training a highly expert gunner, he had developed into a fine all-round soldier, energetic and pushful, undaunted by obstacles, and ever keeping the main issue in view. He had perhaps no great liking for a study of detail, and the trammels of red-tape were certainly more irksome to him than to most. But these traits would be little likely to militate against his success, provided his staff—as he had a right to expect—were competent to take questions of detail off his hands, and those at the War Office were human enough to recognize that an undertaking such as his might necessitate an occasional departure from the letter of the King's Regulations.

On introducing myself, I learnt that the topic of conversation was the condition of the White Sea. The Admiral had been investigating this, and had ascertained that, though the ice was commencing to break up, and H.M.S. *Attentive* had actually succeeded in passing through the western side of the entrance, Archangel itself was still ice-bound. There was thus no immediate prospect of the Mission reaching its destination. This was an unlooked-for contingency, as in normal years Archangel was open to shipping well before the end of June; and it was especially galling to Poole, in view of the increasing hostility towards us shown recently by the Soviet Government. Could the Mission start at once, there was a fair chance of its landing being unopposed; but it was known already that Lenin was yielding to German pressure, and the probability was that, besides endeavouring to eject the Allies from Murmansk, he would seek to prevent an extension of their activities to Archangel. Thus every day's delay in despatching the Mission meant additional time in which the Bolsheviks could make their preparations for opposing it.

The main thing I had learnt whilst listening to this conversation was that Moscow seemed certain to declare against us, and that we might expect to come to loggerheads with the Bolsheviks at any moment.

This of course had always been regarded as a possible eventuality; but now that it looked like becoming an accomplished fact, it brought home to me with a most unpleasant emphasis the magnitude of our task. For if, in addition to Germans and Finns, we were to be called upon to deal with the armed forces of Bolshevik Russia, we were likely to find our hands more than sufficiently occupied. I was anxious, therefore, to learn as soon as possible exactly how the land lay.

Poole accordingly brought his visit to an end, and,

taking me with him, gave me a brief summary of what had occurred since his arrival nearly a month previously.

On reaching Murmansk he found that the navy had landed a small force *on the invitation of Moscow* to assist in preventing the occupation of the port by German or Finnish troops. A detachment from this force had been sent to Kandalaksha, and Russian Red Guards were supposed to be holding the railway farther south.

H.M.S. *Cochrane* was at Petchenga, where she furnished a shore party which had lately driven off an attack by White Finns. At the end of May 400 Royal Marines had arrived, together with a few Royal Engineers for demolition purposes. Some of these had since been sent to Kem.

Early in June Moscow had despatched a special envoy, by name Natzaremus, to confer with him. Natzaremus (described by Poole as " quite a good old bird "), though armed with full powers to conclude an agreement with the Allies, had made as one of his stipulations an official recognition of the Soviet Government by the Allies. This being beyond Poole's powers, the negotiations had produced no result. Natzaremus had, however, given Poole to understand that his Government was determined to defend the northern ports, and was sending up to Murmansk for this purpose two Red Guard divisions as well as the Czechs.[1]

On June 8th he had been informed by members of the Murmansk Council that Lenin had instructed them by telegram to warn the Allies to quit Murmansk, as its occupation by them was in contravention of the

---

[1] Whether or not the Bolshevik Government had any real intention at this time of sending the Czechs northwards must remain a matter of conjecture. But certain it is that within a few hours of Natzaremus making the assertion, Poole was informed by Moscow that fighting was taking place between Czechs and Bolsheviks, and that there was no hope of the former being despatched to Murmansk.

Brest-Litovsk treaty. A little later Trotsky had wired ordering them to eject us by force.

In spite of these telegrams from Moscow, he had received no official intimation of the Soviet Government having broken off diplomatic relations with us, and thus there was officially no state of war between the Bolsheviks and ourselves. For all that, we might take it that the fewer Red Guards who got within striking distance of Murmansk, the better it would be from our point of view. It was bad enough having 500 Russian sailors in the harbour. They were a lawless set, and had recently murdered their Admiral.

We were still on friendly terms with the local Council, and it seemed probable that it would break away from Moscow and throw in its lot with the Allies.

At Archangel there was a strong anti-German party anxiously waiting for us to intervene; but the Bolsheviks were doing their utmost to counteract all pro-Ally tendencies.

As regards our real enemy, Germany, she was undoubtedly pushing troops towards the north; and latest information pointed to a movement of some 15,000 White Finns against the railway at Kandalaksha and Kem.

Poole added that he had endeavoured to enlist local Russians into what he called the " Slavo-British Legion," but had met so far with little success, beyond enrolling some fifty of the officer class. He had had better results with the Poles, of whom about a hundred had joined us, and were to be formed into a battery.

At Kandalaksha were collected 500 scurvy-stricken Red Finns, who had been driven out of their country by the Whites. Their tendencies were probably Bolshevik; but they would certainly be ready to oppose the White Finns, and perhaps the Germans. So he had enlisted them in a " Finn Legion," on an undertaking to serve between the neighbourhood of Kandalaksha and the Finnish frontier. They would be all but useless till they had recovered their health and received some military training. The present distribution of troops, he said, was roughly as follows:

Murmansk :
    150 Royal Marines.
    400 Serbians (nearly all sick).
    150 Russians and Poles (just enlisted).

Kandalaksha :
    French Artillery Group (ill-equipped and many sick).
    Serbian battalion (many unfit).
    Finn Legion (of little use at present).

Kem :
    250 Royal Marines.
    250 of the Serbian battalion.

Petchenga :
    150 landing party from H.M.S. *Cochrane*.

Poole concluded by saying he was likely to be very busy over the political side of the undertaking, and could not leave Murmansk for a time. He suggested therefore that I should make a tour down the line as soon as I had got my newly arrived force settled, and had met the French and Serbian military representatives then at Murmansk.

On returning to the *City of Marseilles*, I remember well jotting down, somewhat in the form of a credit and debit account, the various items of information I had gathered, and regarding it when completed with a certain grim amusement.

It showed that, after deducting the sick and totally untrained, there remained for the defence of Murmansk and Petchenga, and of 350 miles of vulnerable railway, a grand total of approximately 2,500 all ranks. This included my expeditionary force, the naval landing party at Petchenga, and also a possible naval landing party of 400 at Murmansk. This last, however, would only come under my orders when sent ashore,

EARLY IMPRESSIONS

and this would only be to meet some grave emergency threatening the safety of the town itself.

On the other side of the balance sheet appeared the following:

(*a*) In Finland there were over 50,000 Germans, and at least an equal number of White Finns. At a rough estimate 20,000 of the former and 30,000 of the latter might be employed against me. Finns were certainly close to Petchenga already, and 15,000 of them were apparently now on the move against the Murmansk railway.

(*b*) There was a prospect, amounting almost to a certainty, that the two Russian Red Guard divisions spoken of by Natzaremus would be added very shortly to the list of my opponents.

(*c*) Although the local Council might declare for us, there were certain to be strong anti-Ally elements in the town and along the railway—to say nothing of the 500 armed and truculent sailors of the Russian warships in harbour.

Assuredly the enterprise might be regarded with justice as " somewhat in the nature of a gamble."

The odds, however, it seemed to me, were not so overwhelmingly against us as a mere comparison of numbers seemed to indicate.

The problem of the defence of Petchenga I must set aside for the moment, as I could not hope to visit it until I had got a firmer grasp of the situation on the Murmansk side, and had learnt whether it was to be peace or war with Bolshevik Russia. I knew, however, that Petchenga was of secondary importance; that access to it on the land side was a matter of extreme difficulty; and that, in any case, we could not afford to reinforce it at present, except at an urgent call.

The most pressing need was the safeguarding of Murmansk, and this was by no means so hard a task as the enemy's preponderance in strength would seem to imply.

From Kem no single road suitable for military traffic ran northward, and the only serviceable tracks from the Finnish frontier were those debouching on the railway at Kem and Kandalaksha.

During the summer months the boggy tundra would preclude the movement across country of any but small bodies of troops, and thus an enemy advance in strength from the south or south-west must be confined either to the railway or to one or more of the several water-routes leading by lake and river to the Kola Inlet.

The possibility of this latter means of approach being utilized could not be ruled out entirely, but it offered many drawbacks. For there were few facilities on lake or river for the embarkation of a large force, and the rivers, running through a wild and inhospitable tract, were tortuous and rapid. Boats of special construction were needed for their navigation, and the provision of a sufficient number of these would in itself prove, in all likelihood, an insurmountable difficulty.

It could therefore be assumed with fair confidence that, until the winter frost came, any strong movement against Murmansk must be by way of the railway.

This simplified the problem greatly. Holding Murmansk meant holding the railway; and, within limits, the farther south we could hold it, the better for us, provided we could make sure of supplying our men, and of withdrawing them safely if attacked in overwhelming numbers.

Unfortunately this plan entailed splitting up to an alarming degree a force which, even if kept concentrated, would be hard put to it to repel a concerted attack; and thus it infringed one of the first rules of the game of war.

But it was this very fact of the odds being much against us, if we awaited attack in the vicinity of Murmansk, that necessitated the forward policy. For what we had to aim at was, not to prepare the stage for a decisive action in the neighbourhood of Murmansk, but to prevent the possibility of any such action materializing. In other words, our best chance of frustrating a massed attack by Germans and Finns lay in fighting a series of delaying actions, under conditions favourable to ourselves. These conditions would be supplied by the railway and the nature of the country.

The railway crossed innumerable streams and rivers, spanned by bridges up to nearly 200 yards in length—and all were built of wood. A few bundles of straw and dry branches, a liberal supply of paraffin, and a box of matches would suffice for the destruction of any one of them. And their reconstruction, even if unhampered by us, would entail in many cases weeks and perhaps months of labour. For the majority of the rivers were swift-flowing and deep, and many were spanned by no other bridge from source to mouth.

It did not need expert military knowledge to understand how, under such conditions, a small but resolute detachment could hold up the advance of a force many times its own strength, especially as the rivers themselves and the semi-impassable tundra served as useful protection against flanking movements.

Provided therefore we could set up an opposition to the enemy's advance sufficiently far south in the first instance, it should be many long months before he would be able to make any real threat against Murmansk itself.

Had we been operating in a country served with good roads from west to east, it would have been sheer folly to push weak forces hundreds of miles down the rickety railway. But, as already pointed out, there were no tracks connecting Finland with the railway until as far south as Kandalaksha, distant some 50 miles from the Finnish frontier and 150 from Murmansk. Given time, it would certainly be possible for von der Goltz to collect at Kandalaksha a considerable force, and thus the place was marked at once as one of our defensive posts. It was held already, and it looked consequently that, at the worst, we should have 150 miles along which to fight our delaying actions.

Could we, however, venture to push still farther south? The answer appeared to me to be in the affirmative, and that for one specific reason only, namely, that the command of the sea, that asset of inestimable worth, was ours.

From Kandalaksha to Soroka the railway followed approximately the western shore of the White Sea. Thus our left flank would be comparatively secure, and for four or perhaps five months to come our troops could be supplied by water, should the railway in rear of them be cut, and could also be withdrawn, were they in danger of being overwhelmed.

Kem possessed a good harbour, and ships of considerable draught could berth alongside the quay. Also, as in the case of Kandalaksha, the port was connected with Finland by a number of country roads, exceedingly bad, it was true, but possible for military use. There was also the waterway of the River Kem, by which nearly half of the 140 miles to the frontier could be traversed.

Kem was therefore another point of possible German concentration; and none other could be said to exist between it and Kandalaksha.

Thus it seemed that we might rest well contented with the choice of Kandalaksha and Kem as our two main defensive centres on the railway. With these posts held, and strengthened, as I hoped they would be shortly by the arrival of Allied contingents, we should have a reasonable chance of preventing Murmansk falling into German hands, so long as summer conditions prevailed.

All these calculations, with their cheering conclusion, would, however, be upset completely if the Bolsheviks contrived to concentrate a force of any size at or north of Kem, and then commenced hostilities against us. If they succeeded in collecting such a force at

Kem, it would be bad enough; if at Kandalaksha, it would be doubly serious; and if at Murmansk itself, it might well prove the death-blow to all our hopes.

This thought was certainly disquietening; but it did not seem as if any immediate action could be taken. I must, however, proceed down the line at the earliest possible date; make a tour of our defences; and perhaps gather news that would enable me to suggest some means of dealing with this overshadowing threat of Bolshevik hostility.

With this reflection I climbed into my bunk, and was soon asleep.

I was awakened almost at once by the sound of rifle shots close at hand, and it seemed as if Murmansk were not to be tardy in offering us some small excitement.

Though nearly midnight, the sun still shone, and as I reached the deck it was easy to see that the guard posted at the entrance to the quay was " standing to," and that beyond it was collected a crowd of several hundred men.

Another shot or two rang out, but at what target they were aimed it was impossible to say, as no bullet came near us, and the guard gave no sign of being under fire.

It was foolish to run needless risks, so machine guns were manned and reinforcements hurried to the guard. With the reinforcements went a Russian-speaking officer, and he hailed the crowd. After much palavering, during which we were freely cursed, it transpired that the disturbers of our peace were Russian sailors endeavouring to return to their ships. Their boats had apparently been removed—by us, they suspicioned, though this was not the case—and they were signalling to their comrades on board by firing rifle shots over them. They were all armed, but beyond anathematizing us with great vehemence, they made no attempt at violence.

The excitement after all had been of a mild order. But it served at least to indicate the necessity for disciplinary measures in the town, if it were not to become the playground of an armed and swashbuckling mob.

As we turned in once more, eight bells struck. The first day in the land of our venture had ended.

CHAPTER IV

LENIN SHOWS HIS HAND

ONE of my first considerations was necessarily the provision of accommodation for the troops accompanying me. No buildings were available for them in the town, neither could any site suitable for a camp be found in the neighbourhood of the harbour. Thus, on the departure of the *City of Marseilles*, I was compelled, as a temporary measure, to utilize railway-carriages, supplemented by a few tents pitched precariously on the wooden flooring of the quay.

For several months a carriage of the semi-saloon type served as my headquarter office. We could have made shift with this in fair comfort, had we been left to carry on our work undisturbed by visitors. But from the very outset we were swamped by a never-ceasing flow of Russian officials demanding interviews ; and, later on, this flow was augmented by consuls and other representatives of foreign Powers, and by refugees of all nationalities, who had been driven by Bolshevik hostility to quit their employment in central Russia. Unfortunately few were content to be interviewed by one of my staff, and nearly all demanded to see me personally. So long as these could be ushered in one at a time, my " office " answered its purpose well enough ; but the Russian minor officials, such for instance as those connected with the harbour works or railway, came, not singly, but in droves. Any attempt to split them up proved invariably a hopeless task. All would see me or none ; and however great may have been my longing for the latter alternative, the situation demanded that all chance of friction should be avoided. Thus each drove must be admitted. On these occasions the clamour in that small compartment would be almost and the atmosphere quite indescribable.

Towards the solution of the housing problem the local Council certainly rendered such assistance as was in its power. But even log huts cannot be built in a day, and it was impossible to turn inhabitants out of their homes—even in the doubtful event of our wishing to occupy them. The position, however, improved more rapidly than I anticipated. Finishing touches were put to several nearly completed houses, and my few engineers, with such assistance as they were able to obtain, accomplished wonders in jerry building. Thus it was not long before the troops at Murmansk were provided with accommodation that served passably well, at any rate for the summer season.

Of the Russian officials whom I met in these early days, and with whom, as members of the Council, Poole was conducting his negotiations, the more influential were General Zvegintzoff and Commander Vaselago.[1]

Zvegintzoff held the appointment of Commandant of the Red Guards in the Murman Area, and was therefore a man on whose attitude towards us much might depend. I had no opportunity of gauging his military capacity, but there could be no doubt that he possessed brains above the average; and, like most educated Russians, he was a first-rate linguist.

Vaselago was, I believe, an officer of the merchant service. Though seemingly wholehearted in his endeavours to assist us, he did not strike me as endowed with exceptional ability, nor was his manner impressive.

These two, leaders as they were of the local govern-

---

[1] They were joined, after Poole left, by M. Urieff, a man of the people, self-educated and unpolished. But he appealed to me far more than did any other member of the Council. For he was essentially honest and straightforward, and reliance could always be placed on his word. He gave of his best for his country's sake, and I should be glad to think that no evil had befallen him.

ment, found themselves in an unenviable position. For they were called upon to make a decision which was not only of supreme moment for their country, but which for themselves personally might be regarded literally as a matter of life or death. As thinking men, both were by conviction strongly anti-Bolshevik, and both were honestly desirous of thwarting further German aggression. But there were many thousands of influential Russians who, though they held identical views, would not have dared to give expression to them, much less uphold them by any act tantamount to an open defiance of their so-called Government. For then, as now, those who ruled at Moscow could hope to maintain their sway solely by a ruthless massacre of their opponents. Then, as now, clemency was unknown to them.

It was not therefore to be wondered at that our two friends hesitated long before taking any action that would incriminate them definitely. Our display of military strength at Murmansk was still farcical, and there was a risk that our position might at any time become untenable.

Prudence therefore urged them to keep in favour with Moscow—although assuring us privately of their goodwill—until they were convinced that we were prepared to face an open rupture with the Soviet Government, rather than give up our intended policy of denying Murmansk to Germany and of reconstructing the Eastern front.

For this prudence neither could be blamed; nor, so far as I could judge, was there anything in Vaselago's future actions to prove that he wavered in his adhesion to the Allies, once he had thrown in his lot with them. My acquaintance with him was, however, short, as he left Murmansk within a few months, and I saw little more of him.

Of Zvegintzoff's subsequent relations with us it is not easy to speak without risk of doing him an injustice. The very fact that he had been appointed by the Bolsheviks as Commandant of the Murman Area told against him in the eyes of the leading Russian loyalists, who declined throughout to give him their full confidence. It may be that they failed to make due allowance for the position in which he was placed ; for it is possible that his acceptance of the post was the only alternative to banishment or worse. But, whether their lack of trust in him was justified or not, it could not fail to have its influence upon myself, and I felt happier when the local Council was superseded in October by a Deputy-Governor, and Zvegintzoff no longer held a position such as to render it advisable that I should consult with him. He then retired to Soroka, and I heard but little of him till the following spring, when news reached me of a contemplated Bolshevik rising on a large scale. With this rising, rumour had it that Zvegintzoff was connected ; but it seems certain that the report was spread by the Bolsheviks themselves, who knew that he was out of favour, and hoped that the inclusion of his name as a participator might give a magnified impression of the scope of the proposed " coup." Though the Deputy-Governor did not, I think, imagine for a moment that Zvegintzoff was in any way implicated, he considered it best that he should be removed from the south. He sent him accordingly to reside at Petchenga, no greater hardship being imposed upon him than the obligation to remain in that secluded corner, where his presence could not influence the tide of events for good or ill.

When the Reds returned to Murmansk after the Allied evacuation, Zvegintzoff made good his escape from Russia. All his property was confiscated, and I understand that he is now in Paris in business with his brother, an officer who performed most distinguished service for his country during the South Russian campaign.

Poole's attitude towards Zvegintzoff and Vaselago caused us new arrivals considerable amusement. To him they were his pals Sviggens and Vessels, and as such he addressed them. Taking Vaselago by the arm, he would say, " Now, Vessels, when are you going to fix up that agreement with us ? " or to Zvegintzoff, " Hullo, Sviggens, what do those old Red Guards of yours intend doing ? " He treated them rather as a house-master might treat a couple of his prefects ; giving them to understand that they must realize their responsibilities, and act for the good of the house, yet determined none the less that no action taken by them should run contrary to his own preconcerted plans.

Poole's aim was to secure an official undertaking that they would place their resources at our disposal in furtherance of our common cause ; and his bluff and disarming bonhomie, added to his contagious optimism, most certainly paved the way to success. To ensure its attainment, all that was now needed was clear and definite proof that we had no intention of allowing our plans to be upset by any display of force on the part of the Bolshevik Government. And it so happened that this proof was to be forthcoming within a few days as the outcome of my first journey down the railway.

We had arrived at Murmansk on June 23rd, but owing to many minor difficulties, chief of which was the provision of a locomotive fit for the run, it was not until the 27th that I was able to start on my trip.

I was very near to having distinguished company with me. For Murmansk was already commencing to stir the imagination of the great ones of Whitehall, and Sir Eric Geddes, then First Lord of the Admiralty, had thought fit to pay it a hasty visit, camouflaged for some obscure reason as " General Campbell."

Hearing that I was proceeding to Kem, he expressed a wish to join my party, and was with difficulty deterred from doing so—chiefly, I believe, by the impossibility of guaranteeing an exact date for his return.

As events turned out, it was certainly fortunate that he did not come. If he had done so, delay would have been caused by the necessity for providing extra accommodation; and a delay of a single hour might, in the circumstances that arose, have altered the entire situation greatly to our detriment. Even had he expressed himself willing to take as it were pot-luck with us, and share for several days and nights the comfort afforded by a carriage that was brother to a third-class Chatham and Dover compartment of forty years back, his presence would undoubtedly have hampered me in dealing with the problem that was to confront me with such suddenness before the half of our journey was completed. A naval lieutenant with a handy revolver would have had his uses; but a First Lord of the Admiralty could only have been regarded as valuable cargo, the need of safeguarding which might possibly have induced me to take action other than I considered best for the safeguarding of the military situation.

Fortunately I was not faced with any such dilemma. Sir Eric remained on board his cruiser, and started on his return voyage at about the time I was endeavouring to convince a drunken Red Guard officer that two Lewis guns placed in position near the railway track would most assuredly open fire the moment the driver of the train conveying him and his 300 men northwards moved his starting lever.

Our party included Colonel Thornhill, Grove (my brigade major), Clarke (my A.D.C.), and myself. An infantry platoon with a couple of Lewis guns served as escort.

Thornhill was General Poole's chief intelligence officer, and his knowledge of the country and its language, his energy and pluck, proved of outstanding assistance to me during the somewhat critical days that were to follow.

The Murmansk-Petrograd railway calls for a few words of description, if only to rob the reader of any preconceived notion of it, if based solely on his acquaintance with the railway systems of western Europe.

It is of course single. It is also, for the most part, wretchedly ballasted. Its curves are many and prodigious, and, owing to the haste with which it was constructed, cuttings and embankments were scamped. This resulted in frequent inclines, some of them so steep as to be almost unnegotiable by many of the ill-repaired engines, even when drawing light loads. More than once I have travelled in a train which, having failed to surmount some incline, had to slide back again to the level, and wait to raise more steam before making a further attempt.

The number of bridges is almost countless, and all are of wooden piles. Many of those spanning the larger rivers are wonderful engineering feats; but they need constant care and attention, more especially when spring commences to oust winter, and huge masses of ice, swept down by a rushing torrent, buffet and hammer the supporting piers.

It is small wonder, then, that the rate of travel is slow. On the best stretches, at speeds higher than 30 miles an hour, the train rocks so alarmingly as to engender the certain belief that a catastrophe is inevitable. To cover 100 miles in 5 hours is considered satisfactory going; and even those who set the least store on physical comfort, and whose nerves are of the steadiest, soon lose any desire to better this.

The scenery is monotonous to the extreme. Twenty miles through pine forests—then a small clearing, with a siding and rough station buildings. Thirty more miles of forest—and then another similar clearing. And so it goes on.

The only relief is when your train runs slowly alongside, or creeps yet more slowly across, some clear, swift-running river, haunted almost to a certainty by salmon, or at least by many a fine trout, which you picture as rising with a decisive swirl to your red palmer. Then, for the instant, you forget the monotony of your surroundings. Your thoughts fly back to the times when field-boots were replaced by waders and, armed with rod instead of revolver, you spent glorious hours luring hard-fighting trout from some Scottish stream.

Once more, however, the never-ending forest closes round you. You cease to think of trout, and devote yourself to a calculation of how many million trees must have been felled to clear the way for the line, and how many men must have been employed on the work, if it was really completed within sixteen months. Personally I reached the sleepy conclusion that half Russia must have slaved at the job, and that each man, woman, and child must have felled at least one tree per minute.

In winter the outlook is still more dreary and depressing, for on all sides and always is snow-clad desolation; and even the rivers, now frozen to a whitened stillness, refuse to conjure up pleasant dreams of rising fish and screaming reel.

Our journey was slow, but uneventful, until we pulled up at Imandra, a fairly large wayside station some 50 miles north of Kandalaksha.

Here we were shunted on to a siding, though we had been guaranteed a clear run through, as no train of any importance had been notified as proceeding north.

After a delay of twenty minutes or so, enquiries were made of a railway official, who asserted that the engine driver had found it necessary to take in water and replenish his fuel supply, and that we should start again shortly. This statement proved wholly inaccurate, the driver informing us that he needed neither water nor fuel, and was only awaiting the clear-line signal.

By this time a rascally-looking and gesticulating crowd had gathered round the train, and though I knew no word of Russian, it was clear that our arrival was not productive of favourable comment.

It began to look like a deliberate " hold-up," and I therefore asked Thornhill to interview the station-master and insist on our immediate departure. In a few minutes he returned and gave me his report, which was to the effect that the station-master was " an abusive swine "; that he had refused flatly to allow our train to start; and that there was something very fishy about the whole affair.

This necessitated a little rapid thinking. However hostile to us the station-master might be, it looked pretty certain that he was acting on higher instructions. For, even if weapons were available for the loafing crowd around us,[1] he would hardly have dared to hold up on his own authority an armed party, though only forty strong, unless he was sure that we should soon be placed in the position of under-dog. My mind went back to Poole's talk of Natzaremus and his Red Guards, and the most likely solution I could think of was that orders had been issued from Petrograd to keep the line clear for the passage of Red Guards to Murmansk, and that the first batch must be somewhere close at hand.

Now, with the inside knowledge I possessed, I had no intention of allowing an influx of Red Guards into Murmansk, if I could possibly prevent it. Nor had I any wish to meet the first trainload of them at a spot where they would evidently have numerous adherents, and I should be many miles from support. It was certain therefore that my train would have to proceed.

If (supposing my surmise to be correct) the Bolshevik train had not left Kandalaksha, the station-master must telephone to that station and have it detained. If it had already left, he would have to explain the situation to one of the several intervening stations, and have it turned back or held up. We gathered from our driver that there were other sidings between us and Kandalaksha, but that these were seldom used. I determined therefore that unless the oncoming train (if any) had left the last of these, our train must start forthwith;

---

[1] Within a fortnight, several machine guns and a couple of hundred rifles had been unearthed and confiscated at this small centre (see p. 57).

for every mile southward that we covered would be an advantage to us.

This decision reached, it only remained to put it into force.

A revolver at the head of the still cursing stationmaster extracted the necessary permission for the train to start, and the despatch of notification to that effect to Kandalaksha; a stalwart officer, backed by an equally stalwart N.C.O. riding on the footplate, lent needed encouragement to the driver and fireman; and before long we were once more on the move.

As we drew into Kandalaksha, we were all agog to see whether our suspicions would prove justified. They were confirmed to the full. For almost alongside us stood a train packed with Russian soldiers, with engine attached and steam up.

So far we had got the better of the game; but the line northwards was now clear, and the Red Guard contingent might yet give us the slip, if their train made an immediate start. So my escort was tumbled hastily out, and proceeded at once to fall in on parade.

The parade-ground selected was that portion of the permanent way directly in front of the waiting train!

The engine whistle sounded, but my men remained impassive. A second whistle found them still on their chosen parade-ground carrying out an inspection of arms. Sounds of excitement then arose; orders were shouted; and several hundred heads appeared at the carriage windows.

Thornhill hurried in search of the officer in command, and, having found him, informed him politely that I should feel honoured to have a private word with him in my carriage. This invitation, according to Thornhill's report to me, was declined by Spiridornoff, the Russian commander, with a generous flow of expletives, concluding with the assertion that no cursed foreigner was going to prevent him carrying out his instructions.

Truth to tell, I was not devoid of a certain fellow-feeling with him. For in Russia there is a proverb to the effect that the worst Russian is better than the best foreigner; and here was I, most evidently out to obstruct his journey to Murmansk, whither no doubt he had been ordered to proceed with all haste.

I could not, however, allow sympathy to override military necessities. Unless I could get in touch with Poole at Murmansk—which was more than doubtful—and received instructions from him to the contrary, it was, to my mind, essential that the further progress northwards of these Red Guards should be prevented. If I could contrive this by amicable arrangement, so much the better; but contrived it must be, even though it entailed the employment of force.

I suggested to Thornhill that if Spiridornoff would not come to me, I should go to him. But Thornhill would have none of it. Apparently to the Russian mind such action would have been derogatory to my position. This being so, there was nothing for it but to fetch him, and Thornhill, seemingly delighted with his mission, was despatched with half a dozen of my escort to conduct him to me.

At the same time my two Lewis guns were got ready for action, and my handful of men discarded their parade formation for one more suited for possible eventualities. Orders were then despatched to the Serbian detachment and the French artillery, whose quarters were then at some distance from the station, to hold themselves in readiness, the former being instructed to send one company down to me at once.

After a short interval Spiridornoff, with a couple of his officers, appeared at my carriage door. They were ushered in by a smiling Thornhill.

That little scene is printed indelibly on my mind. On one side of the compartment sat Thornhill and myself; on the other Spiridornoff and his companions, all of whom had their revolvers handy on their belts. Spiridornoff indeed was not content with one, for I could see the butt of a second protruding from his pocket. There was little doubt as to the manner in which they had been beguiling the time of their enforced wait at Kandalaksha ; for all exhaled a strong odour of drink, and Spiridornoff evidently found it easier to sit than to stand.

It seemed up to me to begin the conversation, so, with Thornhill interpreting, I explained to Spiridornoff that, whilst I was reluctant to cause him inconvenience, it was incumbent on me to find out how we stood towards each other. Was it, I asked, his intention to co-operate with me against Germany ? If this were so, he could do no good at Murmansk, where my troops had already filled to overflowing all available accommodation, and our common object could be served far better by the Red Guards operating from Kem or Kandalaksha. If, on the other hand, his Government had ceased to be well disposed to us, and had decided to yield to German demands and expel us from the country, it must be perfectly obvious to him that I could not allow him to proceed farther north. Thus, in either eventuality, it was to the interest of the Allies that he should remain for the time being where he was, and this I intended he should do. It must not be supposed that this opening speech of the debate proceeded as smoothly as it reads. Interpositions and angry ejaculations were frequent ; but Thornhill stuck to his job, and contrived at length to make it clear to the Russians that their journey must not be resumed.

There is no need to describe in detail the heated discussion that ensued. Spiridornoff, despite his drunken truculence, was non-committal as regards his Government's intentions towards us. His only point was that the Russians had every right to send troops to Murmansk if they wished to, and that he refused to remain at Kandalaksha. He altered his views somewhat, however, when I told him that the moment his train started my machine guns would open fire, and that, even if it succeeded in getting out of the station, it would be blown to bits by my artillery.

Up to the present I had of course been playing a game that was three parts bluff. For Spiridornoff's men were fully armed; outnumbered my escort by eight to one; and had with them a dozen or more machine guns.

He found himself nevertheless in an awkward predicament. He knew as well as I did that I had reinforcements close at hand. If, then, at the outset, he had attempted to fight his way out, he might indeed have accounted for my small party. But his engine driver would certainly have been shot, and this, apart from the fact that it would have taken some little time to "account for" us to his satisfaction, would have caused sufficient delay to admit of my Serbians putting in an appearance. He would then have found himself in a sorry plight. It is probable too that his instructions did not legislate for any such situation as faced him. I imagine that his orders were simply to report to General Zvegintzoff, no thought of opposition being contemplated.

Had he arranged for his train to steam out directly mine left the line clear for him, I could have done nothing to stop him. He would then have escaped his present quandary, and have carried out his orders without let or hindrance. He made his error and paid for it.

My bluff therefore was favoured by the other man having an exceptionally hard hand to play. Be that as it may, it had secured for me a respite of twenty precious minutes—enough to satisfy me that Serbs and artillery would very shortly be ready, and that Spiridornoff and his men must now await my pleasure before resuming their journey.

So it seemed politic to be conciliatory, and I suggested that I should endeavour to get in touch with and ascertain the views of Zvegintzoff, as Commandant of the Red Guards in the area. To this Spiridornoff gave a grudging assent, so Thornhill and myself went in search of the telephone office. On the way I learnt that the Russians had let drop one important hint during the late discussion, namely, that other Red Guards were following up this leading detachment. If therefore we were to prevent these from leaving Kem, an early start was essential, and we must get through with our telephonic business as speedily as possible.

We tried first to communicate with Poole, but failed. We turned next to Zvegintzoff, and, after a wait that was far longer than I cared for, got him on the line, and laid the situation before him. But he would give no decision, and went no farther than saying that he would try to get an explanation from Petrograd. This perhaps was all that could be expected from a man in his position talking over the telephone; but it was of little value to me. I could do nothing but request him to acquaint Poole of my action, and to tell him that I was proceeding to Kem at once.

To the officer commanding at Kem we sent a message saying that we were starting south immediately.

It must be remembered that these were early days. I had no Corps of Signals, no telephones, no operators. We were therefore dependent entirely on the services of the railway staff, which, so far, had done little to show itself in our favour. The station-master, however, made no objection to the departure of our train, and even promised for us a clear run. This at least was reassuring.

So I informed Spiridornoff that General Zvegintzoff had decided to take no action towards expediting his journey to Murmansk until he had heard from Petrograd—a verbal twist that appeared to me justifiable; increased my escort by fifty Serbians; left the Red Guards under the supervision of the remainder of the detachment; and started for Kem and its unknown possibilities.

North of Petrozavodsk, Kem is by far the most populous town on the railway. It consists in reality of two distinct portions: for its port, Poppoff by name, is distant more than a mile from the town proper.

KEM CATHEDRAL.

(From a photograph by J. Sewell)

Both are busy centres and, gauged by the standard of northern Russia, full of life and movement. Immediately south of the station flows the River Kem, comparable in size with the Thames at Westminster, but with a far swifter current, and rocky, precipitous banks. The railway crosses it by an immense wooden bridge, 200 yards in length and very lofty.

During our eight-hour run we had passed no northward-bound train, so once again luck had been with us. If further Red Guard troops were on the move, they had not yet succeeded in joining their comrades farther north—and that was all to the good. It seemed likely, however, that some at least would have reached Kem, and that there was a good chance of a repetition of our Kandalaksha experiences.

This proved to be the case; for on reaching the station we found it thronged with Red Guards, two trainloads of whom had recently arrived.

We had at Kem a fairly strong detachment numbering over 500, with a naval 12-pounder, and an improvised armoured train; and to these were now added my reinforced escort of nearly 100. There was therefore no doubt regarding our power to detain the Red troops, and the officer in command of them was quick to realize this. He was no fire-eating Spiridornoff, nor did he appear to bear any especial ill-will towards us; and so it was arranged, almost amicably, that his men should be detained pending further developments. There were at a guess some 400 of them, and I caught a glimpse of at least one van packed with machine guns.

I stayed at Kem for some time; for it was to be one of my most important posts, and I wished to glean all the information possible regarding it and its surroundings.

Shortly before starting on my return journey, I learnt that further Red troops, together with an armoured train, were being despatched from Petrozavodsk. I therefore warned the officer commanding at Kem that it might be necessary for him to disarm the Red Guards then at Kem, before the arrival of other troop trains from the south, and that, in any case, he was not to allow any Bolshevik troops to proceed towards Murmansk without definite orders from either General Poole or myself.

I left with him the 50 Serbs whom I had brought from Kandalaksha, and instructions were issued to the railway authorities (and steps taken to see that these should be complied with) that all trains from Petrozavodsk were to be brought to a standstill on the far side of the river. With his 12-pounder gun and the narrow defile of the railway-bridge as the only river-crossing, it would be easy for him to ensure that no more of Natzaremus's men entered the town without his sanction.

We then entrained, and commenced to retrace our path northwards. For it seemed to me imperative that I should get into personal touch with Poole, as soon as circumstances permitted. Events had moved rapidly during the last few days, and I had been compelled to take somewhat drastic action entirely on my own initiative. That it would meet with Poole's approval I was fairly well convinced; but whilst he remained on the Murmansk side, the responsibility was his, and there was just the possibility that I might be putting a spoke in his diplomatic wheel. Also, it was more than likely that the local authorities at Murmansk would have received news such as to set at rest any lingering doubt as to Bolshevik intentions.

On reaching Kandalaksha, however, I was to receive that news myself. From Thornhill's agents we learnt as an undeniable fact that the Red Guards whom I had encountered already were but the advanced guard of a large Bolshevik force, which had been concentrated with the express object of attacking the Allies and driving them from Murmansk.

This was positive information which I could not afford to disregard. Moreover, I must act at once, if we were not to lose the advantage we had already gained.

The first thing was to get through to Kem, and issue instructions for the immediate disarming of the Red Guards already at that place ; for their despatch by train to any locality south of the town that their commander might select ; and for the prevention by force of any further Bolshevik movement north of the River Kem.

The next thing was to arrange for the disarming of Spiridornoff and his men. This little affair I entrusted to Colonel Marsh, one of three senior officers who had accompanied me from England for general employment, and was then in command of the Kandalaksha garrison. He carried it out in the most admirable manner, and it was not long before Spiridornoff and his braves were steaming southwards, weaponless, but well supplied with rations furnished by myself.[1]

This having been accomplished, I sent to Kem an additional reinforcement of two infantry platoons (half my British infantry strength !) and a machine-gun section, which had been hurried down from Murmansk on my orders. Captain Sheppard, who was in command of these, received instructions to stop at certain stations *en route* and disarm the Red Guard detachments which had been located there from some time previously, ostensibly with a view to safeguarding the railway.

The whole scheme worked out successfully. Without a single life having been lost, some 700 to 800 of the advanced troops of what was intended to be an attacking force had been turned back to their base minus machine guns, rifles, and ammunition ; and an ad-

[1] I heard once again of Spiridornoff the following February. According to a prisoner, he was severely wounded when leading a very dashing counter-attack against us after we had captured Segeja. I trust he recovered ; for though a drunken ruffian, he had at least the merit of pluck, and I could bear no grudge against him for having endeavoured to carry out his instructions.

ditional 300 to 400 who had been quartered on the railway, along my line of communication, had joined them.

But the situation facing us had now changed completely. Formerly, although we had good reason to believe that Moscow intended to drive us out of the northern ports, there had been no official break in our relations with the Soviet Government. Now there was rupture, open and unmistakable, whether conveyed to us officially or not—and in bringing this about, I had been instrumental.

Had I been justified?

To me there was no doubt whatever that I had pursued the only possible course consonant with fulfilling my task of keeping Germany out of Murmansk. For this would have been rendered almost impossible had I permitted Red Guard troops, assuredly hostile to us and acting on German instigation, to assemble there, or to occupy in strength either Kem or Kandalaksha. The clash with Bolshevik Russia—little as I desired it—was in any case bound to come. I had but anticipated it by a few days or even hours. But by so doing a grave peril had been averted. If Germany wanted Murmansk, she would have to fight for it herself, with no ally within its gates.

As I had already taken a step bound to break all semblance of friendly relationship between the Soviet and ourselves, it mattered little what further precautionary measures I should take, or what interpretation should be put upon them. This being so, I decided to lessen at once the chances of a Bolshevik rising within the limits of our front.

It was known that many rifles, and probably machine guns also, were in the possession of inhabitants (most of whom were old soldiers), or kept in concealment by minor Russian officials. I therefore ordered that Kem, Kandalaksha, and the intermediate villages should be searched for weapons, and that any found should be confiscated.

At Kem some slight opposition was offered, and fighting resulted, in which one or two Red officials lost their lives; but as a general rule the search parties carried out their work unimpeded.

The outcome far exceeded my expectations. Including the arms taken from the Red Guards, nearly 10,000 rifles, 60 machine guns, and an immense quantity of ammunition were collected.

The turning back of the Red Guards unarmed and the extension of our policy of disarmament to the civil population appeared to convince the Red commander (believed to be Poole's one-time friend Natzaremus) that we were very much in earnest in our intention to oppose his advance. His movement northwards was stopped, and his leading contingents withdrew to Soroka, burning many of the bridges between that place and Kem.

Lenin had shown his hand; but the first trick had gone to us. Moreover, by the destruction of the railway-bridges his underlings had played our game; since, for the moment, it suited me well to know that there was small likelihood of interference from the south.

On my return to Murmansk I found that the course of events had been productive of the results anticipated. The local authorities, headed by Zvegintzoff and Vaselago, had decided definitely and openly to sever relations with Moscow, and espouse the Allied cause.

CHAPTER V

SOME BUSY WEEKS

THE Murmansk Council having now cast aside all pretence of allegiance to Moscow, Poole was enabled to realize his first aim.

An agreement was reached, and signed on July 7th, wherein it was laid down that the Council would render us all assistance in its power to defend Murmansk against Germany, provided the Allies undertook to furnish the necessary funds, and make provision for the food-supply of the Murman Area. The inclusion of these two provisos was, unfortunately, essential; for we were now cut off completely from the remainder of Russia, with no possible hope of obtaining locally either food or money in any way commensurate with our needs. Essential as they unquestionably were, I was nevertheless to find them dangerous stumbling-blocks, cropping up with disconcerting frequency on a road already sufficiently beset with obstacles.

Whatever its unavoidable drawbacks, however, the agreement was at any rate a first step towards the reconstruction of the Russian front, and as such we welcomed it. Undoubtedly too it strengthened my hand; for the local authorities had now burnt their boats, and it was to their interest as much as mine that the aims of both Berlin and Moscow should be thwarted. Definite relations having thus been established with the local Russian officials, Poole was able, with less misgiving, to withdraw from Murmansk the Mission and other troops destined for Archangel, the early occupation of which was now his chief anxiety. But it was not till nearly mid-July that the ice had broken up sufficiently to admit of access to the port, and by then the Bolsheviks had pushed up reinforcements, and were making vigorous preparations for its defence. In these circumstances Poole judged that his available force was too weak to warrant the attempt, and decided to await the arrival of the first of the promised Allied contingents. This proved to be a French Colonial infantry battalion, which reached Murmansk on July 26th.

On the 30th he started, with a total landing-force of about 1,500, including the personnel of the Mission, the French battalion, the Poles—and alas! details "borrowed" from me, chief of which were 100 Royal Marines and a portion of my machine-gun company.

His naval backing comprised H.M.S. *Attentive*, H.M. aircraft-carrier *Nairana*, the French armoured cruiser *Amiral Aube*, and the trawler fleet.

The *Aube* was delayed through striking a submerged wreck, and did not reach the rendezvous; but on the morning of August 1st, *Nairana's* seaplanes and *Attentive's* guns succeeded in silencing the Bolshevik batteries which had opened fire from Modyugski, an island fort guarding the entrance to Archangel channel. The island was then cleared of the enemy, after which no further opposition was offered.

The final phase of the enterprise can be described in the words of Poole's despatch:

"During the night the Bolshevik Government decided to evacuate the town, after having ordered two icebreakers to be sunk in the fairway to block our passage up the channel. On August 2nd the revolution planned by our supporters broke out at 4 a.m. and was completely successful. The Bolshevik Government was overthrown. The new Government cordially invoked our aid, and declared itself pro-Ally, anti-German, and determined not to recognize the Brest-Litovsk treaty. After some delay caused by exploring a passage between the sunken icebreakers, we were fortunate enough to find that there was just sufficient room to allow a passage for the ships. We then made a triumphal procession up the channel to Archangel, being everywhere greeted with enormous enthusiasm."

Poole was now established at Archangel, and I must leave another to tell the subsequent doings of his force. I should like, however, at this point, to give an emphatic denial to a mischievous rumour that reached my ears at a later date. This was to the effect that there was jealousy, and even friction, between Archangel and Murmansk, with the resultant evil of unharmonious working. For this whispered calumny there was no foundation whatever. It is true that, on one or two occasions, a misconception on the part of Poole's staff regarding the conditions on our side resulted in the receipt by me of orders with which it was impossible to comply. But, in view of the difficulties of communication, such misconceptions were perhaps to be looked for, and they most certainly engendered no particle of ill-will. In any case the fault (if such there were) did not rest with Poole, who was a Chief under whom I served most gladly, and between whom and myself there was always a close understanding. When Ironside replaced him, and Murmansk was made independent of Archangel, relationships between the two sides continued to be of the best. Each did its utmost for the common cause, knowing well that success or failure on either side must have its repercussion on the other.

To ensure the greatest possible measure of co-operation, Ironside and myself exchanged visits whenever circumstances permitted ; and it seems almost superfluous to say that from beginning to end of the operations no single incident occurred to mar the harmony of our relations.

Having thus, I trust, scotched a fraudulent bogy, I turn once again to the happenings at Murmansk and along its railway.

I had returned to Murmansk, after the completion

of our first journey down the line, on July 3rd. On the 4th, after twenty-four whirlwind hours, I started once again for the south. I had discussed the situation with Poole and the Murmansk Council, and my policy was now clear. Bolshevik Russia was a recognized enemy, and I had a free hand to take such military measures as were possible to combat a Bolshevik-German-White Finn combination. This called for a more thorough examination of the conditions prevailing many hundreds of miles away than I had been able to make during my initial trip, crowded as that had been with sudden and disconcerting surprises.

I took with me Thornhill and a couple of my staff, but no escort—a convincing proof of our military poverty. Like the previous trip, it did not lack incident; and once again Imandra was the scene of our first excitement.

We were rounding a steep and exaggerated curve just north of the village, when we felt a sudden grinding grip of the brakes, applied as they could only be applied in an emergency. The train rocked and swayed perilously. But it kept the rails, and within some 50 yards came to a standstill with a violent jerk. We had pulled up just short of a huge boulder lying across the track. That it had fallen there by accident was quite inconceivable, and it was clear that a deliberate attempt had been made to derail us.

No damage was done; but, coupled with our previous experience, it seemed time to make a change in the régime at Imandra. Thus, on my arrival at Kandalaksha, troops were sent to the village to carry out a search for arms, and to relieve certain of the leading officials of their appointments. Half a dozen machine guns and 200 rifles were confiscated; and after the station-master (the disgruntled obstructionist of our first trip) and the local commissar had been handed over to the Russian authorities at Murmansk, little further trouble was experienced in that neighbourhood.

After a busy day at Kandalaksha, we embarked for Kem at 1 a.m. on the 6th on the trawler *Sarpedon*, my object being to make a closer study of both ports and of the intervening coast. Had my experience either of the White Sea or of trawlers been more extensive, I feel certain I should have discovered some plausible pretext for continuing our journey by land. But I was unversed in White Sea vagaries, and imagined in my ignorance that a trawler coast-cruise could not surpass in discomfort a bad channel crossing. I learnt my lesson; and though circumstances compelled me to make several further trawler voyages, these were undertaken solely because no alternative method of transport was possible, and assuredly not of my own free will.

At Kem we held our first recruiting meeting, and I was filled with admiration of Thornhill's eloquence. Nominally he was interpreting for me, but judging from his fiery gestures and the manner in which he contrived to play upon the feelings of his audience, I could not repress a suspicion that he added much excellent padding to my simple sentences. However, he knew the Russian, and I did not. And he was certainly successful in riveting the attention of his listeners from start to finish, without provoking any demonstration of hostility towards us.

The immediate response to a call for recruits was not great, nor was this to be expected. But the chance had been taken of explaining the attitude of the Allies to a great gathering at a large industrial centre, and we could only hope that it might lead subsequently to the inhabitants of Kem furnishing practical assistance to their compatriots who had set themselves in opposition to a form of government evidently feared and mistrusted already by the majority of all classes.

Directly after the meeting I received news that induced me to alter completely my intended programme.

As has been narrated already, the Bolshevik troops

who had been turned back south of Kem concentrated for the most part at Soroka. Here they had been joined by others on their way northwards from Petrozavodsk, and had commenced a series of outrages against all suspected of pro-Ally leanings. These, I now learnt, had reached such a pitch that H.M.S. *Attentive* had been despatched to the scene. A detachment of the Finn Legion had also been sent by sea by the O.C. Kandalaksha, who, being out of touch with me whilst on board the *Sarpedon*, had rightly acted on his own initiative.

I decided to push on to Soroka with my two staff officers, as rapidly as the damage done to the railway south of Kem permitted.

Several of the smaller bridges had been repaired sufficiently to admit of the passage of a light engine and coach, and we contrived to creep on to within a few miles of our destination. Here a river-bridge of 80-foot span had been burnt down to the water's level, and we were obliged to abandon the train. The three of us were ferried across the stream by a Russian woman of excellent heart, but of an ugliness so surprising that I am convinced I could identify her even now; and on the far side we were lucky enough to stumble upon a derelict trolly.

Though the manipulation of a decrepit and rust-eaten hand-trolley was not a form of exercise to which any one of us was addicted, we managed for all that to keep its creaking wheels on the move, and eventually made an unheralded and somewhat inglorious entry into the outskirts of Soroka.

This was on July 8th, and I knew that *Attentive* had arrived the previous day. So we gave the town a wide berth, and made direct for the harbour.

Here we were greeted by the welcome sight of our own bluejackets—some formed up on shore, some crowded in a large barge, and others manning a 12-pounder gun. Near at hand, in parade formation, stood some 50 strange-looking ruffians, armed as soldiers, and under the command of a Russian officer who called them to attention as I approached. It was some seconds before I realized that this was the detachment furnished by the Finn Legion.

After I had got the hang of the situation, I inspected them, and was agreeably surprised. I could not of course judge of their fighting quality; but this small body (drawn presumably from the fittest among the Legion) gave every appearance of physical well-being, and, despite their uncouthness, the men had a certain soldierly bearing that filled me with good hope for their future efficiency.

On meeting the naval officer in command of the landing-party I ascertained that the effect of *Attentive's* appearance had been magical. Soroka Bay being exceedingly shallow, she had been compelled to drop anchor several miles distant from the town; but the majority of the Red troops had not even waited for this. No sooner were her funnels visible above the horizon than they had commenced feverish preparations for entrainment; and before Captain Altham had been able to put his landing-parties ashore, they had set fire to a portion of the town and beaten a hasty retreat. During their withdrawal they had destroyed every railway-bridge on the 25-mile section south of Soroka. Some hundreds of the Red Guards had, however, remained behind. They were terrorizing the inhabitants, and doing their utmost to stir up opposition against us. These die-hards had for their centre a large timber-yard on the far side of the bay, and my naval friend was now endeavouring to persuade the Russian harbour-master to tow across to this yard the barge in which his men were ready packed, his own launches not being sufficiently powerful for the purpose. The harbour-master, on his part, was objecting strongly, affirming that there was not enough water to allow of the employment of a harbour tug.

As it was nearly high tide, this excuse could not be entertained. The harbour-master was most evidently suffering from "cold feet"—a malady to which, in the rough-and-tumble game we were playing, no encouragement could be lent. It was therefore made perfectly clear to him that one of his tugs must be made fast to the barge, and that its commander must obey the orders of the naval officer in charge.

Partly because the barge was already crowded, and partly because it seemed advisable to keep the skipper of the tug under close surveillance, my two staff officers and myself boarded the latter; and, within an hour of quitting our railway-trolley, the bluejackets and ourselves were making our way across the harbour with the timber-yard as our goal. As we drew near, we must have afforded an excellent target, but no opposition was offered to our landing, the possibility of bombardment by the naval 12-pounder probably acting as a strong deterrent.

It was only when the timber-yard and adjacent buildings were being searched that a desultory fire was opened. Once more the Bolsheviks favoured discretion, and such as had remained in that part of the town were quick to take initial steps towards joining their companions in the south. As railway-bridges had been destroyed, and few, if any, vehicles were available, we had the satisfaction of knowing they were faced with a 25-mile tramp.

Attentive's men then proceeded to comb out the locality for hidden arms. They did their job most successfully, making a haul of 700 rifles, some 50 cavalry swords, and much ammunition.

An hour or so later I was taken out to *Attentive* for a visit to Captain Altham. From our talk I was able to realize far more clearly than hitherto the immense moral effect of his recent activities along the western shore of the White Sea. They had furnished a sure indication to the Red Guard leaders that the command of the sea was ours, and that, even should they succeed in pressing on to Murmansk, their communications would be open wide to our attack, and their coastal towns at our mercy. On looking back, too, it seemed well within the bounds of possibility that their influence had caused the Red commander at Kem to raise so little demur at the measures I was forced to impose upon him.

I could not remain on board for long. But when I learnt later of Altham's splendid services on the Archangel front, it caused me little surprise. He was so evidently a man of action—sound, keen, and thorough.

Soroka having been cleared of the Reds, it became necessary to consider the question of its occupation. For it was one of our guiding principles throughout the operations never to attempt the eviction of Bolshevik troops from any populous centre unless we were prepared to occupy it ourselves.

For this there were obvious reasons. For one thing, a withdrawal would certainly have been regarded as a sign of weakness. For another, it would have left the inhabitants open to reprisals; since there were always some whom the Bolsheviks eyed with suspicion, and were only too ready to " put out of the way " should an occasion offer—and a charge, whether trumped up or otherwise, of having assisted the Allies afforded just the opportunity needed. In addition, recruitment for the local forces must always be kept in view; and it was only by rendering life secure in the larger towns, and making our influence felt there, that we could hope to induce Russians to enlist in any numbers.

A garrison therefore must be found for Soroka; and this was done by the despatch from Kem of half the detachment of the invaluable but long-suffering Serbian battalion (whose motto should certainly have been " Ubique " throughout the period of my operations), followed by the armoured train as soon as the railway had been repaired.

This early advance beyond the limits of our original front is of note, as being the first of a long series of forward pushes made almost entirely with a view to securing recruits for Russian units, and ending in our penetration as far south as Lijma, on the shores of Lake Onega, over 550 miles from our base at Murmansk.

An engine and carriage being forthcoming at Soroka station, our return journey to the destroyed river-bridge was made in orthodox fashion; but on nearing its site we could see no sign of the coach in which we had travelled down. A closer examination showed that it had been allowed to run down the incline, and was now reposing half-submerged in the river-bed. This little contretemps, unlike the incident near Imandra, could in all probability be attributed to mere carelessness. But it was none the less annoying, causing as it did considerable inconvenience to each of us individually, and much loss of valuable time.

There was still work to do at Kem and elsewhere, and it was not until July 14th that we brought our wanderings to an end at Murmansk. Here, as the result of my own experiences, and of reports received from Thornhill's agents, I made it my first concern to extend my policy of disarmament to the whole of the region north of Kandalaksha. It was carried out with little show of opposition and, as far as could be gathered, met with general approval amongst the inhabitants.

By the middle of July—that is to say, within a little over three weeks from the date of our arrival—we were thus established along the railway from Murmansk to Soroka, in fair security against any probable Bolshevik attack.

It was, however, with the Germans and the White Finns co-operating with them that we were mainly concerned. The clearance of organized Red troops from the railway was but a preliminary step, leaving us more free to deal with our chief enemy.

It is not easy to understand why General von der Goltz stayed his hand during these first few difficult weeks. Raiding parties from Finland had reached the railway a month back, but had been withdrawn with nothing accomplished. Had these been reinforced, and a real threat made to one or other of our posts, or even a hold secured on any unguarded portion of the line, our position would have been rendered far from happy. Certainly we should have been unable to deal piecemeal with the various Red Guard contingents; and our weak garrisons would consequently have been liable to a combined Red Guard and Finnish-cum-German attack.

Possibly von der Goltz relied on Bolshevik troops pulling his chestnuts out of the fire. Or it may have been that he experienced greater difficulty than he anticipated in preparing his White Finn auxiliaries to take the field. More likely than either of these, however, was the probability of our naval and military strength having been greatly exaggerated in the reports of his agents, for there is ever a tendency in such reports to an over-estimate of numbers. In the early autumn, for example, though my whole force had not then reached a total of 6,000, papers were found on a German agent instructing him to ascertain the number of divisions on the Murmansk side, together with the names of their respective commanders.

Whatever the considerations influencing him may have been, the action taken by von der Goltz was, from our point of view, highly satisfactory. Within a fortnight of our landing, all formed bodies of German and Finnish troops had been withdrawn to near the Finnish frontier.

We were thus afforded a most welcome breathing-space, of which every advantage must be taken.

After our occupation of Soroka, Poole had handed over to me entire control of all operations in the Murman Area, and had placed at my disposal the services of several officers who had belonged originally to the Archangel Mission. These officers were at once entrusted with the task of training and expanding local units already raised (such as the Slavo-British and Finn Legions), and of organizing a fresh unit—the Karelian Regiment.[1]

The development of these formations, their value in the earlier stages of our enterprise, and the grave anxiety they occasioned me subsequently, must be dealt with later. My chief concern for the moment was to enlist and give rudimentary training to sufficient numbers to ensure the establishment of an effective outpost system pushed out towards the frontier of Finland. This was accomplished within a surprisingly short period, the Finn Legion at Kandalaksha and the Karelian Regiment at Kem soon reaching a strength enabling them to watch all likely lines of advance and, later on, to take a chief part in repelling attacks by considerable bodies of White Finns under German leadership.

Thus, throughout the Murman Area, things had so far gone well with us—far better indeed than our most sanguine expectations could have led us to believe possible three short weeks previously.

For a time there could be no danger of a serious attack either from the south or west; while each day brought nearer the arrival of promised Allied reinforcements,[2] and enabled us to make further progress in raising and training our newly formed units. Moreover, the various officers appointed to command defensive posts had by now obtained a good grasp of the situation confronting them, and the foundations had been laid already of an administrative system which, though I could not regard it with satisfaction,

---

[1] Karelia is the name given to the tract of country lying roughly between the railway and Finland, from Kandalaksha on the north to Lake Onega on the south. Though coming originally from the interior of Russia, its people have developed a most independent spirit, regarding themselves almost as a nation apart, and showing subservience to Russia solely from force of circumstances. The Karelian Regiment was open for enlistment to Karelians only, and its strength rose eventually to over 4,000.

[2] The days, however, proved to be many, no reinforcements reaching me for nearly two months.

seemed the best of which my limited resources permitted.

I decided therefore to accept the opportunity now offered of making my contemplated trip to Petchenga, as Admiral Kemp was proceeding thither on a visit to H.M.S. *Cochrane*, and had invited me to accompany him on his yacht.

On this occasion, thanks to the Admiral's kind-hearted hospitality, my sea-voyage proved one of comfort and even luxury.

Petchenga is a tiny village close to the shore of an almost land-locked bay. With the exception of the village huts, the only habitation within many miles is a substantially built monastery at the extreme head of the harbour. At this time the Petchenga defences were entrusted entirely to H.M.S. *Cochrane*, which lay at anchor near the centre of the bay. She furnished a strong landing party, having for its headquarters the monastery, around which field works had been constructed. These had been held successfully against a recent attack by a White Finn raiding party.

The chief impression I formed of the place was that of extreme isolation. There were no roads leading to it from any direction—nothing but a few tortuous tracks, little better than footpaths, winding through the scattered scrub that clothed the hillsides as far as the eye could reach. The best of these ran to the Norwegian frontier a few miles to the west. The nearest railway centre in Finland I knew to be over 250 miles distant. In the bay itself there were no shipping facilities whatever—no wharves, no quay; nothing but the smallest of wooden jetties for the use of fishing-boats. And even this could not be utilized at low water. At such times the shore must be reached by wading through long stretches of deep and tenacious mud.

The whole appearance of the bay and its surroundings filled me with a sense of deep relief. For it seemed to me impossible to believe that Germany would consider it worth her while to make any sustained attempt to obtain and hold a footing on its desolate shores. How could her gain compensate for the effort required? To capture Petchenga, and hold it after capture, needed the employment of military strength far greater than that of a mere Finn raid. It would demand the equipment and despatch of an organized force, with guns, engineering material, and an immense quantity of supplies, since none of the last named could be obtained on the spot. What this would have entailed, with the nearest railhead 250 miles away, and no roads available for other than the lightest of wheel transport, was fairly easy to calculate; and one hour's examination of the locality convinced me that von der Goltz would not waste men and material in a real effort to establish himself at Petchenga.

Had the place held out any attractions as a submarine base, I might have been left in some doubt. But to my mind it was inconceivable that such a base could have been established at that wild spot without years of toil and concentrated labour, which must include the construction of 250 miles of railway. During the summer the bay was no doubt ideal in many ways as a harbour of refuge for U-boats. But, as such only, could it have had any outstanding strategic value, with no sea base within 1,700 miles?

In winter, its utilization by submarines was out of the question.

In these circumstances, would Germany be likely to fritter away her resources by an attempt to capture a place which afforded nothing more than a sheltered anchorage for her submarines during a few summer months of each year, quite apart from the fact that the summer of 1918 was already slipping away? Or would her submarines dare to take advantage of such shelter, were even the smallest of Allied garrisons in the vicinity?

To me it seemed certain that if Germany were really bent on acquiring a North Russian base, she should and would concentrate against Murmansk. With Murmansk in her possession, Petchenga, if she desired it, was hers for the asking. Consequently I, for my part, should be ill-advised to weaken unduly my Murmansk force in order to strengthen Petchenga.

I left Petchenga therefore, after that first visit, with any fear of its occupation by Germany almost set at rest. Finns, acting under German pressure, might possibly endeavour to capture it and, if only for the sake of our prestige, their attempt must be frustrated. But I doubted both the practicability of and the desire for any determined effort on their part, and was quite satisfied that the existing naval garrison, strengthened perhaps by a small reinforcement from Murmansk, and backed by *Cochrane's* guns, would suffice to cope with any attack likely to be made.

These views regarding the possible utilization of Petchenga as a submarine base are, I am well aware, totally at variance with those then held at the Admiralty. But I adhere to them unhesitatingly.

Towards the end of August, when there was every indication of a strong German movement against Murmansk, I informed the War Office that the occupation of Petchenga was of purely subsidiary importance, and that I recommended evacuating it and concentrating on the defence of Murmansk, as I was unable to spare troops for the protection of both. I was informed in reply that the Admiralty laid great stress on holding Petchenga and that, to enable me to defend both it and Murmansk, reinforcements on a considerable scale were to be sent me.

Again, in one of my official despatches, I spoke of Petchenga as being ice-bound during the winter. This despatch was returned to me with the remark that the Admiralty regarded Petchenga as ice-free, and asking me whether I could modify the statement. I felt unable to comply, as my contention was backed by the strongest of evidence. Local opinion was with me in maintaining that, as a general rule, nothing but an ice-breaker could force an entrance between January and March; whilst my own experience went to show that two feet of ice covered Petchenga Bay during the winter of 1918–19. More than this, I had been informed by an officer of H.M.S. *Cochrane* that the ship had damaged her bows when breaking through the ice during the previous spring. Whether this was so, I am of course unable to say; but the remark served at least to corroborate my view that Petchenga was totally unsuited for harbouring submarines during the winter months.

However divergent my views may have been from those entertained in Whitehall, I know that I returned to Murmansk feeling that the burden of one particular responsibility was very appreciably lightened.

It may be thought that in this and the previous chapter I have laid over-much stress on the hurried comings and goings of early times, and also that I have overloaded my account of them with my own personal experiences.

But the decisions and actions taken during these first few weeks had a permanent effect on the whole course of future operations; and had things gone otherwise than they did in this brief period, it is quite possible that our efforts to prevent a German occupation of Murmansk might have failed.

For the frequent references to my own doings I shall, I hope, be pardoned by those who can visualize the situation. Until Allied reinforcements should reach me, or a very considerable body of local troops be raised, trained, and equipped, I could not hope to commence military operations in the usually accepted meaning of the phrase. All I could do in the first instance was to make sure that my garrisons were so disposed as to afford the best hope of obstructing a German advance. This was a matter to be determined by myself, and called for a personal examination of each locality.

Again, the all-important decision as to whether Red Guards were to be allowed to concentrate at or near Murmansk was one that could not be delegated to any subordinate. It must be taken either by Poole himself, or by me as his representative on the spot; and, owing to an almost entire lack of reliable means of communication, it so fell out that I was forced to decide and act.

Thus the story of how we first came to loggerheads with the Bolsheviks, and how the vanguard of their army was expelled, was bound to be little more than the story of the hasty journeyings of myself and the few who accompanied me. Of these few, a word must be said, if only in token of my appreciation of their services.

Apart from Colonel Thornhill, who was lent to me temporarily, they comprised Captain J. Grove (brigade major), Major G. Steele (staff-captain), and Captain C. Clarke (A.D.C.). I feel sure that none of these will consider himself aggrieved when I say that no single one of them could be described at that time as an officer of wide experience, accustomed to handle big problems. But the keenness and efficiency with which they tackled their respective tasks, their stout-hearted loyalty and unfailing cheerfulness, were magnificent.

For long periods they lacked both rest and sleep; for there was no appreciable distinction between day and night, and it seemed ever to befall that we reached a certain destination or were confronted by some new and unexpected development at about the hour of midnight. Had darkness surrounded us, we might perhaps have felt justified in awaiting the break of dawn. But always it was broad daylight, and each hour of the twenty-four was as suitable for work as any other. Swift-moving events, too, demanded action equally swift. Thus delay seemed unthinkable, and sleep must be deferred—perhaps for a further dozen hours or more.

Yet my small staff never failed to be bright and cheery. One incident, absurdly trivial though it was, will never escape my memory.

We had had no sleep for over thirty hours, and had returned to our comfortless railway-compartment for a short rest, utterly worn out after an exceptionally strenuous and anxious time. Whilst entering the carriage, a projecting nail caught my tunic, ripping in it a nine-inch gash. The tunic was new, but I almost repented of my pardonable expletive when I heard my A.D.C., himself so dog-weary that he could scarcely stand, mutter with a whimsical smile, "There's the end of a perfect day."

CHAPTER VI

ADMINISTRATIVE TROUBLES

MY visit to Petchenga had completed the survey of the area occupied by my troops, and I was satisfied that the military dispositions were, in general, those best suited to the strength of my force.

But I had to keep in view two important considerations. Firstly, I must be prepared to accommodate not only the Allied reinforcements promised me, but also the ever-increasing numbers enlisting in local units.

Secondly, the arrival of winter would necessitate changed dispositions; for, from November onwards, the whole country would be passable for troops suitably equipped, and I could rely no longer on the railway being the main, if not the sole, line of enemy advance.

But both the augmentation of my force and the future alteration of dispositions meant building; and building entailed the employment of Russian workers, who would naturally expect a fair remuneration for their labours.

As a case in point, my plans in connexion with the local defence of Murmansk (see Chapter VII) included the construction of a fortified line in the neighbourhood of Kola, which lies at the head of the inlet, six miles from Murmansk. As there was not sufficient accommodation in the vicinity to house my contemplated garrison, I proposed to erect hutments for 1,000 men.

I was especially anxious that this piece of work should be commenced at once and completed as rapidly as possible; since even if the defences should still be incomplete, the huts would be required for the reinforcements I was expecting, suitable quarters in Murmansk itself being non-existent. So I approached the Russian official (Makedonski by name), who held a position corresponding more or less with that of a borough engineer. He was all for taking the job into his own hands, asserting that it would be the easiest thing in the world for him to find the necessary labour, as he had no doubt about the men coming forward, if it were understood that they were working for, and being paid by, their own authorities. I therefore acquiesced, stipulating only that my own engineers should furnish the supervising staff.

At the end of a week I learnt that, out of the 80 to 100 workers I required, only five had put in an appearance. On seeking out M. Makedonski I was told that the railway was claiming all available labour, but that their demands were now slackening, and that I should get the men I wanted within a few days.

At the end of the second week, looking for great things, I went to Kola to see how the building was progressing. There I was told that the maximum number of Russians ever turning up for work had been eight, and that of these only two had remained on for more than a couple of days. Such progress as had been made was the result of the labours of my own R.E.

This was getting serious. So, taking Makedonski under my wing, I interviewed the local Council.

I explained that, unless labour were forthcoming at once, I should have to cable to England asking for the despatch of reinforcements to be postponed; and this appeared to strike home.

The Council severely censured a protesting Makedonski, who was now given a free hand to collect all the workmen he could, his demands to take precedence of all others.

As a result 20 men were forthcoming, but even these declined to continue work after a week, as their wages were in arrears.

This was more serious still. I had no money myself, but it was essential that accommodation should be provided.

I therefore told my R.E. officer to act on his own, and to rope in every man he could. He was to give the guarantee of the British Government that the money to pay wages would be forthcoming, and tell the men that, though they might have to wait for a week or so, their pay was absolutely assured. The response was immediate, and I had as many workers as I needed for a fortnight.

But my frantic cables home for money had produced no result. I had not a penny wherewith to pay well-earned wages, and quite naturally my builders declined to continue giving their labour for nothing.

They struck work, and neither threats nor cajoling could induce more than a bare half-dozen to remain.

I have mentioned this one case only, but it was symptomatic of what was going on throughout the whole of the Murman Area; and for weeks on end building operations were brought to a complete standstill—all for the lack of a little ready money.

As could have been expected too, with no funds available for the payment of wages, the builders were not the only operatives to go on strike.

On August 15th the whole of the railway employees from Murmansk to Soroka struck work, and refused to run a single train until they had received their full arrears of pay. Most certainly they had my sympathy. For the customary supply of roubles from the south had been cut off six weeks previously, and the local treasury chest did not contain sufficient to meet the demands of even one week's wage-bills. Thus they had received for many weeks past an almost negligible percentage of the pay to which they were entitled, and in all probability found it none too easy to obtain a sufficiency of food for themselves and their families.

The local authorities, having failed in their efforts to induce the men to resume work, appealed to me, on the grounds that the Allies had given an undertaking to provide money and food, and that I, as military commander, was the one chiefly concerned in the maintenance of rail communication.

The position was not hopeful. I had no railway engineers, and no railway troops; and were I to use force to compel the Russian staff to work the trains essential for military purposes, it was almost certain that sabotage would result, bridges be destroyed, and locomotives deliberately put out of action.

For me to pay the men's wages, and regard this payment in the light of a loan to the local government, was out of the question, as I had no money.

Even the thought of the hundreds of barrels of pickled herrings in far-away Vardo, so kindly placed at my disposal by the Treasury in lieu of cash, afforded me no encouragement. Something must be done, however; and as the strikers had arranged for a mass meeting at which to consider their future action, I gave out that I proposed to address them, and lay the situation before them frankly.

I was warned that many of the men were in an ugly mood, but it seemed to me wisest to avoid any display of force or of over-anxiety. So my A.D.C. and myself cantered across to the outskirts of the town where the meeting was being held. We were of course unarmed, and no troops were allowed to attend.

It was certainly a sullen and unprepossessing crowd that awaited my appearance, but the 500 of them gave me at least a patient hearing.

I began by saying that the whole situation was ruled by the fact that the Allies were still at war with Germany, whom Russia had fought so valiantly, and would still be fighting but for the treachery of her alien leaders.

We were in the Murman Area solely because our campaign against Germany necessitated it, but its permanent occupation was the last thing we desired. We must and should remain, however, so long as there was a danger of the Germans gaining a foothold at Murmansk.

We owed a great debt to Russia as our former ally, and we had no wish to wage war against her present Government, however rotten we might consider it. Germany was the only enemy we wanted to fight, and nothing would please me better than to be allowed to carry on that fight unhampered by Moscow. Lenin and Trotsky had, however, decided to ally themselves with Germany—doubtless to their own great profit. Could I be blamed therefore for taking steps to minimize the help they wished to give to our enemy?

It was quite true that the action I had taken had resulted in Murmansk being cut off from interior Russia, and that consequently no money to pay their wages could be expected from railway headquarters. This possibility had, however, been foreseen by my Government, which had undertaken to supply their local authorities with the necessary financial assistance. This assistance could not be forthcoming in a day or a week, but come it most assuredly would.

In the meantime they could make their choice. Either they could return to work, knowing that funds would be available shortly to enable their authorities to pay the wages due to them, and that the Allies would arrange for the food-supply both of themselves and their families—or else they could continue the strike.

If they were fools enough to choose the latter alternative, I cared little or nothing. My garrisons were already well supplied, and I was quite well able to furnish them by sea with all essential requirements. If necessary, I would even go the length of obtaining from England sufficient personnel to work the railway myself—and then their jobs would be gone.

The only people to suffer therefore would be themselves and their fellow-Russians down the line, who would soon be reduced to starvation, were no trains run.

For not only would I make it my personal concern to see that no man who failed to return to work the following day should receive his back pay when money was available, but I would ensure that rations from a food-ship expected shortly from England were issued only to those actually carrying out work regarded as useful by the Murmansk Council.

I was well aware that there were German agents among them doing their best to stir up strife between us. Some of these were known to me, and would soon be laid by the heels; but I was astonished that Russians should be led by the nose by these emissaries of a Power that had brought such miseries upon them. Would it not be far better to work in harmony with their old allies?

There must be no shilly-shallying. The choice must be made at once. For myself it was almost a matter of indifference what they decided; but for them the continuance of the strike would mean long-drawn-out privation for every Russian civilian in the Murman Area.

I added that I did not think they would be so misguided as to endeavour to damage the line, even if a conclusion were reached to continue the strike; since a broken railway would entail all their compatriots from Murmansk to Soroka being cut off from every necessity of life. I wanted, however, to give them fair warning that any man caught in an attempt at sabotage would be regarded by me as being in German employ, and would consequently receive but short shrift.

This harangue, purposely somewhat bombastic, and perhaps straining the truth at points, was interpreted for me by one of the many British refugees who had fled for shelter to Murmansk. At first he spoke glibly enough, but half-way through his fluency began to desert him, and once or twice he came almost to a standstill.

I asked him if I were speaking too fast or too colloquially. " No," he replied; " but do you really wish me to repeat exactly what you say, or to give your words a more conciliatory turn ? "

The cause of his hesitation was out! But I had to tell him that he was on no account to tone anything down; that the responsibility was mine; and that much might depend on the strikers being convinced that we had no fear either of them or their action.

Apparently he accepted this, for he continued with but little faltering; and the next day much of my address was repeated to me with smiles by a member of the Council. This official added that my audience had taken my words in surprisingly good part: they were hard words, they had said, but quite possibly they had deserved them—all perhaps but those which insinuated that they were under German influence. These they had resented deeply.

The mentality of the Russian working classes is quaint in its seeming simplicity, but unfathomable nevertheless to all but their own kith and kin.

On the conclusion of my speech there were consultations between the strike leaders; but, pursuing my line of seeming indifference, I rode off without waiting to hear the result of their deliberations.

The following morning work on the railway was resumed. For the time being, at any rate, industrial peace had been restored. But I had pledged myself publicly that money for the payment of wages would reach the local Council shortly. When would it be forthcoming ?

Could I have looked into the future, the hopes I then held of being able to maintain good relations with the railway, quay, and other workers would have been most rudely shattered.

The monetary situation went from bad to worse. For month after month the Allies failed completely to fulfil their obligations under the Agreement of July 7th; and the good name of Great Britain became utterly besmirched in the eyes of the Russian working man.

Strike followed strike in heartbreaking succession. Material taken over by me for urgent military services could not be paid for. And, perhaps worst of all, my pledged word, accepted at first as the one thing on which reliance could be placed implicitly in that land of crooked dealing, became the target of jeers and curses. It was only by going cap in hand to Russian officials, or to one or other of the foreign representatives at Archangel, that I was able to scrape together the occasional small sums by means of which I found it just, and only just, possible to weather the monetary storms that threatened time and again to cast our venture's ship upon the rocks of failure.

By November the position had become so desperate that I was compelled to return to England in order to make a last effort to place my finances on a more satisfactory footing. How I fared is told in Chapter XII.

The failure of my efforts to obtain money could not be attributed in any way to the War Office authorities, who lent me invariably their encouragement and all assistance within their power. Neither could they be held responsible for the long delay that arose before the first shipload of food-stuffs for the civil population reached Murmansk.

America had undertaken to arrange for this supply, but she let us down badly; and as week followed week, without the arrival of the long-promised foodships, discontent and mistrust increased throughout the whole district—and with them my difficulties.

The situation was only saved by our own Government drawing upon British food-stocks, and hurrying out supplies in British ships, at that time badly needed elsewhere. This was only one amongst many instances of our energy and wholeheartedness compensating, so far as it was possible to do so, for the dilatory shortcomings of some other Power associated with us in the enterprise.

Having thus put a feather in England's cap, I must,

on the other hand, voice what all of us at Murmansk regarded as a very legitimate grievance, for which our own people alone could be held responsible.

We had landed on June 23rd, but it was not until August 20th that we received our first mail! For those who know the soldier on service, and have witnessed the arrival of a mail-bag at unit headquarters, this bald statement of fact requires neither amplification nor comment.

Enough, however, has now been said on such depressing subjects as lack of money, food, and mails, and I turn to the more cheerful side of the picture.

As already stated, the War Office was doing its best to meet my needs. My overworked staff was gradually increased; additional instructors for local units arrived; and a few much-needed specialists were provided.

Our journeyings on the railway, too, were no longer undertaken in needless discomfort, for we were now provided with a special and luxurious coach, built originally for the Grand Duke Nicholas, and fitted with every modern improvement.

Besides this, the accommodation of the troops was slowly improving, and though my staff and myself were still housed in railway-carriages at the end of September, a substantial log building earmarked for headquarters was nearing completion, and we were sure of being in occupation of it before the short autumn should give place to winter.

Life in Murmansk itself, moreover, had been rendered more peaceful and secure by the eviction of the more turbulent of the Russian sailors and others of anti-Ally leaning, who were not content to keep their views to themselves. These had been taken under escort down the line, and dumped in the No-man's-land south of Soroka, with three days' rations by their side. Without a doubt the majority were enlisted in the Red Army, and fought against us in the months to come.

A further cause for congratulation was that the

GENERAL HEADQUARTERS AT MURMANSK.

cable from Peterhead to Alexandrovsk and thence to Murmansk, was functioning well. The Russian operatives at Alexandrovsk had given trouble at first; but the establishment of a small military detachment as a " supervisory " staff soon cured their *malaise*, and there was now little fault to find with either the accuracy or speed of transmission of cable messages to and from London.

The military situation also, though not devoid of anxiety, gave cause for comparative satisfaction, and it was greatly improved by the results of the operations in Karelia, the story of which is told in a succeeding chapter.

Thus the outlook was not all black. Anxiety was ever present, and comforts were few. But there was more than sufficient work to occupy the time of all, and fortunately my headquarter family was blessed for the most part with a sense of humour—ever a saving grace, but of incalculable value in the wild uncivilization of Arctic Russia.

CHAPTER VII

DEFENCE SCHEME FOR MURMANSK PORT

As my Preface shows, this volume is not intended as a military treatise, and detailed descriptions of engagements and plans of operation will find no place in it. It is, however, probable that of those who trouble to turn its pages, the majority will have had some first-hand experience of war's schooling; and to such, a brief and general indication of our scheme for the local defence of Murmansk and its port may prove of passing interest.

There is one point not to be lost sight of, namely, that the defence scheme for the immediate protection of our base was worked out and put in hand solely to meet the eventuality of German forces breaking through to the northern sea-board, and endeavouring to oust us from Murmansk itself.

When opposed by Bolsheviks alone, the danger of any such break-through did not enter seriously into my calculations; and my dispositions were altered completely when the shadow of a German offensive darkened my horizon no longer.

A commencement was made on the scheme towards the close of July, but progress at first proved exasperatingly slow. For it was only with the greatest difficulty that even a few dozen men could be spared for work upon it, and, as can be gathered from what I have said already, the Russian labour obtainable was practically negligible. Later, thanks to the gradual augmentation of my force and to assistance rendered by the navy in the construction of certain works close at hand, more satisfactory results were obtained; and though the system never reached full completion it had pro-

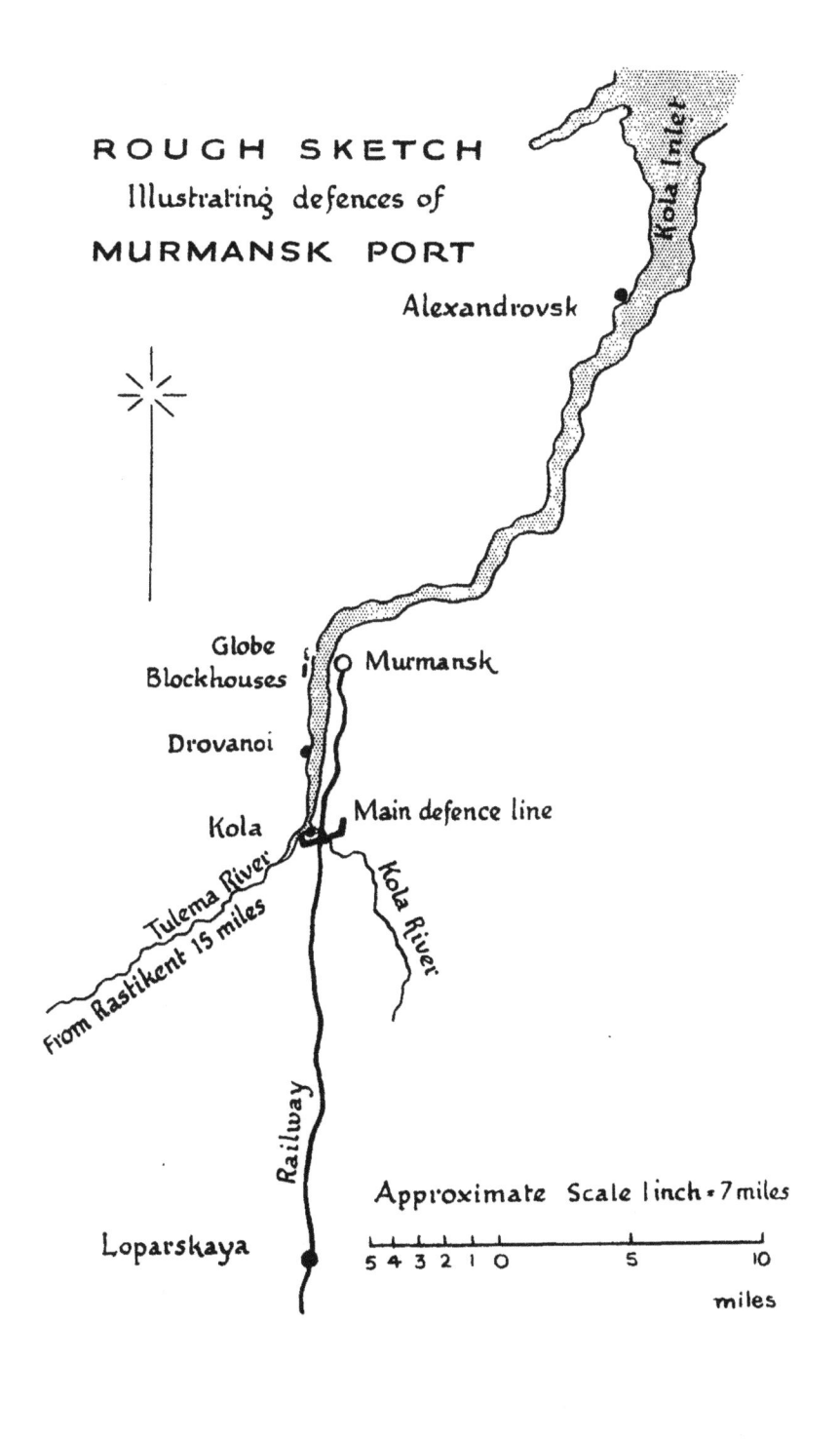

ROUGH SKETCH
Illustrating defences of
MURMANSK PORT

Kola Inlet

Alexandrovsk

Globe Blockhouses

Murmansk

Drovanoi

Kola

Main defence line

Tulema River

From Rastikent 15 miles

Kola River

Railway

Loparskaya

Approximate Scale 1 inch = 7 miles

5 4 3 2 1 0   5   10
miles

DEFENCE SCHEME FOR MURMANSK PORT

gressed sufficiently far by early October to warrant its utilization had occasion demanded it.

Though my first concern was naturally the provision of defences barring such lines of advance as were negotiable in summer (namely, the railway and Tulema River), it was obviously essential that the system as a whole should be mapped out from the start in such a way that it should serve its purpose equally well in winter, when cross-country movement must be reckoned with. This, taken in conjunction with an almost complete ignorance of what additional troops I might expect, did not tend to simplify my calculations. Some assumption as regards possible strength must, however, be made, and I fixed upon 3,000 as the highest figure to which the local defence garrison could hope to attain, this figure being inclusive of naval landing parties.

With so small a force, one thing at least was certain. Any project for a scheme of all-round fortification could be dismissed at once; since its perimeter must be in such close proximity to town and harbour as to risk both being subjected not only to enemy gun fire, but even to rifle fire also.

The best that could be done was to hold strongly a few selected vantage-points sufficiently far removed to preclude the enemy from bringing effective fire to bear on the port, unless we were first evicted from them, and to rely mainly on the active employment of mobile reserves.

Immediately after our arrival an observation party had been sent to the hamlet of Rastikent, about 30 miles up the Tulema River, which, together with the lakes through which it flowed, constituted one of the possible lines of enemy advance during the summer months. Movement against us by this route was hardly probable, as it would be beset with many difficulties; and, with my paucity of troops, I could do no more than seek to obtain early news of any attempt to make use of it, should that unlikely contingency arise. The only other, and by far the more practicable, line of approach was the railway. In order to check an advance along this, an outpost was established at Loparskaya, a station some 25 miles down the line. Here huts were erected for a garrison of a hundred, and small defence works constructed. The place offered fair facilities for resistance, and was in close proximity to several river-bridges with spans of 50 to 100 feet. The rôle of its garrison was to push back hostile reconnoitring parties, and delay the enemy for as long as safety permitted. On withdrawal in the face of an attack in force, all bridges were to be burnt—a sure means of lessening appreciably the rapidity of an enemy's subsequent advance.

The main line of defence was at Kola, commanding the junction point of the railway and Tulema River, and was planned with a view to its being held by a garrison of 2,000. The most careful reconnaissance failed to discover any positions having really satisfactory fields of fire either for gun or rifle; but the general line was so selected as to have its flanks reasonably secure, and to afford adequate protection for reserves. This last I regarded as a matter of first importance, for even in summer it was possible for the enemy to fall upon Murmansk by a détour to the east, and in winter a move along the western shore of the inlet was feasible also. It was my intention to employ my Kola reserve to attack in flank or rear any force attempting such encircling movements.

It is true that an enemy would find it a difficult undertaking to force the crossing of the inlet from the west anywhere in the neighbourhood of Murmansk (where its average width is at least 1,500 yards); but the town itself, including the quay and ships in harbour, would be at the mercy of any high-angle-fire guns which he might be able to bring to that side; for such guns, owing to the configuration of the ground, would be immune from the fire of the guns of the Allied ships.

Thus any hostile advance on the far side of the

DEFENCE SCHEME FOR MURMANSK PORT 85

inlet must be prevented equally with an attempt to reach Murmansk by an easterly move round the flank of our Kola line.

But here I was confronted with a difficulty. The Tulema River, where it debouches into the inlet at Kola, was 200 yards broad, and unbridged; its current was always swift; and in winter, blocks of ice, many of them of sufficient size and weight to stave in the gunwales of a stout rowing-boat, were borne down in swirling confusion by its swift-flowing tide.

The transfer of the whole or even a half of the Kola reserve to the western side of the water would prove consequently no easy matter, and must occupy a very considerable time.

With a view to mitigating this unavoidable drawback, two small defence systems of the bridgehead type (named by us the " Globe " blockhouses) were constructed on the western shore of the inlet, in close proximity to Murmansk, with the object of covering the landing on that bank of reinforcements from Murmansk sufficient to hold the enemy in check until such time as my Kola reserve should be able to cross the mouth of the Tulema.

As a further safeguard, when winter conditions were approaching, and I was able more easily to spare troops for the purpose, an infantry company destined to be trained for mobile work on skis was quartered at Drovanoi, a village west of the inlet, almost midway between Kola and Murmansk. This detachment would be useful for reconnaissance and, if driven back by numbers, could retire on the " Globe " blockhouses, or could even be withdrawn by water, as the village boasted a serviceable quay utilizable at any state of tide, and comparatively well sheltered from all but close-range fire.

At Murmansk itself I was compelled to retain permanently an all-too-large proportion of my troops for the purpose of furnishing standing working parties necessitated by lack of civilian labour, and the numerous guards essential to cope with persistent attempts at looting made by hooligan Russian gangs. I had also to keep in constant readiness a force of sufficient strength to quell local disturbances, which, during the whole of our time at Murmansk, constituted a very real source of danger.

On the above troops, together with such landing parties as could be provided by the Allied naval forces, I relied as my general reserve.

No commander could be satisfied completely with these arrangements, and I most certainly was not; especially as time and labour did not permit of any but the most primitive artificial strengthening of the various systems of works. Little indeed was, or could be, taken in hand, beyond essentials.

Therefore, whilst hoping that my preparations and dispositions would enable me to beat off such a German attack as I conceived might be launched against us, I felt bound to take every step possible to ensure my retaining a footing at some spot adjacent to the Kola Inlet, should I be forced to evacuate Murmansk; for thus I might still be in a position to prevent the port being utilized as a submarine base. There could be small doubt as to the locality best suited for the purpose, if it came to making a final stand. Alexandrovsk was indicated at once. It was the landing-place of the Peterhead cable, and I should therefore be able to maintain communication with England and Archangel; the anchorage facilities were such as to promise better co-operation with the navy than could be ensured elsewhere; and a limited amount of accommodation and storage room was ready available.

Alexandrovsk was scheduled accordingly as the rallying-point for all troops, should we be driven from Murmansk, and supplies, stores, and ammunition sufficient for 2,000 men for one month were collected there. Additional stores were also loaded on sailing-ships and lighters, ready for conveyance to our new base, should the necessity arise; reconnaissances were

ALEXANDROVSK AND THE KOLA INLET.

Medium sized vessels can break their way through the ice even in mid-winter, and their tracks can be noted.

DEFENCE SCHEME FOR MURMANSK PORT 87

made, and a defence scheme mapped out ; and plans were drawn up for transporting to the rallying-place such troops as might have been pushed back along the eastern side of the inlet.

This whole scheme of preparation, though seemingly perhaps a small thing when glanced at in the comfort of an easy-chair, entailed nevertheless a mass of work for my (at first) lilliputian staff and the weak personnel of my administrative services. It meant too that the rank and file were employed almost unceasingly on working parties of many and diverse natures—a type of occupation never congenial to the soldier on service, and more than ever unwelcome amidst surroundings devoid of comfort and lacking nearly every facility for recreation.

There could, however, be no alternative, save that of trusting to luck to pull us through, should the storm burst upon us. I had therefore to harden my heart and, though at times it went sorely against the grain, act the part of a relentless task-master, bent on extracting from every officer and man the best of which he was capable.

All responded splendidly to the demands made upon them, exorbitant perhaps as these may have seemed ; and it was owing to their unflagging exertions that my scheme of defence reached at least such a stage on its road to completion that I felt reasonably confident of being able to put the plans I had evolved into operation with a fair prospect of success, should they ever be called upon to stand the test.

CHAPTER VIII

OPERATIONS IN KARELIA

DURING the second week of August reports reached me of large enemy concentrations along the Finnish frontier, at points most suitable for descents upon the railway. It seemed that my period of respite was over, and that Germans and Finns were about to make a real bid for Murmansk, with Kandalaksha and Kem as their first objectives.

Up to this date I had received no increase in Allied fighting strength, and apparently none could be expected for some weeks. France, alone of our Allies, had answered promptly the call made upon her, and her first contingent had already sailed with Poole to Archangel.

In spite of this, however, we had undoubtedly strengthened our position.

True, the Slavo-British Legion was not prospering as I could have wished. It still numbered less than 200, and the class of recruit was indifferent. But both the Finn Legion and Karelian Regiment had made marvellous progress. Recruiting had been brisk, and the few British N.C.O.s whom I had been able to spare as instructors had done splendid work with the material at their disposal. The men were willing and, as was only to be expected after nearly four years of almost universal war and turmoil, it was found that some at least were not unversed in the elementary duties of a soldier.

The Finn Legion now numbered some 800, of whom 500 were fit to take the field, and included the personnel of a mountain battery which was rapidly gaining in efficiency. The strength of the Legion, too, seemed

OPERATIONS IN KARELIA 89

likely to increase still further, as a hurried visit to Archangel had shown me that it harboured a considerable body of Finnish refugees. These, with Poole's sanction and help, were to be shipped across to me.

Even more satisfactory was the growth of the Karelian Regiment. Recruits were pouring in, and its enlisted strength was nearly 1,200. Of these, over half could be considered fit for military operations, and each week the number would be swelled.

Well as they had carried out their job, the British officers and N.C.O.s responsible for the recruitment and training of these two units were not workers of miracles. Thus it is needless to say that neither Finns nor Karelians would have been welcomed by any brigade commander on the Western front. Judged by the standard in France, they were in fact totally ignorant of modern warfare, and their ideas of discipline were more than vague. But they could use their rifles in a fairly workmanlike way; were ready to obey orders according to their lights; and were accustomed to travel with a minimum of food and impedimenta. Moreover, as they were fed, clothed, and housed on a scale contrasting vividly with the want and privation of many months past, they were fully content with their lot. Added to this, the Finns were thirsting for a chance of paying off old scores on the Whites, who had driven them with such ruthless ferocity from their homes; whilst the Karelians, staunchest of patriots, would be fighting to rid their country of an invader.

In addition to my diminutive Allied force, I had therefore some 1,200 partially trained local troops available for operations in the field, and these I determined to employ at once.

Had their training been even less advanced, I should still have felt constrained to utilize them. For at this juncture the pursuance of an active policy appeared imperative, and it could only be put into effect by drawing upon all available material.

My efforts had always been directed with one main

object in view, namely, that of preventing Germany from obtaining a footing at Murmansk; and now, more than ever, all other considerations must be made subservient to this.

It could not be denied that our embroilment with the Bolsheviks was disconcerting, for it increased my difficulties by compelling me to employ a portion of my meagre force otherwise than against our chief enemy. But it was a side-issue, and must be treated as such. What mattered above all else was this seeming German threat against Murmansk, and how best I could deal with it.

Now, it had always appeared to me that von der Goltz's inaction up to the present could be explained in part by an exaggerated impression of Allied strength. If this had been so at the start, it was possible that he saw as yet no reason to revise his estimate. For the advent of supply ships and the comings and goings of the Royal Navy were lending Murmansk an increasing air of activity; whilst the Bolsheviks would be unlikely to belittle the strength of the force which had compelled them to evacuate hurriedly the whole Murman Area.

Any such misapprehensions as he may have entertained, it was of course in my interest to foster; but more than rumours and reports were needed if he were to be kept in continued ignorance of our real weakness. He must have actual or implied evidence that we were ready and willing to try conclusions with his army—and this evidence I proposed to afford him.

Orders were issued accordingly to the officers commanding at Kandalaksha and Kem to prepare mobile columns for operations towards the Finnish frontier. These were to be composed mainly of the Finn Legion and Karelian Regiment respectively, with such backing of Allied troops as could be spared.

During the progress of these contemplated operations I was anxious to be relieved, so far as circumstances permitted, of any anxiety regarding the safety of Petchenga. I decided therefore to reinforce the existing naval garrison by drawing on the fittest of the 400 Serbians who had been convalescing at Murmansk. It was found that 200 had recovered sufficiently to admit of their employment on garrison duty, and were in fact likely to benefit by a transfer to the more salubrious surroundings of Petchenga. Later on, detachments of these men were trained in the use of our 4·5 howitzer and the French ·75, and the defences of Petchenga much strengthened by the inclusion of a section of each type of gun—an example of the adaptability of the Serbian soldier and of the make-shifts to which necessity drove us.

The remaining Serbs at Murmansk were too sick to hold out any hopeful prospect of early recovery, and were shipped to England.

Before giving any account of the doings of the columns which moved from Kandalaksha and Kem against von der Goltz's men, I propose first to follow the fortunes of a three weeks' dash made southward from Soroka by 150 British and Serbian troops.

At this time my intelligence service was in embryo. The few trustworthy agents originally employed by Thornhill had been transferred to Archangel, and their replacement had not been an easy matter. Such information as was now forthcoming from the men taken on in their stead was scanty and, as experience had taught me, far from reliable.

Thus my knowledge of what was taking place beyond the limits of my patrol system was almost negligible. For all I knew, there might be thousands of Bolsheviks with a dozen batteries endeavouring to work their way northwards by the indifferent but passable track leading from Povynetz (on Lake Onega) to Sumski Posad, and thence to Soroka. In fact, such reports as I had received pointed to Bolshevik concentrations along this route.

As I had no aircraft to assist me in clearing up the

situation[1], the only alternative to remaining in ignorance of what was happening was to push out a reconnaissance on an extended scale. It certainly involved risks; for it meant despatching into the blue what must necessarily be a tiny force, which might quite possibly have to face great odds, and which, once it had left Sumski Posad, would have no means of communicating with me. Also, its retreat might well be cut off, as a highway runs along the southern shore of the White Sea from the town of Onega, and I was completely in the dark as to Bolshevik movements between that place and Soroka.

The risk appeared, however, warranted. For it was the only certain method of acquiring information sufficiently authentic to enable me to judge whether, and for how long, I could afford to regard the Bolshevik menace with equanimity, and devote myself entirely to opposing a German-Finnish move from Finland. Further than this, I was well aware that Bolsheviks and Germans kept close touch, and one of my chief aims was to broadcast an impression of strength. If, then, the news that I was advancing southwards were passed on, it was likely to lead to the assumption that I had a sufficiency of troops at my disposal to warrant an offensive on two fronts.

As events turned out, the risk proved justified. Captain Sheppard of my infantry company, who had volunteered to command the party, led it with great gallantry. His British platoon displayed magnificent pluck and endurance; whilst the Serbians, stouthearted and full of guile, showed themselves exactly suited for a venturesome enterprise of this nature. The Bolsheviks were nonplussed at every turn. First encountered some 20 miles south of Sumski Posad, they were driven back 10 miles on to their supports.

---

[1] Later on, one of *Nairana's* seaplanes was placed occasionally at my disposal, but the dense forests made it almost impossible to gather any detailed information, outside the limits of the railway track.

These were attacked boldly, and after suffering heavy casualties beat a rapid retreat, leaving behind them quantities of stores and ammunition. They were followed up for another 20 miles, and, according to reports reaching me later, withdrew eventually to the shelter of Povynetz. The Bolshevik force was estimated at an infantry battalion, with 200 mounted men, but it was without artillery.

This in itself was a great thing to have learnt at little loss. In addition, it was most unlikely that the Red troops in that area, after the rough handling they had received, would make any further aggressive effort for some time to come.

I lived too in the hope that something more had been accomplished. Captain Sheppard took with him false orders, in which mention was made of large formations, and of the contemplated assumption of an Allied offensive on a big scale on all fronts. It was hoped that these orders would fall eventually into German hands, with the Bolsheviks as intermediaries; and plans (discovered subsequently to have proved successful) were worked out with this in view. They were compiled, therefore, with scrupulous care. As I drafted them, I was reminded strongly of Staff College days, when I spent laborious hours writing operation orders for forces equally large and equally fictitious, praying that Richard Haking's[1] red pencil would display a not too devastating disregard for the appearance of my neatly written sheets.

By this time the columns from Kandalaksha and Kem were commencing to fight their way through Karelia towards the Finnish frontier, for they had not covered many miles before encountering opposition.

I have no wish to exaggerate the magnitude of their operations. Compared with even the smallest offensive

---

[1] Now General Sir R. C. B. Haking, G.B.E., K.C.B., K.C.M.G. Then an instructor at Camberley, to whom hundreds of Staff College graduates are largely indebted for any success they may have won.

action in France or Flanders, they could be regarded as nothing more than a prolonged military picnic—a mere series of skirmishes, fought by half-trained local levies in a waste of forest, lake, and bog. But the results they achieved were, none the less, outstanding. But for their bold action in face of tremendous difficulties, it is fairly certain that Finns, with German support, would have succeeded in establishing themselves on the railway. Not only would this have entailed an immediate withdrawal of all garrisons to the south, and a probable farewell to every hope of our assisting in building up a new Russian front, but Germany would have taken an immense stride forward towards the occupation of Murmansk. As events turned out we should, in all likelihood, have been able to retard her advance up the railway sufficiently long to prevent Murmansk proving of any value to her. But the collapse of the Central Powers in November was an eventuality totally unforeseen. In August the assumption was that the Allies could make no decisive effort to end the war before 1919; and thus the fall in September or October of either Kem or Kandalaksha could only be contemplated as an untoward disaster, imperilling gravely the safety of Murmansk.

The possibility of this disaster was put well into the background by the operations of two small columns of semi-barbaric auxiliaries, led with resolution and determined to overcome all obstacles.

Both columns set out during the third week in August, and from the very start both experienced extreme difficulty in maintaining an adequate supply system.

Such tracks as were available proved even worse than reports had indicated, and it soon became evident that any type of wheel transport was almost valueless. The idea of utilizing pack transport in its place had to be abandoned, as no trained animals were available, and there was no pack equipment in the country. The only solution was to make use of such waterways as existed and, when these failed, to fall back on carriers.

The Karelians made full use of the River Kem for some 60 miles. But there was a shortage of suitable boats, and the swiftness of the current made light loading essential. It was, too, a most difficult matter to ensure the protection of convoys.

In connexion with this conveyance of supplies by river, an incident occurred which is probably without parallel in our military annals.

Karelian women had taken upon themselves to supplement the crews of ration-boats, and in this they were not to be denied. They were excellent waterwomen, and had a fixed determination to assist their menfolk in driving out the Finns. One and all argued, with some show of reason, that in times of peace they had always been accustomed to row the boats carrying food for men who were away from home, and that surely it was of more importance that they should do so now, when their men were at the front.

On one occasion two women formed the sole crew of a ration-boat, and had started ahead of their escort. They were spotted by three Finn soldiers, who put out in a boat to intercept them—and a naval action followed. The Finns were armed, and opened fire; but their marksmanship was bad.

The Karelian women had never heard of Nelson, but they acted as, in all probability, he would have done. They promptly turned their boat; drove hard and straight at the enemy craft; and struck it amidships.

The Finns, taken utterly by surprise by this unlooked-for attack, were hard put to it to prevent their boat capsizing; and profiting by this, the Karelian women proceeded to belabour them with their oars. All three Finns were placed *hors de combat*, two being knocked overboard and drowned.

However unprecedented and irregular it might be, I felt that devotion such as this should not go unrewarded, and a little later I decorated both women with our Military Medal. There were, I think, no two prouder ladies in North Russia that day than this couple of brave Karelian W.A.A.C.s.

The Kandalaksha column, having no river at its disposal, was in even greater straits than the column based on Kem. Fortunately, however, a string of lakes lay more or less parallel with its line of advance, and on each of these all available boats were collected and utilized. Between the lakes, stores had to be carried by hand, much of the work being done by the troops themselves, owing to the scarcity of civilian carriers.

Thus the difficulties confronting both columns were sufficiently great, even when their numbers were small and their respective bases within a score or so of miles. But the Kandalaksha column reached a strength of over a thousand, and the Kem column more than double that figure before the close of the operations ; and, with every advance, their lines of communication were lengthened, thus adding ever-increasing difficulties to the solution of the supply problem. That these were overcome, and an unbroken series of victories gained, speaks volumes for the grit and determination of Finns and Karelians alike, and for the fine fighting qualities of the handful of British officers and N.C.O.s who led them.

The Kem column, operating along the northern bank of the Kem River, soon found itself in opposition to Finnish White Guards. It pushed stubbornly on, driving its opponents back in a number of minor engagements, and forcing them to withdraw to their advanced base at Ukhtinskaya. Here, on September 11th, the enemy was completely routed in a miniature pitched battle.

For some time the issue remained in doubt; but the Karelians contrived to carry out a turning movement across country believed to be impassable, and this movement decided the day. Ukhtinskaya, with all its war stores, including much ammunition, many rifles, and several trench mortars and machine guns, fell into our hands.

Despite the fact that German officers and N.C.O.s were counted amongst the killed, it is probable that no German unit was employed in this encounter. It is more likely that von der Goltz, pursuing the same policy as myself, had refrained from throwing in his own regulars, and had merely entrusted the control of the operations to German officers, with a sprinkling of N.C.O.s to assist them.

The success met with by the Kem column was due to sound administrative arrangements, coupled with the able leadership of its commander, Lieutenant-Colonel Woods, who had raised and trained the Karelian Regiment, and was entirely responsible for its efficiency in the field.

Meanwhile the Kandalaksha column, under Major Burton, a Canadian officer, had been making slow but steady headway. It moved firstly direct towards the frontier, and came in contact with White Finns during the second day's march. Weeks of desultory fighting followed, in which the soldiers of the Finn Legion proved themselves more than a match for their White compatriots, who, after many reverses, took refuge eventually behind the shelter of their frontier. The column then turned south-west in order to gain touch with the Karelians from Kem, and also to clear the intervening country of certain White Finn troops reported to be concentrating near Lake Pyavozero. A small but decisive action was fought on the western shore of that lake, and the last-formed enemy body in northern Karelia was driven in rout across the Finnish border-line.

Central Karelia was not similarly cleared until early in October, when the Kem column gained another victory 130 miles west of Kem, and close to the frontier. This almost rivalled Ukhtinskaya, the enemy losing between 200 and 300 in killed alone, and the booty including 600 rifles, a number of machine guns and trench mortars, large quantities of ammunition and stores, some 30 boats, and several hundred pairs of ski.

These striking and opportune successes meant much for the Allied cause. It was not that the losses inflicted had been so great as to preclude further enemy efforts; for, though heavy in proportion to the strength of the forces engaged, it is doubtful whether they totalled 2,000 throughout the whole area. What counted most was the moral effect of two offensives, each conducted with unremitting vigour, and each having to its credit an unbroken series of victories.

What the German plan may have been must remain a matter of conjecture. But throughout August and the early half of September persistent reports reached me of German preparations near the Finnish frontier, and these were substantiated by information sent me from the War Office. Possibly they were spread solely as a " blind "; but this was improbable, unless von der Goltz had already abandoned all idea of a breakthrough to Murmansk. It was more likely that his Finn auxiliaries had been sent forward to feel the way for him and obtain, if possible, a footing on the railway. Had they met with success, the chances were that they would have been followed up by German troops, and a determined effort made to drive us from the Murman Area.

The White Finn Guards, however, so far from gaining a hold on the railway, had been defeated time and again, and ejected from Karelia with substantial losses.

If therefore it was intended to drive us from the railway—a necessary preliminary, until the frost came, to any attempt on Murmansk—it must have become evident to the German Command that this could not be achieved by Finns alone. The employment of German troops was clearly called for, and this I most certainly expected.

But, as the outcome of our operations, I was far better placed to meet this more formidable threat than I had been in early August. To begin with, the strength of my local forces had been more than doubled, and nearly 3,000 could be relied upon to give a good account of themselves in the field. Moreover, lines of communication towards the frontier had been established, and it would be possible to commence putting up an organized opposition to a German advance at distances varying from 30 to 100 miles from the railway—in itself a distinct gain, when the time-factor was all-important. Then, too, Ukhtinskaya had been fought and won by the Karelians, and the Finn Legion had gained many minor successes; so that von der Goltz's White Finns, after having been badly mauled and driven back continuously for weeks, would be unlikely to show any great enthusiasm for an offensive. Besides this, the country would be almost unknown to German soldiers; transport arrangements for a European force of any size would need elaborate preparations; and the ground lent itself to the guerrilla type of warfare favoured by my levies.

I could therefore regard the outcome of the Karelian operations with no little satisfaction and much thankfulness.

For several months, at least, the safety of Murmansk was ensured.

CHAPTER IX

STILL AT WAR WITH GERMANY

In dealing with the operations in Karelia I have, for the sake of clarity, treated them apart from other happenings, and have followed their course briefly up to as late as the beginning of October.

Though the victories gained ultimately by both columns taking part in them relieved my mind of the fear of any immediate threat to Murmansk, the period immediately subsequent to their setting out was for me one of exceptional anxiety.

During the latter half of August both Christiania and Stockholm reported that the Germans were preparing for a sudden blow against the railway, in which Finnish troops were to co-operate. The German strength in Finland was given as 55,000, of whom 6,000 were believed to be concentrating in the neighbourhood of Ukhtinskaya; and information from other sources pointed to a large Finn force being collected near the frontier, if not already in Karelia.

At this time my columns were beginning to push their way slowly forward, but were meeting with continuous opposition, and had as yet gained no signal success.

When despatching them, I had hoped that they would force back the White Finns known to be in Karelia, and by a bold front lead von der Goltz to believe that mine was a really powerful force, and thus perhaps induce him to abandon his designs for an offensive campaign. But now it would seem that his plans were ripe already, and that we might expect him to commence an attack in strength at any moment.

And against it how would my raw auxiliaries fare?

Most certainly the possibility of both columns meeting with reverses could not be overlooked and, if pressed closely by German troops in force, such reverses might well become routs.

I could not reinforce either column. Ought I, therefore, to order the retirement of one or both, or to stand by my original decision?

This question could only be answered by seeking a reply to one of far graver importance. With the enemy in such preponderating strength as reported, was I justified in maintaining any garrison south of Kandalaksha, in view of the near approach of winter conditions?

If these garrisons were to remain, then the columns most undoubtedly must remain out also. If, on the other hand, it were decided to evacuate Kem and Soroka, then the withdrawal towards Kandalaksha of both columns might prove the only sound solution.

The larger question must therefore be settled first, and it involved the consideration of many pros and cons.

In the first place, lest the end of August should be regarded as a somewhat early date on which to give thought to winter, I must point out that we experienced a slight fall of snow so soon as August 6th; that late September and early October brought many days of snow and hard frost; that on October 26th the thermometer fell to zero, and the naval authorities declined to send to Kem a vessel conveying reinforcements, for fear of the ice preventing her return to Murmansk; and that H.M.S. *Cochrane* was brought back from Petchenga at the end of the same month lest she might get frozen in. Thus we could not reckon for certain on being able to withdraw our southerly garrisons by sea later than mid-October.

Towards the close of August I was faced therefore with this position. If the reports with which I had been furnished were correct (as I saw no reason to doubt), it seemed almost certain that my two columns must be driven back eventually. The stouter the resistance they offered, the longer would the enemy be kept in check—but the nearer the time would be brought when I must cease to rely on our command of the sea as an aid to extricating my troops at Soroka and Kem. And, unless they were withdrawn by sea, how could they be saved at all, if any point on the railway were captured and held by Germans or Finns?

It came in fact to this. Apart from my being absolutely sure of preventing the enemy ever gaining a hold on the railway (which I was not), provision for the safety of my men at Soroka and Kem would be more easy if our forces in Karelia were thrust back within a couple of weeks than if they kept German and Finn at bay for as many months, and then met with defeat.

It was evident, therefore, that I should be playing the safer game were I to order the Kem column to retire at once, and to transport it to Kandalaksha together with all troops to the south, whilst there was yet time. The Kandalaksha column could then be strengthened greatly, and Kandalaksha itself (the main gateway to Murmansk) made doubly secure.

Dealing with the situation purely from the point of view of military operations between von der Goltz's troops and mine, little could, in fact, be said in favour of retaining our hold on any place south of Kandalaksha, when once the White Sea was closed to shipping. In the face of such odds as were reported to be against us, it would merely be asking for trouble; and, with my eyes set ever on the safeguarding of Murmansk, I was inclined at first to take military exigencies alone into consideration, and to follow the line dictated by them.

But further deliberation, and consultation with Poole, produced on my mind a more vivid impression of the grave objections inherent to any withdrawal.

It would be opposed vehemently by all Russian officials at Murmansk and down the line who at present were by way at least of co-operating with us, and would be regarded by them as an unpardonable breach of faith. So much so, that it was quite possible many would become actively hostile.

For the inhabitants of Kem, Soroka, and numerous smaller towns it would entail unutterable calamity. The Reds would return at once; and I, for one, did not care to contemplate the savage ferocity with which most certainly they would set about purging the evacuated area of all suspected of having shown friendly feeling towards us.

The hope, too, must go of taking our share in reconstructing a Russian front against Germany. For, apart from forfeiting the confidence of the Murmansk Council, we should lose practically the whole recruiting-ground from which it was expected to secure enlistments for the new Russian army.

It was doubtful, moreover, whether the Karelians would consent to transfer to Kandalaksha. There was indeed little chance of this unless their families were moved also; and lack of accommodation prohibited any such project.

Thus, though the retention of our southern posts might be strategically unsound, withdrawal from them would result in such political and economic disaster as would be likely to outweigh the handicap imposed on me by their continued occupation.

Between the two alternatives there could be no question of compromise. Either I must fight on for as long as I could, in accordance with the plan of operations already in train, or I must withdraw my southern garrisons almost at once.

The conclusion reached finally, and approved by Poole, was that there should be no withdrawal. This point settled, everything must hinge on the fortunes of the columns in Karelia.

So long as they could hold their own, and block the approaches to Kem and Kandalaksha, Murmansk would be safe whilst summer lasted. But it would not be safe when winter conditions obtained, and cross-country movement became feasible. Neither the columns nor the retention of our southern garrisons could then ensure the immunity of Murmansk against attack.

Provision must therefore be made for holding the defensive line constructed in proximity of the port itself; and this called for additional troops, my lowest estimate of the number required being 2,000.

I was aware that the Italian Expeditionary Force, some 1,200 strong, was due to arrive shortly; and I could count on a naval landing party of 300 to 400 being added in emergency to my general reserve. But these left me still several hundreds short of my absolute minimum.

How could these be found, since I had no expectation of further reinforcements, and could not spare from his present duties a single man of my existing force?

To me it appeared that there was only one solution, namely, the complete evacuation of Petchenga.

I have told in Chapter V how my first visit to the place went far to convince me that Germany would be unlikely to put forth any great effort to occupy Petchenga; and it seemed to me that its loss to us, now that winter was approaching, would be an almost negligible factor in the struggle. True, if we quitted it, White Finns would probably usurp our place. But what could they do, beyond sitting there and gazing on what, in a couple of months or so, must be a field of ice surrounded by unbroken desolation? Some prestige we might lose; but that would be of small account compared with the safety of Murmansk.

There was, in my opinion, no danger whatever of Germany finding the bay of the slightest use for her submarines until the following April at earliest, and even then it could prove of no value save as a temporary resting-place, which, with its narrow and easily blocked exit, was not likely to find favour as such.

Its garrison now included an R.E. Section (half my total of Royal Engineers), 200 Serbian infantry, two sections of field guns manned by Serbs, and several

British officers who would be of great use on the Murmansk side. Counting *Cochrane's* landing party, it numbered over 500.

Had my strength been sufficient to spare these troops, it would of course have been desirable to retain our hold on Petchenga. But Murmansk was in danger, and Murmansk was of ten times more value to the Allies than was Petchenga. Thus Petchenga must be evacuated, and its garrison utilized for the defence of Murmansk.

That at least was my conclusion, wrong perhaps, and certainly at variance with Admiralty views; but formed as the result of personal observation and local enquiry.

I therefore informed Poole and the War Office on August 25th that I did not consider myself strong enough to hold both Murmansk and Petchenga; that the latter was, in my opinion, of very minor importance; and that I recommended withdrawing its garrison, and devoting all my efforts to ensuring the safety of Murmansk.

My cable caused no little perturbation in London, Paris, and elsewhere.

Admiralty objections to an evacuation of Petchenga were unqualified, and these carried the day. I was told that the maintenance of our hold on the place was regarded as of vital importance, and that, to enable me to maintain that hold, the Government was prepared to send me reinforcements. What was the minimum additional strength I considered essential?

This was a difficult question to answer. The much-quoted " fog of war " was for me a dense and blinding smoke cloud. The fighting quality of 80 per cent. of my troops was still a matter of complete uncertainty; the measures likely to be taken by the Bolsheviks to evict us were equally so; the extent and thoroughness of von der Goltz's preparations were entirely problematical; and I was quite unable to judge how far the seeming goodwill of the local Council would be countered by anti-Allied activities throughout the whole Murman Area.

Basing my calculations on the estimate of German strength being approximately correct, and regarding everything else in the light most favourable to ourselves, I felt that optimism would outrun my judgment if I asked for less than a minimum of :

>   1 infantry brigade,
>   3 batteries of field artillery,
>   2 machine gun companies,
>   1 trench mortar battery.

Once again the War Office played up to me magnificently, and my estimate was accepted without demur. The troops were to be drawn from the Home Defence forces.

But shipping difficulties were great. The first contingent did not reach me till September 26th, and, owing to various accidents, the last, which comprised brigade headquarters and two infantry battalions (a large percentage of the whole), did not arrive until two months later—a fortnight after the signing of the Armistice, and long after all danger of a German attack was at an end.

In consequence of these delays, the first half of September was not without its anxious moments, in spite of the arrival on the 3rd of the Italian Expeditionary Force. This was, of course, a most welcome addition to my strength, but unfortunately the climate affected the Italians adversely from the start, and my very limited hospital accommodation was soon taxed severely.

It was only from the 17th, when the news of the Karelian victory at Ukhtinskaya reached me, that I began to feel real confidence in our power to frustrate German aims.

This confidence grew with each succeeding week; for in France and Macedonia the seemingly impossible was happening. The Allies were starting their great effort to bring the war to a conclusive end, at least six months earlier than had been deemed possible, and were meeting with undeniable success. The pressure exerted by them in the west, coupled with the launching of our Balkan offensive, would assuredly make their influence felt even in distant Murmansk; for it was a fair assumption that German troops would be recalled from Finland to meet the urgent demands of other more decisive theatres.

The favourable turn thus taken by events does not, however, lessen one whit the debt we owe to my few thousand auxiliaries who, in a time of great need, had set out to confront an enemy whose strength, though unknown, was by every indication far greater than their own, and who, by the vigour and relentlessness of their advance, had set at rest for the time being any fears of a German occupation of Murmansk.

In support of this, facts must speak.

An Allied offensive in France on a grandiose scale was to me absolutely unexpected; and in framing my plans I had to assume that I should be called upon to hold my own until at least the following spring.

September and October were marked for me as critical, in view of the reported magnitude of German preparations. Yet the first shipload of the British reinforcements for which I had asked did not reach me till the end of September, and the majority not before the close of November, when winter had already set in.

What, then, would have been my position, say in October, if the unlooked-for had not occurred in France, and if my Karelian columns, meeting with defeat instead of success, had allowed German troops to secure a footing on the railway? With Petchenga still to be held, and the Italians as my sole reinforcement, it could hardly have been regarded as reassuring.

In point of fact, I was to find myself forced to strengthen Petchenga by despatching thither a portion of the first British unit from England immediately it landed at Murmansk.

On September 28th, whilst on a visit of inspection at Petchenga, I learnt from the garrison commander that his outposts near the Norwegian frontier had been driven in by Finnish troops, reported to be the advanced guard of a large force.

There had been for weeks past, as on the Murmansk side, persistent rumours of a contemplated enemy attack; so, as telephonic communication between the outposts and Petchenga had been cut, I decided to run no uncalled-for risk, and to bring over at once the reinforcements I had earmarked for the garrison, in order that it should be self-contained during winter, when the difficulties of sending additional troops would be all but insurmountable.

I felt enabled to do this without great misgiving, as our columns in Karelia were advancing steadily, and at that time I had no reason to anticipate that two months would elapse before the bulk of my remaining British reinforcements would be disembarked.

Cochrane's wireless was therefore utilized to despatch an order for half the 11th Sussex Regiment, and one machine-gun company to leave at once for Petchenga. They had only just got ashore at Murmansk, but were hurried again on board the s.s. *Cameron*, and landed at Petchenga within thirty-six hours.

Meanwhile, however, the Petchenga outposts had rallied, and had succeeded in driving back the enemy without calling for support; and though the Finnish advanced troops remained in contact with our covering force for some days, they made no further attempt to push home an attack.

Peace reigned subsequently at Petchenga and in its neighbourhood. But this was not to be foretold, and I was constrained to retain the garrison at its reinforced strength. A fortnight later I even felt it necessary to add a detachment of 60 French skiers for patrol work, since, without some such mobile force, the garrison commander could receive no warning of possible enemy movement, after the snow had once begun to lie.

STILL AT WAR WITH GERMANY 109

Thus nearly the whole of my first batch of British reinforcements (or its equivalent in strength) was swallowed up in a far-distant wilderness. But I had little choice about the matter. My orders to safeguard the place were implicit, and *Cochrane* was due to be withdrawn within a few weeks.

As the October days passed, however, it became increasingly evident that the German army in Finland was being reduced. For, as was expected, the urgent necessity for replacing casualties elsewhere was compelling the German Command to detach troops from that front.

The withdrawal had begun in September, but became greatly accentuated in October. By the middle of that month von der Goltz's army was so denuded as to preclude all thoughts of aggressive action on his part; and before its close, we had every reason to hope that our main purpose had been accomplished.

November 11th made that hope a certainty.

Those who still regard our intervention in Russia as a grotesque and unjustifiable venture—its inception an outrage, and its outcome failure—are, as I have already said, either wilfully blind, or else biased to such a degree as to render them incapable of a true vision. Despite reiteration, I must once again assert most emphatically that, in gauging the success or failure of the enterprise as originally planned, our subsequent embroilment with Bolshevik Russia must be regarded as a thing apart. At the outset, not only did Moscow raise no objection to our action, but even sanctioned the landing of Allied troops for the defence of Murmansk. Obviously, too, it was all to our interest that there should be no break in our semi-friendly relations with the Soviet authorities, since our only object was to prosecute the war against Germany.

That the rupture occurred was owing solely to the machinations of Germany's tool Lenin.

Whether it was politic, despite this rupture having been forced upon us, to continue operations against the Bolsheviks after the overthrow of Germany, is an entirely different question. That we were more than justified in doing so I shall endeavour to show later; but for the present my purpose is to demonstrate that those who initiated the scheme of intervention, and who did so as a strategic move against Germany, and that alone, have every right to congratulate themselves on the success of their bold conception.

I am concerned only with the activities of the Murmansk force; but even this force, laughably small though it was, achieved sufficient to warrant its employment.

It is beyond doubt that Germany hoped to establish a base for her submarines at Murmansk. Had she succeeded in this, it is certain she would have taken an increased toll of our Atlantic shipping, which at that time included scores of transports conveying American troops to Europe. For the ocean route from Murmansk to the Atlantic was free of minefields, and the area to be patrolled by our anti-submarine craft would have been extended so enormously as to banish all hope of efficient counter-measures to cope with the new danger.

Had Germany been left to carry out her designs unimpeded, it may be assumed fairly that, by early autumn at latest, Murmansk would have been in her hands, and her submarines stealing down the Kola Inlet, with confident expectations of a clear and undisputed passage to their favourite hunting-grounds off the south-western shores of Ireland. Murmansk, however, did not fall into German hands. The Murmansk force had barred the way.

But the safeguarding of Murmansk was not the only piece of work for which the Murmansk force could claim its share of credit.

Russia's collapse in 1917 had enabled Germany to make a wholesale withdrawal of troops from that front. Beginning in September 1917, it continued without interruption until the end of May 1918. During these nine months 54 German infantry divisions were recalled from the east, and thrown into the scale against the sorely pressed Allies in western theatres. But the stream ceased abruptly with the first landing of the Allies at Murmansk. During June, July, and August no single unit was sent from east to west. For these three months the Murmansk force tied down the whole German army in Finland, and put a stop to the transfer to France of the probable equivalent of from three to four enemy divisions.

This figure is not based on conjecture. It is known that the German strength in Finland at that time was roughly 55,000. It is known, too, that withdrawals from the east during the three previous months totalled ten divisions, whilst eight were withdrawn in September and October, when Germany was forced to abandon her attempt on the North Russian ports and to throw in every available man to help stem the tide of Allied advances in the Balkans and France.

It can be calculated therefore with reasonable accuracy that our efforts in the Murman Area prevented some 40,000 reinforcements being sent by Germany to Macedonia and the Western front during the summer of 1918. Had these been despatched before September, they could have reached France in time to play their part in the culminating battles of October. As it was, their withdrawal was postponed until it was too late for them to exert any influence on the decisive struggle.

Not only, therefore, had the Murmansk force been instrumental in defeating German attempts to secure a footing on the North Russian seaboard, but it had succeeded in pinning down to Finland large numbers of German troops, who could otherwise have been employed against the Allies elsewhere, at a time when the war's final issue was still shrouded in uncertainty, and none could say how much or how little was needed to tip the scale of fate.

These were undeniable achievements, and, in face of them, the opinions of those who contend that the Murmansk enterprise was misguided and unforgivable can bear no possible weight.

A mere handful of Britishers and Allies, despatched to almost unknown Arctic wilds, had done more to assist in the overthrow of Germany than could have been accomplished by many times their number employed in any other theatre of the war.

In their success alone, the strategic policy of Allied intervention in Russian received ample vindication.

CHAPTER X

A PERIOD OF TRANSITION

In the last few chapters I have confined myself almost entirely to military considerations, paying chief regard to their influence on the campaign against Germany; and the story of our operations has now been told up to the time of the Armistice. As a record of the simultaneous doings of many small forces, it is necessarily somewhat involved. Thus, in order that it might be followed the more easily, I have avoided purposely, during its narration, all allusions to extraneous matters such as our relations with the Allied Powers associated with us, changes in command, and the gradual transition of my force from a weak detachment (devoid of nearly every requirement essential for the conduct of war) to a fairly efficient fighting machine.

I purpose therefore to retrace my steps, and deal with certain aspects of the general situation, as they unfolded themselves during the period of the operations already described.

I have told how I cabled to the War Office on August 25th, stating that I considered myself too weak to hold Petchenga as well as Murmansk; how the Admiralty insisted on its retention; and how, in consequence, a decision was reached to send me 5,000 additional British troops.

The cable mentioned was not, however, the first occasion on which I had described frankly both to the War Office and Poole the military situation on the Murmansk side, and its needs, as I saw them. For it had always appeared to me that nothing would be gained by failing to depict in its true colouring the problem confronting us. If my force were to be given a fair chance of accomplishing its work it should, in my opinion, be strengthened—and this I said. If, however, reinforcements were out of the question, I was perfectly ready to carry on with the troops at my disposal. There would still be a reasonable hope of success, and we should continue in any case to serve the useful purpose of pinning down the German forces in Finland.

But a few thousand extra men would make all the difference between hazy hope and well-grounded confidence. And, after all, why should I not have them, if it could be managed without detriment to the Western front? Were the reasons for withholding them good and sufficient, in view of what was at stake?

Replies to these questions were not the concern of England alone. The enterprise was one to which the Allied and Associated Powers as a whole had given their approval, together with a promise of co-operation; and its broad policy had been determined by the Supreme War Council. With the War Council therefore must rest the decision as to whether or not additional troops should be sent me, and, if sent, from what source they should be drawn.

From the very first I had been given to understand that I could not expect reinforcements in any strength from England. In our grim determination to avert defeat we had grudged nothing. All that our Empire could offer had been given without stint or reservation; and in every zone we were carrying already even more than our full share of the war burden, both by sea and land. The consequent drain on our resources had been stupendous, and by now our man-power reserve was almost completely exhausted. Italy was sending 1,200, and no more could be expected of her. Sorely-tried France, whilst others were dallying, had sent the battalion which had made possible the occupation of Archangel. She was also finding for me a company of " skieurs," and had even consented to replace entirely the personnel of the artillery group which had worked its way north from Rumania, and had lost much of its efficiency through sickness and hardship. We could hardly look to her for more.

But what of America? She had a million under arms and, when summer came, the number considered fit to take the field was already so large that it was impracticable to accommodate and feed in France the full monthly contingents she was prepared to furnish. Consequent on this, tens of thousands were being held up in concentration camps either in England or the States.

It was certain, therefore, that America was in a position to lend substantial aid, and that too with little, if any, appreciable loss of power to the Allies in the decisive theatre.

True, I had gathered from the outset that we could not rely on America taking her proportionate share in our enterprise. But after our initial successes at Archangel and Murmansk had paved the way to checkmating German endeavours in North Russia, and had made the reconstruction of the Eastern front something approaching a feasible project, it did not seem unreasonable to hope that, out of her plenitude, she would be prepared to furnish the relatively insignificant number of troops required to obviate any possibility of a setback, and to render practicable the accomplishment of a great strategic aim.

But however reasonable the hope, it was not to be fulfilled. Despite Allied pressure, the United States Government declined to provide more than the three infantry battalions and three engineer companies originally promised. Even these, although the policy of intervention had been agreed upon in early June, did not arrive at Archangel until September 4th—too late to enable Poole to profit by an almost heaven-sent opportunity, offered in August, of the Archangel force gaining touch with the pro-Ally Czecho-Russian army of Siberia.

On the Murmansk side no American troops were landed before the following April, when two railway companies were sent me, after many urgent requests by our own Government. Until then, the only American support available for me was an emergency landing-party of 100 marines from the U.S.S. *Olympia*, a small cruiser which had arrived in North Russian waters the preceding June, and was based on Murmansk.

This lack of effective co-operation on the part of the United States can, I think, be ascribed almost wholly to the attitude adopted by President Wilson, who, totally devoid of strategic insight, refused to be guided by those who had made war their lifelong study, and had been responsible during four tumultuous years for the conduct of a world-wide conflict.

Many American soldiers there must have been shrewd and longsighted enough to see what America herself stood to gain in the struggle against Germany upon which she was just entering, by ensuring success in Russia. But apparently their views were treated with scant consideration. One instance of this came within my personal experience. Towards the end of July I met at Murmansk many foreign representatives who had been forced to quit Russia as the result of Bolshevik hostility. Among them were French and American military attachés, with whom I was in close touch for several days. These spoke exceedingly strongly regarding the necessity for additional troops at Murmansk, basing their contention on knowledge of German and Finn preparations acquired by them in Central Russia.

The American attachés in particular were emphatic on this point, asserting that, if their Government had any conception of the true state of affairs, it would send at once (say) 20,000 troops, which would be a mere flea-bite from America's monthly contingent to France, but would make every difference to my chances of safeguarding Murmansk and Petchenga.

These officers, when passing through England,

A PERIOD OF TRANSITION 117

expressed their views to our own authorities exactly as they had expressed them to me, and our Government did its utmost to back them up. But it availed nothing. America declined to send additional troops to North Russia.

This was sad hearing; but sadder still was the fact that the American attachés, trained soldiers who had based their conclusions on first-hand information, were hauled over the coals severely by their own War Department for daring to give expression to an honest conviction, in the hope that it might prove of benefit to the Allied cause.

One thing was now abundantly clear. America was determined to avoid pulling her weight in Russia, and I, at least, could expect no assistance from her, as her sole contingent was to be allocated to Archangel. As already stated, meagre as it was compared with America's resources, it failed to reach that port until nearly three months after the promise of despatch. This in itself must have proved a grave disappointment to Poole; but there was more to come. For the American Government had practically limited the scope of action of its contingent to the defensive. It was to be permitted to undertake the guarding of stores, and the preservation of life and order in Archangel and its vicinity; but a strong hint was given that its employment in offensive operations against the Bolsheviks (the sole enemy opposed to Poole) would meet with little favour at Washington, and was therefore to be avoided, unless military exigencies demanded it imperatively. Poole no doubt needed guards, watchmen, police, and working parties, and presumably used the Americans chiefly as such. But I was glad he had made no suggestion of exchanging the 3,000–4,000 of them for my 1,000 Serbians, sturdy fighters all, on whose employment the Government of a stout-hearted little State had placed no restrictions.

It is illuminating to note how history repeated itself at Shanghai in the spring of 1927. I quote two extracts from articles by the special correspondent of *The Times* appearing in its issue of March 3rd, 1927. The italics are mine :

" In defending British life and property the British troops will not permit retreating Chinese troops to enter the defended area, and will resist attacks by Chinese forces. The French and Italians have adopted the same policy. The American marines will protect American lives and property within the Settlement, *but will not help to defend the Settlement boundary against Chinese regular forces.*"

" To-day the United States is disembarking marines who will be used to protect American life and property, but not to resist the Regular Chinese forces. *The United States, therefore, will take no share in the defences of the Settlement boundary, but, behind the British, French, and Italian forces, will guard its own nationals. This restricted rôle meets with little favour among American residents.*"

There was no resident American population at Murmansk, but I hope and believe that the half-hearted policy adopted by the United States Government in North Russia, and of which that of 1927 in China was a replica, found little to commend it amongst those Americans who were in any way conversant with North Russian affairs.

It may perhaps seem that I have gone out of my way to shed an unfavourable light upon the part played by America in the Allied attempt to reconstitute the Russian front. No Government, however, whether home or foreign, can expect to be immune from criticism ; and doubtless, if America had thrown herself heart and soul into the enterprise, a chorus of protest against their Administration would have been raised by scores of her less well-informed citizens, to which the " Hands off Russia " fraternity in England would have added its voice most gladly. Thus, as I am endeavouring to give an accurate account of the swaying fortunes of our venture, there seems no valid reason for withholding facts well known to me and many others both in Russia and elsewhere. For no word of mine is likely to be regarded as carrying sufficient weight to bruise American susceptibilities, and, more than this, I am convinced that, of those Americans who took a thoughtful interest in the Russian undertaking, eight out of every ten would agree that they had little cause for pride in the policy pursued by their Government.

But I have a further reason for laying stress on the unwillingness of the United States to take a more proportionate share in our operations.

It is an unfortunate fact, even more apparent in recent years than formerly, that in England there is always to be found a party searching for and welcoming every opportunity for belittling the efforts of their own Government and their own countrymen. The extremists of this party rise to further heights. They proclaim from the housetops their sympathy with and readiness to support any Government or faction whose aim it is to strike a blow at England's welfare; and the greater the nation's peril, the more vociferous becomes their condemnation of every action taken to ensure their country's safety. On such all argument is wasted.

But, setting aside extremists, there are many to whom the decrying of their own land, and all pertaining to it, is little more than an unpleasing habit, springing from weak-kneed imitation and thoughtless ignorance. These I am anxious to convince that the failure of Germany's designs in Russia was due solely to the steadfastness of purpose of the British Government, and to the promptitude with which we shouldered burdens essential to be borne, but shirked by the one Power most capable of supporting them.

For such American troops as came under my actual command at a later period I have nothing but praise.

My two companies of railway engineers were of first-class material, and proved invaluable. My only complaint is the difficulty I experienced in persuading them to conform with the orders of their Government. For their great desire was to push forward to the front, and many, I know, contrived to gain positions in the firing-line during several small encounters. This keenness, alas! could not meet with my official commendation, as my instructions prohibited me from employing them in active operations.

But if America failed the Allies in North Russia, the British Empire did not.

When the emergency had to be faced at the close of August, England rose to the occasion grandly. The weakening of the Home Defence Force by 5,000 men was a serious matter, and must have given rise to considerable perturbation. But the despatch of reinforcements was deemed essential—and therefore they must be found. If no other Power were able or willing to provide them, then England would do so, however great the sacrifice, and despite the fact that her Government must have felt that others were better placed to make the effort.

But even before this, Britain and her Dominions were striving their hardest to meet North Russian needs. Though the crisis in France might preclude the despatch of formed units, everything else possible was done.[1] Sledges and dogs, skis and polar equipment, were ordered in readiness for a winter campaign. Canada prepared a contingent of 150, all of them men experienced in Arctic conditions, and accustomed to handle sledges and dog-teams. The personnel of my medical, supply, and ordnance services was largely

---

[1] With the sole exception perhaps of the provision of aircraft. I received no machines until December, and those arriving then, besides being of an unsuitable type, were in sore need of repairs which it was impossible to carry out locally. Out of the six that reached me, only three could be rendered serviceable, in spite of the herculean efforts of the R.A.F. personnel.

increased; my headquarter staff augmented; and training instructors, telegraphists, and other specialists reached me in ever-growing numbers. These last included a few railway engineers; and how welcome these proved can be gathered from the following incident.

Towards the end of August, just at the time when a German move against the railway appeared imminent, and the possibility arose of having to withdraw my southern garrisons by rail, there was a recrudescence of unrest among the railway workers. The main cause, once again, was the discontent aroused by the inability of either their own authorities or myself to pay to the employees their overdue wages. This discontent, fanned by Bolshevik propaganda, had resulted already in a local strike on the Murmansk—Kandalaksha Section, and it seemed more likely than not that another general strike would be declared, affecting the whole length of line under my control. This might well prove the precursor of disaster, in the event of Germany pushing home her threatened attack; but it was hard to see what effective steps I could take.

If I endeavoured to force a resumption of work, it might very possibly lead to sabotage and a further extension of the strike. I must of course redouble my endeavours to obtain sufficient ready cash to satisfy immediate demands; but this would take time, even if my efforts chanced at last to meet with success—and something must be done at once.

Enquiries were made amongst the British troops at Murmansk, and these elicited the fact that there were five men who had been in railway employment in England, and who considered that, at a pinch, they could drive a Russian engine. This was good; but I wanted them at Kandalaksha or farther south, and the question was how to get them there. The idea of taking an engine from the local yard had to be dismissed, as this most certainly would entail the use of force, and thus precipitate an extension of the trouble.

By a lucky chance another means was found. Some weeks previously we had laid hands on an old Ford car, and thinking that this might prove of use for short journeys on the line, my engineers had fitted to it new axles and flanged wheels. The alterations had been carried out on the Russian repair ship *Xenia*, and the car had just emerged with moderate satisfaction from its preliminary trials. I decided to utilize the car, and Clarke, my A.D.C., volunteered as chauffeur.

It was a drive of 150 miles through the wildest type of country, and quite on the cards that the party would meet with opposition from the strikers or their Bolshevik sympathizers. Thus every precaution must be taken.

A plentiful supply of rations and ammunition was put on board ; and just before midnight Clarke started his engine, and the hybrid machine drew out, all too noisily, from the quay siding towards the main line. The strikers, however, had posted no pickets, and its departure was apparently unnoticed. This was lucky, as, in the gloom, manipulation of the many points was not a simple matter, and we passed some jumpy minutes before the main track was reached, and Clarke, waving a cheery farewell, slipped into top and, gathering pace rapidly, rounded the first bend and disappeared from view.

For the six of them, with their arms and equipment, ammunition and stores, packed tightly in the body of a small touring car, there was small chance of any comfort during the ten-hour run. In addition to this, there must have been many moments of tense anxiety. Between Kola and Kandalaksha (over 140 miles) there was only one detachment of Allied troops ; and thus Clarke and his companions must rely solely on their own wit and courage to get them through. Bridges might be found destroyed ; strikers might endeavour to hold them up at any of the score of stations ; or a breakdown might occur. Even the last of these (a far from impossible contingency) would have serious consequences both for them and me, since it would mean the failure of my amateur engine-drivers to reach Kandalaksha, and leave the party stranded on an unused railway track, amidst dense forests, and in all likelihood far removed from any human habitation.

It was therefore with profound relief that I received news of the safe arrival of the Ford and its occupants. Though the reception given them at certain stations had not been marked by friendly enthusiasm, no actual attempt had been made to bar their progress. It might, however, have been a different matter had the railwaymen known that each of the five passengers in that quaint-looking vehicle was a potential strike-breaker.

Three of the volunteer drivers went on to Kem, and I thus had the satisfaction of knowing that, come what might, it should at any rate prove possible to run a limited train service, in the event of the evacuation of my southern posts being forced upon me.

The strike on this occasion did not extend beyond Kandalaksha, and it so happened that I was able to settle it within a week, by borrowing from the French Ambassador at Archangel sufficient roubles to induce the railway employees to believe that it was worth their while to return to work.

But it had been a near thing ; and the whole incident serves to show why, of all the specialists sent out to me, the railway engineers were the most gladly received. Their number indeed was small, but even so, their advent lessened appreciably one of my main preoccupations.

. . . . .

During the period June to October I had been acting nominally under the orders of Poole as commander-in-chief in North Russia. But he had left me a free hand in the conduct of local operations, and I was empowered to communicate direct with the War Office, it being left to my discretion which of the more important of my cables home should be repeated to him.

This system had its drawbacks, especially as regards administrative affairs; but I had always seen eye to eye with Poole on all large questions, and knew that I was acting much as he would have acted had he been in direct control at Murmansk. Thus there had been no real cause for dissatisfaction with my position, and I had never felt called upon to set my views at variance with those enunciated by him, until it came to his request to the War Office, made early in October, that the whole of the 5,000 British reinforcements promised me as the result of my cable of August 25th should be diverted to Archangel. If this were sanctioned, the entire structure of my winter plans would crash; it would be impossible to provide an adequate garrison for Petchenga; and the number of British troops maintained down country must be so reduced as to endanger both Soroka and Kem.

The change, moreover, seemed to me strategically faulty; and as its approval would affect me so directly and so extensively, I could do nothing less than express my opinion upon it both to the War Office and Poole. This I did to each by cable, and also, later on, personally to Poole, as he passed through Murmansk on October 15th on his way to London, whither he was proceeding to explain his proposals, and report on the general situation.

It must be remembered that in October the German menace against Murmansk and Petchenga, though admittedly greatly reduced, was not altogether a thing of the past, and the future was entirely nebulous. There was certainly a hope of compelling the Central Powers to sue for peace at an early date, but of this none could be sure; and even should the hope materialize, there remained the question of our policy in Russia. Should we withdraw if and when peace was concluded with Germany and Austria? No decision on this point had been arrived at, and, so far as I could gather, there was every indication that we should be bound to remain until at any rate the summer of 1919. On this assumption, it was beyond doubt that I should have to face at least an eight-months' campaign against Bolshevik Russia, during which the Soviet Government would have ample opportunity for reorganizing its military forces, and might at any time launch a strong attack against me. In such an event, as I had already begun to grasp, I could place but scanty reliance on my Karelians, whilst the Finn Legion with its Red leanings, so far from opposing the Bolsheviks, would probably go over to them *en masse* at the first propitious moment. Added to this, I had failed to secure more than a handful of Russian recruits; and though mobilization was spoken of, the population was small, and most of the men of military age were required for work on the railway and at the various ports. Thus, before a Russian army of any material assistance to me could be built up, it would be necessary to extend the area from which recruits could be drawn. This would be totally impracticable, were I to be deprived of the whole of the promised reinforcements from home; and so far from opening up new recruiting-grounds, the evacuation of territory already occupied would probably be forced upon me, with all the political chaos such an evacuation would entail.

Assuming, therefore, that hostilities with the Bolsheviks would not be brought to a close with the defeat of Germany, it seemed to me that we should be courting disaster unless a portion of the British reinforcements were retained on the Murmansk side.

On the same assumption, the strategic advantage to be secured by locking up an extra 5,000 British troops at Archangel during seven winter months was far from evident. All hope of the Archangel force gaining touch with the Czecho-Slovaks, and thus fulfilling its main task, had vanished; and beyond encouraging the anti-Bolshevik movement, it could accomplish little until the Dwina was free of ice the following June. Even then it must be doubtful whether its action would result in gain commensurate with the risk involved, unless the anti-Red Siberian army had by that time recovered from its reverses and met with almost miraculous success.

The one outstanding reason for sending reliable troops to Archangel at once was of course that, after a few weeks, no further reinforcements could reach it by sea, and, as was the case with Murmansk, it might have to sustain a heavy Bolshevik attack.

But the number of Allied troops at Archangel was already greatly in excess of that at Murmansk, and the length of their lines of communication was infinitesimal compared with mine. Moreover, Archangel was a populous centre, and some 5,000 Russians had now been enlisted, whilst a mobilization order should result in the recruitment of at least 20,000 more.

A further stiffening of British troops was undoubtedly desirable, and if Poole's demand had been for the transfer to Archangel of half or even more of those due to me from England, I should have made no demur. But if all were taken, apart from the straits to which I should be reduced, Archangel itself would be liable to suffer. For it would be wholly impossible for me to keep open the overland route from Soroka to Onega (along the southern shore of the White Sea), by which alone reinforcements could reach Archangel during the winter months, and along which 2,000 Britishers were in fact despatched by me in midwinter at Ironside's urgent call.

With the object of making clear my attitude in this divergence of opinion between Poole and myself, I give an extract from a private letter written by me on October 12th, 1918, to General P. de B. Radcliffe, then Director of Military Operations at the War Office, with whom I maintained a regular correspondence which, though entirely unofficial, proved frequently of mutual benefit :

"At the moment I am naturally somewhat anxious as to what is going to happen to my reinforcements. Poole's wire home (repeated to me) came as a great surprise, as he had not said a word to me before, suggesting in any way that my Infantry Brigade and guns should be diverted to him; nor had he even asked me how I intended to employ my troops under the altered conditions.

"I shall of course be very disappointed if all the troops on whom I was relying are sent to Archangel; moreover, in my opinion, it would be wrong both strategically and administratively. Presuming there is a continuance of hostilities with the Bolsheviks, surely the probability of my advancing on Petrozavodsk, and thus threatening Zvanka and the Petrograd—Vologda railway would make them more unhappy than the shutting up for the winter at Archangel and its vicinity of an additional 5,000 troops. Then, too, it is much easier for me to cater for the needs of these extra men in winter, than it will be at ice-bound Archangel. I imagine, though, that Poole wants them for his spring operations, which he hopes to begin before the ice clears from the White Sea entrance.

"It will not be very pleasant for me if I lose such a large number of men; for I shall have to send *some* infantry to Petchenga in addition to the Serbian detachment, and I must also guard against raids at Alexandrovsk, Drovanoi, and Kola, besides keeping a small force at Murmansk. Also, in winter, I'm bound to use troops for guarding vulnerable spots on the railway, and thus it won't be possible for me to have any troops at Soroka, or any but a small British detachment with local troops at Kem. Again, the impression made on the inhabitants will be bad, as they were very nervous over the prospect of my withdrawing troops from the south, and overjoyed when they learnt that I was making arrangements for the possible accommodation of extra troops at the southern posts instead of reducing them.

"However, the final decision must rest with you people at home, and you may be quite sure that I shall take it smiling whatever it is."

It would seem that Poole did not succeed in convincing Whitehall that he had sufficient grounds for his request. On October 22nd I was instructed to despatch to Archangel one infantry battalion, one battery, and one machine-gun company; but the decision to allot the remainder of the reinforcements to Murmansk still held good.

Poole himself did not return to North Russia, and Ironside, who had been sent out a fortnight previously as his chief of staff, succeeded to the Archangel command.

Shortly afterwards Murmansk was made entirely independent of Archangel, both Ironside and myself acting under direct instructions from the War Office.

Undoubtedly this was a step in the right direction. Hitherto responsibility for operations in the Murman Area had rested entirely with myself, but administrative control had been, and was still, vested in general headquarters at Archangel. Such a system did not make for smooth working. Conditions on the two sides were utterly dissimilar, and those pertaining at Murmansk were a closed book to the Archangel staff.

The drawbacks inseparable from the arrangement, enhanced as they were by untrustworthy communications, had been made only too evident to me for many months past; but I had hesitated to represent them, as I wished to avoid any possibility of appearing averse from being subordinate to Poole. Beyond pointing out that it would be essential to confer on me certain of the powers of a commander-in-chief during the winter, when written matter could not get through to Archangel, I had made no attempt therefore to urge the separation of the two forces. But in October an accumulation of unfortunate instructions and decisions emanating from the administrative staff at Archangel led me to conclude that the handicap imposed on me by the existing scheme was not only needlessly irksome, but fraught also with danger.

As it was not easy for me to express my views officially, I decided to put the case before Radcliffe in one of my periodical letters, leaving him to decide whether any action was politic or expedient.

I wrote to him accordingly on October 31st as follows:

" One of the points I wanted to discuss at home [1] was the separation of this Command from Archangel. I feel most tremendously strongly about it, and I'm certain no one who knows me will entertain the idea that I want the separation from personal motives. It is simply that, to my mind, the present system is objectless and harmful, and it would be almost as bad—though not quite—were Archangel to be under Murmansk. I say 'not quite' because cable communication between here and England is much more rapid and reliable than between Archangel and England, and written correspondence can reach here during the whole year. This would enable the pith of important letters to be sent on by cable or W.T. if this place happened to be the G.H.Q. of the whole Expedition. But I don't want this, as I consider one man cannot run both shows successfully.

" During the past ten days I've had many instances of orders received from Archangel with which it is quite impossible to comply, and which would never have been sent if any of the conditions here were known at Archangel.

" This has been the case especially as regards medical matters. For instance, I was ordered to send a stationary hospital of 200 beds to Archangel, when all I've got in the whole place is one General Hospital. Then

[1] Just previously I had requested and obtained permission for a quick trip home, as the speediest way of settling many important points—especially the provision of money; but a sudden outbreak of disaffection at Murmansk had necessitated its postponement.

I was ordered to send all the French medical officers who were in the French Section of my General Hospital (which is chock full), leaving me with none here, and forcing me to withdraw French doctors from their proper French units down the line. When I pointed this out, I was told to comply, the words ' this is final ' being added ! Then too I get a wire saying they are evacuating to *me* at Murmansk 120 hospital cases. Most are ' sitting ' cases, it is true, but my own hospital is absolutely full, and I've no place whatever to put them into. Setting aside the fact that they ought of course to have been evacuated from Archangel direct home, it simply shows complete ignorance of my position here.

" Again, I was most anxious to get the Liverpool battalion down the line to Kem and Soroka. The railway was smashed at the time, and so I took the chance of sending them by sea, with three months' reserve of supplies. The ship had to go to Archangel *en route* to drop the howitzer battery for that side, but I let them know how keen I was to get the battalion to Kem as early as possible. Nevertheless they collared the battalion, and upset all my arrangements. I was already committed to Soroka, and am none too strong in the south. Now I have no prospect of reinforcing before three weeks, though there is a lot of sabotage, and the Bolsheviks are supposed to be organizing an advance against me. Added to this, by holding up the supplies on board the ship at Archangel, my southern garrisons only just escaped having to go on half-rations.

" A further instance. I lent 100 marines to *Elope*[1] when they started for Archangel, and was promised them back in a fortnight. That was three months ago, and though I've asked for them continually I have not got them yet. I am told now that I cannot have them till I send winter clothing for them to travel in—and yet they send me 120 hospital cases in an ordinary boat without their winter garments.

[1] Code name for Archangel Mission.

" There are dozens of other cases I could quote, many of them quite small in themselves, but all leading to delay with no compensating advantages, and sometimes to the feeling that due consideration is not being paid to this force—for we are all idiotically human. As a tiny example, out of the total number of ' immediate awards ' allotted to North Russia, I have been sub-allotted only one-sixth, though my force is two-thirds that of Archangel.

" Don't imagine that I'm grumbling because I individually happen to be under Archangel. I agitate solely because I'm convinced that the formation of two independent commands is the only solution for North Russia."

The letter from which the above extract is taken cannot have reached Radcliffe before November 3rd or 4th. On November 5th notification of my independence of Archangel was despatched. It was therefore fairly certain that the expediency of reconstituting the North Russian force as two separate commands had been recognized for some time previously by the General Staff at home.

. . . .

The autumn of 1918 thus saw two important innovations—the assumption of the Archangel command by Ironside, and the inauguration of a new régime abolishing the post of Commander-in-Chief, North Russian Expeditionary Force, and substituting in its stead that of two Commanders-in-Chief, with general headquarters at Archangel and Murmansk respectively.

Other outstanding changes also occurred at about this period.

Rear-Admiral Kemp returned to England, and was relieved by Rear-Admiral John Green, most cheery of companions, and always ready to lend a helping hand.

The local Soviet was abolished, and M. Yermoloff

arrived from Archangel to take over civil control as Deputy-Governor of the Murman Area.

My force was reorganized on a divisional basis, with Brigadier-Generals M. N. Turner and F. G. Marsh in respective command of its two infantry brigades (236th and 237th).

A Canadian company, under Lieutenant-Colonel Leckie, and a French " ski " company joined me—both likely to be of immense service during the coming months.

Sir Ernest Shackleton, together with half a dozen officers who had been associated with him in his Antarctic expeditions, arrived, and commenced to put in train the special preparations needed in connexion with my winter mobile columns. And Lieutenant-Colonel E. O. Lewin, the value of whose subsequent work it would be difficult to overrate, took over duties as my Chief of Staff.

The above form some indication of the great metamorphosis in North Russian affairs brought about during the months of October and November.

The sudden spurt in the growth of my force was, of course, due principally to the arrival from home of the reinforcements promised me at the end of August, when I was confronted with the threat of a German attack in such strength as to necessitate either my withdrawal from Petchenga or the strengthening of my command. As mentioned previously, I was called upon to send some of these additional troops to Archangel in October, and others did not arrive until the end of November, when the Great War had reached its end already. But at the commencement of December I had under my orders nearly 7,000 Britishers, over 3,000 Allies (French, Serbian, and Italian), and more than 4,000 Karelians, Finns, and Russians—a grand total of close on 15,000, of whom 10,000 were combatant troops.

Apart, therefore, from other changes of importance, the autumn months had seen the strength of the

ADMIRAL GREEN WITH THE AUTHOR.

Murmansk force almost doubled ; its staff brought to full requirements ; and its efficiency increased by the inclusion of detachments already trained for movement over snow and ice.

Doubtless, campaigning during an Arctic winter (should it be in store for us) would be fraught with difficulties ; but, with expert advice at my elbow, and other changes for the better born of this period of autumn transition, I felt I had good grounds for believing that we should not fail to overcome them successfully.

CHAPTER XI

AFTER THE ARMISTICE

As has been stressed already, Allied intervention in Russia was a strategic measure aimed wholly against the Central Powers. Clearly, therefore, it was deprived at once of its original purpose by the signing of the Armistice on November 11th.

It may thus be asked, with much show of reason, why our troops were not withdrawn straightway from Archangel and Murmansk, and Allied military operations in Russia brought to an immediate close.

The main reasons are twofold.

In the first place, the approach of winter had made the evacuation of Archangel impracticable before the following spring. In a few weeks, or perhaps days, the port would be ice-bound; and even had an order for withdrawal been issued at the very hour that hostilities terminated in France, no reliance could have been placed on its completion during the short remaining period when the White Sea would yet be open to navigation. And, as Archangel relied entirely upon Murmansk for the maintenance of her communications, and as no reinforcements could reach her during winter except via Murmansk, it was certain that, if Archangel were held, Murmansk must be held also.

But there was a second consideration which, as touching our moral obligations, was weightier still.

It was unthinkable that we should desert and leave to their fate the many loyal Russians who had risked all by supporting the Allies.

For, be it remembered, these Russians were patriots, and not seekers after personal gain; and they had rejoined the Allied cause in order to assist in countering German aggression and to maintain inviolate their country's soil. For them the honour of their land was a thing held dear.

For three years of unsurpassed trial Russia had fought as our Ally; and her terrible sacrifices in the autumn of 1914 had gone far to save France—and with France, England and our Empire.

But she had given an undertaking to conclude no separate peace, and her solemn pledge had been set at naught by a band of foreign adventurers whose usurpation of power, far from being in accord with the people's will, had been the fruit of German intrigue, plucked the more easily by reason of the privations of a stricken army and a nation's war-weary apathy. Russia's honour had thus been dragged through the mire; but it might yet be cleansed—and this was the aim of those Russians who once again ranged themselves beside their one-time Allies.

That they were actuated also by an additional motive cannot be denied. To them, as to practically every Russian endowed with reasoning power, the Bolshevik rule was abhorrent, and its continuance presaged for their country misery and ruin unspeakable. Was it therefore strange that they should long to see its overthrow, and that they should embrace the chance, offered by our break with Moscow, of swelling the number of those who were demonstrating already to the world that they refused to recognize as their rulers Lenin and his alien associates?

As patriots they were ready to fight to save Russia from the enemy without. Equally as patriots they would fight to cast from power those who sought to destroy her from within.

The corollary was natural. They had dared to oppose Russia's dictators, and were thus branded as rebels, with probable torture and certain death in store for them, should they fall into Bolshevik hands. And this fate assuredly awaited them early, if they were deprived at once of Allied backing. For, though the anti-Bolshevik movement was making promising headway at that time both east and south, its growth was necessarily restricted in the thinly populated confines of the far north. Here the strength of the loyalist force could increase but slowly, and only as fresh territory came under its influence. In its isolation, it formed at present an easy prey for the blood-lusting wolves of Moscow.

Thus, should we now leave unaided those who had sided with us, their outlook would be hopeless. There was, moreover, no possibility of removing to a place of safety all such as might wish to quit the country; since the White Sea entrance would be blocked by ice long before the necessary shipping could be made available.

If, therefore, the Allies were to escape the accusation of deserting those who had stood by them in an hour of urgent need, it was incumbent on them to continue their support temporarily, and thus offer the northern loyalists a reasonable prospect of so strengthening their position that they should be able ultimately to hold their own, whilst the anti-Soviet armies elsewhere staged the main efforts directed against the authors of Russia's disruption.

The Allies had contracted a debt of honour; and the debt must be paid, however great the inconveniences, and however loud the protests of those who might hold of small account their country's unwritten bond.

Two objections to an immediate evacuation of Russia's northern ports have been disclosed—one material, the other moral—and each in itself of sufficient weight to turn the scale against a policy of instant withdrawal. But other circumstances combined to militate also against any decision to recall our troops.

We could have issued no withdrawal order without the consent of every interested Power; and the same can be said of France, Italy, Japan, Serbia, and America.

It was a joint enterprise, and the steps to be taken in the changed conditions resultant on the Armistice must be settled in conclave by all the partners in the undertaking.

Of conclaves, indeed, during that month of November there were many; but the problems confronting these, as the outcome of Germany's defeat, were so overwhelming in their immensity as to cause the question of immediate action in Russia to dwindle into comparative insignificance.

It was too much to expect the world's statesmen to busy themselves with an unpopular side-issue, at a time when their thoughts were centred on ensuring that the revised maps of Europe, Asia, and Africa should so be coloured as to meet the aspirations of their respective peoples.

Small wonder then that the days immediately subsequent to the Armistice saw no conclusion reached as regards the attitude towards Russia to be adopted by the Allies in face of altered circumstances. And, lacking such a conclusion, there could be no withdrawal, even had an Arctic winter and the obligations of honour permitted it.

There may be those who hold that Russian affairs should have received more urgent attention at this period, however great the press of other matters; and their criticism would, in some degree, be justified. It could not, however, be levelled against our own Government, which advanced constantly (both to the Supreme War Council and afterwards to the Peace Conference) the need for a settled policy in respect of the whole question of Allied intervention.

Having thus explained why, after Germany's collapse, Allied troops were not recalled at once from Russia, I, in my turn, would ask a question.

Even if all the reasons already given against withdrawal are set aside completely, had the Allies no justification for continuing their campaign against the Bolsheviks?

In considering the reply to this question, it must be recollected firstly that the Bolsheviks, and not ourselves, were the original aggressors.

Their Government had not only acquiesced in the despatch of an Allied force to North Russia, but had even asked for Allied assistance at Murmansk. As showing this, General Poole states explicitly in his first despatch that " our troops were landed at Murmansk to defend the port, *on the invitation of the Soviet Government of Moscow* "; and he adds that Natzaremus, a Soviet Commissioner, was sent to him with the object of arranging for a common defence of the town.

It is therefore preposterous to assert that ours was an invading force, or that we had any wish to make war on Bolshevik Russia. It was only later—and presumably as the outcome of German pressure—that Lenin shifted his ground and, after ordering the local authorities at Murmansk to eject us, proceeded to hurry Red troops northwards to aid in enforcing his order. The first hostile move was made therefore by the Moscow Soviet, on which must rest responsibility for the situation it created. The move, too, was traitorous. For no intimation was sent to any one of the Allied Governments of an intention to break off former relations, which, officially at least, had so far been friendly. We were to be attacked at Murmansk without warning, after our help had been solicited to safeguard the port. That we were able to forestall the move cannot alter the indisputable fact that the Bolsheviks had planned an act of war against us. Surely therefore three Great Powers cannot be censured for picking up the gauntlet thus flung at their feet or, having picked it up, for selecting their own time to terminate the quarrel.

Again—and here I tread, I know, on controversial ground—is it beyond the bounds of reason to urge that some measure of justification can be claimed for helping those who strove to establish an honest and stable Government in place of a régime such as Russian Bolshevism ?

That Russia's self-elected rulers followed then, and have followed ever since, methods so brutal and barbaric as to rob them of any iota of claim to represent a civilized Government, must be apparent to all save the wilfully blind.

The proof indeed is overpowering. The bloody butchery of the Czar and his family ; the wanton murder of our own naval attaché ; the wholesale slaughtering of thousands upon thousands of the upper and middle classes—priests and women included —without trial, and on concocted charges, illustrate but incompletely the savagery of Lenin and his satellites. But as facts they are incontestable, and in themselves sufficient to place beyond the pale of civilization those who held then, and still hold, their despotic sway over Russia's luckless millions. There is no call for the added testimony of myself, or of those who were with me in the Murman Area for sixteen months ; though even in that remote corner, frequent and indisputable evidence of Bolshevik ruthlessness and inhumanity came within our knowledge.

But had the Soviet Government confined itself to spreading misery and ruin throughout its own country, it might perhaps have been urged that this was solely Russia's affair, and could concern no outside Government. Even in the early days of 1918, however, Moscow had proclaimed her intention of working unremittingly to sow the seeds of communism in every foreign land ; and the harvest for which she tilled and sowed was universal revolution. Can it be held for one moment that it was not the concern of France, Italy, England, and indeed of every nation of good repute, to stay the hands of those who would scatter broadcast the seeds of such a crop ?

My arguments and contentions, unless they are to be classed as inaccurate and weightless, sum up therefore as follows :

(i) Withdrawal from North Russia immediately after the Armistice was impossible, owing to climatic conditions.

(ii) It was inconceivable, in view of the fate that must have awaited them, that we should desert the loyal Russians who had sided with us.

(iii) Great Britain could not have recalled her troops at once in any case, as the undertaking was an Allied one; and, despite her efforts to obtain a decision as regards the policy to be pursued in Russia, it was not till the following March that evacuation was agreed to by all the interested Powers.

(iv) The prosecution of the campaign against the Bolsheviks can be said to receive a further meed of justification in that :

(*a*) The Bolsheviks themselves were responsible for the initiation of hostilities.

(*b*) Russia's leaders had not been chosen by the people. Their rule was hated, and they owed their retention of power solely to the terror inspired by systematic bloodshed and massacre. As history can relate, semi-civilized States have before this been brought to account by some civilized neighbour for excesses less repellent than those practised by the Bolshevik Government.

(*c*) This Government, moreover, had asserted openly that it purposed the encouragement of world-wide revolution and anarchy.

In face of the above, it would seem almost more within reason to ask why the Allies made no greater effort to stamp out Bolshevism, and thus avert the danger threatening them and civilization at large, rather than why the operations against the Soviet were not brought to a close.

The explanation, if somewhat humiliating, is simple, and can be applied to all Allied Governments.

Much as they might desire to make an end of Bolshevism, it was obvious that this would call for further considerable sacrifices—and these they were not prepared to face in the circumstances ruling in 1918–19. Any attempt might well alienate the sympathies of political friends, and would certainly arouse to fever pitch the animosity of opponents. They had had their fill of war; coffers were empty; and perhaps in time Russia herself might save the situation for them. From its very nature, too, the campaign could arouse but little enthusiasm, and would be likely to provide socialist malcontents with an added pretext for fomenting insubordination and disaffection amongst the armed forces.

The objections to a concerted and determined effort to overthrow the Bolshevik régime were, of a certainty, many and great. But would they, I wonder, have been considered insuperable if, in 1918–19, the book of the future had been open for Governments to read? In the struggle, lives would have been lost and money poured out; but it is morally certain that the sum of all casualties would have totalled but a fraction of the toll of life exacted by Bolshevik Russia during the past nine years; whilst the monetary cost would have been almost paltry compared with the hundreds of millions lost during the same period, owing to labour conflicts and dislocated trade, attributable solely to communist activities.

Judging, moreover, from what I saw and gathered, there is reason to believe that the effort demanded would have proved less excessive and less prolonged than is assumed generally. Lenin's government was supported wholeheartedly by but a few hundreds; the peasants had commenced to realize already that the new tyranny surpassed that of the Czars in its brutality and injustice; and the Red army, bolstered up by foreign mercenaries such as Letts and Chinese, was ill-led, undisciplined, badly equipped, and devoid of enthusiasm.

The loyalist forces were, it is true, far from efficient. But they formed an immense nucleus of fighting material, and were capable in themselves of bearing the main brunt of the campaign, if properly equipped, and given a stiffening of disciplined units. Their eventual failure, I am convinced, was due largely to the adverse moral effect produced on all ranks by the withdrawal of Allied support, and to the encouragement which the recall of our troops lent to the Red Commanders.

The precise strength of Allied backing likely to have been required in 1918 to ensure an early and decisive issue can be of course a matter of conjecture only. I can go no farther than to say that I have debated the point with soldiers at least as well qualified as most to form an estimate, and that the conclusion we reached was that an army of 100,000, provided there were joint naval action in the Baltic and Black Sea, would have sufficed, within six months or less, to secure the hurried abdication of Lenin and his Government.

At the time, a price such as this seemed too high to pay. But can we hold honestly the same opinion now, when we review the happenings of the last few years? Throughout them, the internal affairs of nearly every nation have been marked by constant turmoil and strife, whose initiation and furtherance can be traced unmistakably to Moscow. The poisonous tentacles of communism, reaching out across land and sea, have fastened their grip on five continents; and always and everywhere, insurrection and riot, strikes and disorders, disloyalty and atheism, are blessed and nurtured by Russia's avowed apostles of civil war and disruption.

Bolshevism, save to ill-balanced minds, stands revealed as the most malign of all influences at work in the present-day world. Of its conversion to a more sane and humanitarian creed there seems, unhappily, but little hope; and its overthrow by armed intervention from without cannot now be looked for. Is there then no cause for regret that the opportunity for crushing it, once and for all, should not have been grasped, at a time when its store of resources was small, its tenure insecure, and the co-operation of strong loyalist forces assured ?

To me at Murmansk, the considerations set forth above were of little more than academic interest. I was well aware that winter conditions would prohibit a withdrawal from Archangel; and if Allied troops were still to remain there, as remain they must, the retention of our hold on Murmansk was an obvious military necessity. I was certain therefore that my force would not be recalled as yet, whatever final decision the Allies might reach. Whether, when arrived at, it should prove to be in favour of evacuation as soon as circumstances permitted, or of intervention on a far larger scale, it could not alter my position for the time being to any material degree. A state of war with the Bolsheviks still existed, and seemingly must continue to exist, so long as we remained in Russian territory. Up to the present, such action as I had taken against them had been solely with a view to preventing them from hampering my operations against von der Goltz; now, unless our own safety were endangered, I should fight them only in order to assist the loyalists in their endeavour to establish themselves more firmly in the Murman Area: but fight them I must, if occasion demanded, just as I had fought them previously. The one great change that mattered was the passing of the German threat, and with it the fear of any attack in strength from the west.

Although, therefore, owing to the havering of the Allies, it was some months before I received any definite instructions, my course of action was sufficiently clear. I must consider the interests of the anti-Soviet movement in my own area as my chief concern, and do my best to enable it to stand alone as speedily as possible.

This, however, was hardly likely to prove a simple matter. A prime necessity was the raising of a Russian army capable of putting up a really effective resistance to the Bolsheviks; and the first thing was to get the men. So far, with the exception of the Karelians, the number volunteering for service had not exceeded 400, and these had been enrolled in the Slavo-British Legion. It was a poor response to my call, but one that could occasion no surprise under existing conditions. For throughout the whole occupied area there were but few able-bodied men of Russian birth who were not employed in one or other of the various local services, and thus debarred from voluntary enlistment; whilst, in addition, the close proximity of the Bolshevik forces, and the activities of their agents, did not tend to encourage recruitment at such centres as Kem and Soroka.

At Murmansk there was certainly an unemployed population of considerable size; but it consisted mainly of Koreans, Chinese, and other foreign riff-raff, always ready to join in acts of lawlessness, and causing constant trouble, but unrecruitable for any Allied or Russian unit.

There was, to my mind, only one hope of creating a Russian fighting force at all proportionate to the numbers actually available for military service; and this was the issue of an order for general mobilization. Yermoloff, the newly appointed Deputy-Governor, was in full agreement with me; so recruitment for my Slavo-British Legion was closed, and after some delay, caused by the need for referring the question to the Provisional Government of the Northern Province at Archangel, mobilization was put in force.[1] At the start, though registration was universal, mobilization was enforced on a limited scale only; and this was a wise decision, in view of the shortage of officers.

[1] A Provisional Government had been formed at Archangel, with jurisdiction over what was called the " Northern Province," which was to include the old Archangel Province, and such additional territory as might be occupied by the Allied and loyalist forces. At its head was a Governor-General (afterwards General de Millar), and under him M. Yermoloff administered the Murman Area as Deputy-Governor.

AFTER THE ARMISTICE

On the whole the scheme worked smoothly and well. As was to be expected, it revealed a superfluity of railway employees, consequent on the running of a much-restricted service; and most of these would have preferred remaining in comfortable half-time billets to joining up as recruits. But, speaking broadly, it was far less unpopular than most of us anticipated.

Yermoloff expressed himself as confident that complete mobilization would produce, from the area I occupied already, a force of not less than 5,000. This I regarded as a sanguine expectation; but, even were it to be fulfilled, a force of such strength, after making the large deductions necessary for administrative services and the guarding of communications, could not be relied upon to hold its own unaided.

I foresaw therefore that there was every likelihood of my being compelled to open up fresh recruiting-ground; and this could be done only by driving southward the Red troops now opposed to me.

As mobilization progressed, my conclusion was strengthened; for the evidence of each succeeding week pointed with increasing certainty to the total of enlistments falling well short of the number hoped for. Actually, the area between Murmansk and Soroka yielded about 3,500 recruits. To these might have been added the 400 of the Slavo-British Legion; but, with curious perversity, the men opposed stubbornly any idea of transfer, asserting that they preferred to serve under British officers.

A southerly advance was thus indicated, as the sole means of swelling the ranks of the slow-growing Russian army. It would serve also to render Soroka more secure, and help to annul the Red influence at present pervading it—matters of great importance, since Soroka must be the starting-point of any reinforcements proceeding by route-march to Archangel. But a commencement could not be made at once. New dispositions must first be completed, and these included the withdrawal of a portion of the Petchenga garrison (the strength of which could now be reduced with safety) and a redistribution of troops along the railway to meet winter requirements. Arctic equipment, too, must be issued; sledge transport provided; and the men of my newly formed mobile columns trained in the use of skis.

But I had other cares beyond the certainty of a renewal of hostilities against the Bolsheviks.

Large numbers of Finnish White Guards remained concentrated near the eastern border of Finland, and strong parties had once again entered portions of Russian Karelia. Against these I had no intention of undertaking serious operations; but I learnt that they were bent on revenge on my Karelians and Finn Legion, and were likely to attempt raids on undefended villages. Thus they needed careful watching.

I was also under the continued necessity of guarding against insurrection and riot within the limits of occupation. There existed still a strong undercurrent of Bolshevism, evidenced by agitations and strikes, and by persistent efforts to create trouble between the Allies and the local population. This culminated at times in demonstrations of active hostility, such as the destruction of railway-bridges and attempts to derail trains. Special steps must be taken to prevent a recurrence of these during the winter, when the difficulties of bridge-repairing would be accentuated, and there would be no hope of maintaining communication with the south by sea. Nearly every case of disturbance occurring hitherto had been traceable to the work of trained propagandists sent from Moscow, many of whom had been smuggled in amongst batches of former Russian prisoners of war returning to their homes. It was my original proposal to prohibit the return of all such war prisoners; but Yermoloff did not consider himself justified in agreeing to this, in view of the demand for recruits for the young Russian army. Anti-Allied propaganda therefore had every chance of flourishing amidst an underpaid, poverty-stricken, and ignorant population, with its underlying stratum of foreign ruffianism. It was the more dangerous, too, by reason of the changing attitude of my Finn Legion, the men of which had been evicted from Finland for Red activities, and were now showing ever-increasing signs of sympathy with their brother-Reds of Russia. Time, therefore, did not promise to hang heavy on my hands, even though I need give no further thought to von der Goltz and his men.

In the last few pages I have made more than one passing reference to M. Yermoloff; but I have said no word as yet of the changed relations between the local government and myself, brought about by his assumption of the office of Deputy-Governor.

When I learnt first in October that his early appointment was to be expected, I realized at once that here was a new factor likely to exercise a strong influence for good or ill.

The Murmansk Council, which had been a party to Poole's original Agreement of July 7th, and with which I had conducted all my negotiations up to the present, would be abolished, and my future dealings would be with the new Governor. Would the change prove beneficial or the reverse?

Though the members of the Council had evinced frequent signs of weakness and vacillation, and had been fearful of approving any steps in connection with civil control likely to produce unpopular results, I had contrived to reach a workable understanding with them.

Discovering, after a short experience, that it was useless to approach them as mentors, I had adopted the tactics of putting my plans into operation first, and consulting them afterwards. This appeared to suit them; for they could feel fairly safe, whatever the issue. Should all go well, they would acquire credit; and should a hitch occur, they could give out that I had forced their hands.

The outcome had been a gradual transference of

civil control from them to me; and when it was made known in October that the Council was to be replaced by a Deputy-Governor, its members ceased to take further interest in their duties. Thus, for a month or more prior to the arrival of M. Yermoloff early in November, I had been acting, to all intents and purposes, in the dual capacity of Governor and Commander-in-Chief.

It was not an ideal arrangement; but it served at least to keep timorous lethargy in the background, and to set going many schemes of improvement which, had the decision rested with the Council, would never have been initiated. It admitted, too, of an outward semblance of harmony and co-operation between the civil authorities and myself.

But, in all probability, a newly appointed Governor would see things in a light very different from that of the late Council. If he were worth his salt, he would wish to shoulder the whole responsibility of his office, and would not be content to see many of his functions usurped by a military commander. He would have constructive ideas of his own, and desire to carry them out in his own way. In short, instead of allowing himself to be led, he would, unless a weakling, be likely to resent any interference with matters relating to his own sphere of work.

Heaven knows, I wanted no weakling. Necessity, not choice, had driven me to play a predominating part in civil affairs, and I would hand over control of them more than gladly to any Russian Administrator—if he were the right man.

But would the new Governor show himself "the right man"? If he were courageous, sound, and businesslike, and ready to support me as, in such circumstances, I was prepared to support him, his appointment should prove a god-send. If, on the other hand, he were either a timorous nonentity or a bureaucratic obstructionist, it would be better by far that existing conditions should remain unaltered.

SOME BRITISH AND FOREIGN OFFICERS.

On balcony from left to right: Admiral McCully (United States Navy), Admiral Green, General Maynard, M. Yermoloff (Deputy-Governor) and Colonel Sifola (Commanding Italian Expeditionary Force).

It was therefore with feelings deeper than those of mere curiosity that I awaited his advent.

It had been intended that he should assume duty in mid-October, but he had declined—and rightly so, in my judgment—to take over his appointment unless provided with funds wherewith to pay a portion of the wages due to Government employees. He had asked for 5,000,000 roubles, but, as this sum could not be provided, had agreed eventually to come with 1,000,000 only, though the amount actually owing to workmen was twenty times as large.

He arrived on November 5th, and on the following day I had my first interview with him.

It is not easy to describe my early impressions of Yermoloff, but I remember well that they were not over-favourable.

Short and sallow-faced, with sandy-brown hair and indifferent features, appearances were all against him. His manner, too, was neither impressive nor cordial. Not once did he smile; not once did he show the tiniest trace of enthusiasm. In his seeming sullenness, I likened him to some pale-faced city clerk, ordered suddenly, and much against his will, to clear a rat-infested barn.

A landowner in a small way, he came from Novgorod, and had held minor offices under the old régime. And he looked just such an one, and nothing more. Of indications of fitness for the difficult and danger-strewn task he was about to take up, there were none.

All of which serves to show how far astray one may be led by first impressions.

Were I now to be asked my opinion of Yermoloff, I should say unhesitatingly that if ever man possessed a lion's heart, it was he. Duty and love of Russia were his gods. Unassuming, he paid no court to popularity, and shunned the display usually dear to Russian hearts. Responsibility he never shirked, and though his rule was stern, as it had need to be, none could question its justice. Honest, straightforward, and utterly self-effacing, he worked unfalteringly for his country's good, without a thought for personal advancement or his own well-being.

Yet, at that initial meeting, I had little hope that " the right man " had come to me !

I can account for my faulty judgment only by ascribing it to lack of imagination on my part. I ought to have pictured myself in his place. A shy man, reserved and acutely sensitive, he stood amongst complete strangers, not one of whom was of his own race. Like every other Russian situated as he was, he had lost all his worldly goods, and his apparel bore an unflattering resemblance to that of an out-of-work farm hand. He knew no word of any language but his own ; thus my smattering of French was useless, and every sentence we uttered needed interpretation—a type of conversation not conducive to easy freedom. Untravelled Russians too can seldom bring themselves to take a foreigner on trust ; and Yermoloff, I believe, had never quitted his own land. It was also quite possible that reports received by him from late officials were not unstinting in our praise. Added to all, he was tackling a thankless task, the successful outcome of which depended primarily on a sufficiency of ready cash. And of this he had but the smallest fraction of what was needed.

Had I been thus imaginative, I might have gauged earlier the sterling value of the true man. But, fortunately, it was not long before I discovered the need for revising my original estimate. As our acquaintance ripened, each day showed me more clearly that I was dealing with one whose ability was beyond discussion, and on whom I could rely confidently to work for our common end. His mask of moroseness was put aside, revealing him with a sense of quiet humour, strangely attractive, and especially welcome when trouble was upon us and our outlook dark. From the date of his appointment to the end of our operations, we travelled our stony road together without discord, he lending me his willing assistance throughout.

The debt I owe him is immense, but can, alas! never be repaid. Poor Yermoloff! Great-hearted patriot and loyal friend, he has passed long since to the Great Beyond.

When we evacuated Murmansk, he was given the opportunity of accompanying us, but refused to leave Russia.

The rest of his story I learnt from one well placed to hear it, whose word I cannot doubt.

As is widely known, the opposition to the Bolsheviks put up by the loyal forces crumbled soon after our departure. The triumphant Reds pushed north, and regained possession of Murmansk, their entry being accompanied by their wonted excesses. Yermoloff, not deigning to flee, was captured, put into chains, and forced to work as a coolie on the quay. To escape the fate he knew to be inevitable, he flung himself into the water, shackled as he was, hoping thus to meet his end. But he was dragged out, beaten almost to death, and afterwards despatched inland, there to undergo a mock trial. He was sentenced to death and shot.

Having chosen his path, he had followed it fearlessly to its last and fatal turn.

CHAPTER XII

PREPARING FOR WINTER OPERATIONS

I HAVE told how M. Yermoloff agreed, under pressure, to accept the Deputy-Governorship of the Murman Area with a sum of 1,000,000 roubles only at his disposal, although his requirements to meet wage-bills alone amounted to 20,000,000. Both he and I knew only too well that it would be impossible to put an end to labour unrest, or for him to carry out necessary administrative changes, unless additional money were forthcoming. He, for his part, did his best to obtain a further grant from Archangel, whilst I continued my efforts to induce the Treasury to supply me with ready cash. Yermoloff met with scanty success; I with none.

In the meantime, no repairs were being carried out in the railway workshops, as the men refused to work without pay. In consequence of this, breakdowns and accidents [1] were of almost daily occurrence; and the number of engines fit to run became so reduced as to prove insufficient for the service essential for military needs. Discontent, too, amongst the railwaymen seemed to be reaching its culminating-point; for attempts to blow up trains and destroy bridges became more and more frequent.

The full story of our monetary troubles is too long to tell, and I have devoted to them already a portion of Chapter VI. But a few salient points must be given now, if only to make it clear why I felt compelled to

[1] As an example, an accident, due to engine defects, occurred to a train conveying two companies of the 11th Sussex Regiment from Murmansk to Kandalaksha. It resulted in twenty casualties, several men being killed.

PREPARING FOR WINTER OPERATIONS

leave my command and return to England at a somewhat critical juncture.

By August the necessity of making provision for money payments in North Russia had been grasped by the Treasury. As there was in the country no cash, and an exceedingly limited supply of rouble notes, the choice lay between providing British notes and launching a special new currency. The latter alternative was selected. But an argument commenced as to whether the new notes should bear a guarantee, and weeks passed into months without any tangible result being achieved.

On August 17th the War Office suggested that British currency notes should be sent me, to tide over the time until the new currency were available. I jumped at this, and asked for £150,000. Treasury intervention, however, brought this proposal to nothing.

In November the crisis became so acute that I cabled home on the 9th requesting that £150,000 should be sent out by fast destroyer, but was put off with promises of an immediate circulation of the new currency. These did not materialize, so I sent a further message asking for the despatch of the £150,000 at once. This produced some effect, and I was informed by cable that H.M.S. *Dublin* was leaving England with the sum asked for.

Here indeed was cause for jubilation. To all appearance we were out of the wood at last, and we shouted accordingly.

But our shouts, alas! proved premature. The wood with its thorny undergrowth encompassed us still.

The first cable was followed a few hours later by a second, emanating from the Treasury. In it I was told that on no account whatever was any issue of British notes to be made without sanction. It also gave me to understand that my demand was regarded as ridiculous.

The situation as it then existed is described frankly

in two private letters written by me on November 16th and 17th to General Radcliffe at the War Office. The first was despatched just prior to receipt of the news of *Dublin's* departure, the second (as is very evident) shortly after reading the Treasury cable of prohibition and admonishment. From these I give the following extracts, from which my feelings at the time can be gauged with fair accuracy :

"*November 16th*, 1918.

" As you know, I'm not and never have been an alarmist. But I should be absolutely wrong not to tell you quite clearly that the political situation here is exceedingly serious. This is owing solely to the failure to supply me with money and an adequate ration for the civilian population.

" Months and months ago I pointed out that it would be necessary to give some sort of guarantee for the rouble notes which we were going to have printed in England, but no notice was taken of my opinion. Later it was found essential to give such a guarantee, and endless delay followed.

" All this time I was struggling on, trying to make two or three million roubles answer the purpose of the twenty million required.

" We were under treaty obligation to supply money, yet I could do nothing. Serious discontent arose, culminating in more than one far-reaching strike. If I hadn't shown an absolutely firm front then, it is probable that our operations here would have had to come to a close.

" Also, I had promises from home that the new notes would arrive from England before the end of August, and I told the workmen in consequence that by the beginning of September their own Government would be in a position to pay them at least a portion of their back wages. They were commencing to mistrust our promises then ; but week after week and month after month have passed with our promises still unfulfilled,

PREPARING FOR WINTER OPERATIONS 155

and the workmen have long ago reached the end of their tether of patience. The word of a Britisher fairly stinks in their nostrils—and I don't wonder at it.

" It is hardly to be believed, but we actually cannot pay for material which we have had to demand for buildings and other purposes. And we are the richest nation in the world."

"*November 17th,* 1918.

" It really is the limit. Yesterday I got the cable about the £150,000 coming out in a destroyer, but it was followed immediately by another cable saying that I was on no account to use it, and putting me under a long catechism on behalf of the Treasury.

" I replied as fully as I could in a lengthy cable, and I don't mind admitting that I was boiling over with indignation the whole time. Apparently the Treasury think (*a*) that I'm a damned fool, (*b*) that it doesn't matter how many lives are needlessly risked, or how far the success of the whole show here is endangered, so long as they can save a few miserable thousand pounds. By heavens, it's enough to make a practical man on the spot weep to hear of £150,000 described as an excessive figure. I wish to God I could put a few of the Treasury pundits 400 miles down my railway for a week or so to see how they would like it, during the present state of the feeling against us."

On November 22nd *Dublin* arrived, carrying, in addition to the £150,000 which I could not touch without sanction, the first consignment of the special new issue of Russian currency notes, which were to be forwarded to Archangel by icebreaker. These latter were found to be engraved with the Russian Royal coat-of-arms, and N. II.—and they were dated 1918 ! Accordingly, to the best of my belief, none were ever put into circulation.

On the very day of *Dublin's* arrival the War Office did, as a matter of fact, authorize me to expend £25,000 " if the situation became extremely critical," adding that 12,000,000 roubles would be available from Archangel shortly.

From this it was evident that even the War Office, which had stood by me so well, did not really grasp how serious the situation was, and had been for some time. Also I had grown very sceptical regarding the fulfilment of promises of money from Archangel : and if the 12,000,000 roubles were to come from the stock of new notes bearing the coat-of-arms of Nicholas II, and dated 1918, I doubted whether the workers of Murmansk would hear the crinkle of a single one of them. I decided therefore on a hasty run to England, obtained the necessary permission, and was taken home by *Dublin* on her return journey.

Shackleton and Steele accompanied me, as there were matters connected with winter gear calling for the former's attention in London, and I had need of a staff officer to assist me in the adjustment of a large number of administrative questions.

At Murmansk, autumn had yielded place already to winter. Not till shortly before midday did the sun commence his lazy climb above the horizon, sinking again within a few hours behind the encircling hill-tops, as if exhausted with his effort ; the thermometer had fallen more than once to well below zero ; tundra and forest alike had assumed their mantle of white ; and our bell-decked sledge-horses battled their way to the quayside on November 24th through a scurry of driving snow.

Temptation to enlarge on that trip to England grips my pen, but space forbids, and I must bring myself to limit rigorously the setting down of such matters as are extraneous to my story. As regards the voyage itself, suffice to say that all three of us felt exactly as if we had been schoolboys starting home for the holidays—and, I believe, behaved as such ; that the goodwill and hospitality of *Dublin's* officers could not have been excelled ; that the dreary twilight of the

PREPARING FOR WINTER OPERATIONS 157

North Cape was replaced by glorious sunshine as we neared the Scottish coast; and that, with a carriage cushion as table, we played cut-throat bridge nearly the whole way from Thurso to London.

During my stay in England much was accomplished, and I had every reason to be glad that I had been allowed the opportunity of bringing the true state of affairs home personally to those who held the reins in Whitehall.

As was natural, most of my business was with the heads of military branches at the War Office. Here I was in constant attendance, and besides being successful in getting certain important details put on a more satisfactory footing, I had the advantage of interviews with Lord Milner (then Secretary of State for War), General Mannerheim (whose election as President of Finland was probable in the near future), General de Millar (Governor-General designate of the Northern Province), and many others closely interested in Russian affairs.

My talk with General Mannerheim did not afford me great encouragement. For, as was only to be expected, he was much averse from the return to Finland of any "Reds" who had been driven from the country; and the soldiers of my Finn Legion, though they had done good work for me when Germany was our enemy, were most indubitably "Red." As such, one of my problems was how to get rid of them, and I was building chiefly on the hope of their repatriation. This hope, I now gathered, was of the flimsiest, and only great pressure on the part of our Foreign Office could put it on the road to fulfilment. As Lord Milner himself was aware of this, there was nothing I could do beyond urging the need for the opening of negotiations, as soon as General Mannerheim (if elected) took over his Presidential duties.

Other considerations, however, were all of secondary importance compared with the urgency for setting to rights my financial position.

I had need of no reminder on this point, but I got it nevertheless on the day after I reached London, in the shape of a cable from Lewin. He informed me that Russian Treasury Bonds (nicknamed " Confidence " Bonds) for a sum of 3,000,000 roubles had been sent from Archangel, but that these, besides being regarded with much mistrust, were for the most part in large denominations, such as 10,000 and 5,000 roubles. Thus they were of little use for paying wages, even so far as their face value went. He also told me that Mr. Lindley (our Chargé d'Affaires at Archangel) could give no definite news regarding the date of issue of the new currency. This last piece of negative information he had felt bound to pass on to Yermoloff, who regarded the situation consequently as one of extreme gravity, and whose resignation he feared, unless money were forthcoming at once. Would I, he concluded, use every endeavour to obtain authority for the issue of the whole £150,000 worth of British notes, and cable the sanction ?

Armed with this cable, and fortified by the companionship of General Radcliffe, I proceeded to the Treasury. I did my utmost to convince the official whom we interviewed that I was not making mountains out of molehills, and that there was a very real danger of disaster, unless a percentage of back wages were handed to the Murmansk railwaymen within the next few days. All I could get out of him, however, after much talk about the division of expenses between France, America, and ourselves, was that the end of December at latest would see the establishment of the new currency and of a standard rouble ; and that, until then, I must carry on as best I could, as it was impossible to sanction the lump expenditure of so extravagant a sum as £150,000.

This was more serious even than Vardo herrings being offered me in lieu of cash when first I went out. But I could not repress a smile as I glanced at Radcliffe. For I felt certain that his thoughts, as well as mine,

PREPARING FOR WINTER OPERATIONS 159

were reverting to the letter I had written him a few days before I left Murmansk, in which I expressed a pious wish that a few of the Treasury pundits might be transported 400 miles down my railway, there to taste for a week or so the delights of a Bolshevik environment. For all that it was no laughing matter. I could not wait until the close of the year, and of this there was no shadow of doubt. It would imperil the whole undertaking, and lead, almost to a certainty, to the needless sacrifice of good lives. Placed in the scale against this was the expenditure now of a few thousand pounds which, unless we were going to repudiate our bond, must be incurred in any case at a subsequent date, whether as pounds, shillings, and pence or new-fangled rouble notes.

I do not see, therefore, that I could have acted otherwise than I did.

I told the Treasury representative that I was exceedingly sorry; but that if his help was to be confined to an oft-repeated promise of assistance in a month's time, it was my intention to return to the War Office at once, and despatch a cable to my Chief of Staff authorizing him to expend the whole £150,000 if, in his opinion, the situation demanded it. I was, I assured him, quite prepared to face the chance of being hanged afterwards by the military authorities.

I suppose that the dictum of a Treasury official is seldom disputed, and, the Treasury being the guardian of the public purse, it is probably as well that such should be the case. Obviously our inimical friend was startled. The discussion had reached a phase out of all accord with Treasury precedent. Turning quickly he remarked, "That means you are holding a pistol at my head," and then to Radcliffe, "Isn't that your view, General Radcliffe?"

Now, this was hardly fair on Radcliffe. He could not be expected either to testify to the fact that I was playing highwayman at the Treasury, or to associate himself officially with my determination to utilize the money now at Murmansk, regardless of consequences.

He was, however, equal to the occasion, and his answer, I think, could hardly have been framed better: "I'm not at all sure that both you and I wouldn't have done the same, if in General Maynard's place."

The advocacy of a Director of Military Operations is not to be despised. In this case, at any rate, it led to a resumption of the argument on more conciliatory lines. Much of the old path was trodden afresh, but at every step it became more certain that we were gaining ground. I, to my great amusement, was more or less ignored; but Radcliffe fought nobly, and the capitulation came after the exact interval needed for the preservation of dignity. "Well, if the General Staff make such a point of it, we can hardly take the responsibility of going contrary to their wishes."

Lewin got his cable, and that too without the endangering of my neck.

More than this: early in 1919 a new currency was established successfully, and my financial worries became nightmares of the past.

By the middle of December little of what I hoped to accomplish at home remained undone, and I felt it was time to arrange for our return. I found, however, that an immediate start was out of the question, as I was told that at least ten days must elapse before the sailing of the first Murmansk-bound ship. Thus it was not until Christmas Day that we embarked at Invergordon. Here we had a most pleasing surprise, for H.M.S. *Dublin* was in port, and Shackleton, Steele, and myself spent some cheery hours with the good friends of our homeward journey.

The most enthusiastic of sea-lovers could not have described our voyage as a pleasure trip. Our vessel was a tublike craft, lamentably slow, cockroach-ridden and leaky; we were much overcrowded; and, after the first thirty-six hours' steaming, the day gloom of Arctic midwinter fell upon us, and no single ray of sunshine came to brighten our desolate surroundings.

Amongst my fellow-passengers was Brigadier-General G. D. Price, who was to take over command of the 237th Brigade, Marsh, its late commander, having been invalided to England.

General de Millar was also with us. We had many talks together, and our acquaintance stood me in good stead at a later date, when a volume of correspondence passed between us relative to the building up of the Russian army raised on my side. He never wavered in his conviction that Russia would breast successfully the cataclysmal flood now threatening to engulf her. He relied, he said, on the innate patriotism of the peasant classes ; but he realized that they were easily led, and that much would depend on an early expansion of anti-Bolshevik influences. The next few months would be all-important. His one desire, therefore, was to get through to Archangel and take over his Governorship as speedily as possible, and he left Murmansk by ice-breaker immediately after our arrival.

The reports I received on reaching my headquarters were, on the whole, satisfactory.

Shortly after my departure, an attempt had been made to murder Yermoloff, and secret agents had overheard much talk of a general rising against his authority; but the distribution of wage-money, made possible by my cabled sanction to utilize the £150,000 of British notes, had produced a marked effect, and, for the time being, the political atmosphere was comparatively calm.

There had been trouble, too, with the Finn Legion, the men demanding that we should make terms with the Finnish Government on their behalf, these to include an amnesty and permission to return to their homes. Some of them had threatened to cross the border—but had been told that this was prohibited, and that any attempt might prejudice fatally the negotiations we hoped to initiate.

Preparations for winter work had been pushed forward. Laplanders, who inhabited the remote regions of the Kola Peninsula, and were never seen in any village near the railway during the summer months, had contracted to supply 600 reindeer sledges. Seven mobile columns, each about 200 strong, had been equipped, and their training in the use of ski and snow-shoe and in the management of sledge transport was making progress, under the general guidance of Commander Victor Campbell of Antarctic fame. Sufficient accommodation had also been provided for all garrisons.

This last item of news was a tremendous relief to my mind; for, owing largely to make-shift heating appliances, many houses used as barracks had been destroyed by fire, and my building programme had been hampered in many ways. One of these was the method in which a large number of double-sided Nissen huts had been loaded for shipment. The first consignment of these was received early in October, but it consisted of identical sections of some 80 different huts, so that, whilst it was possible to erect a portion of each, no single hut could be made ready for occupation. The sections required to complete the huts did not reach me till mid-November. This plan might have economized storage space in a ship's hold; but it put an end to hut construction for nearly six weeks, and all but compelled me to alter the disposition of my garrisons.

Shortly after I had resumed command, Yermoloff impressed upon me the desirability of endeavouring to drive the Bolsheviks southwards. The Russians, he told me, had now a mobilized force of about 2,500; but this was less than half his original estimate, and if it were to be increased to any material extent, not only must conscription be enforced more rigidly, but fresh recruiting areas must be tapped. I was not, however, prepared as yet to recommence operations, unless forced to do so by enemy action.

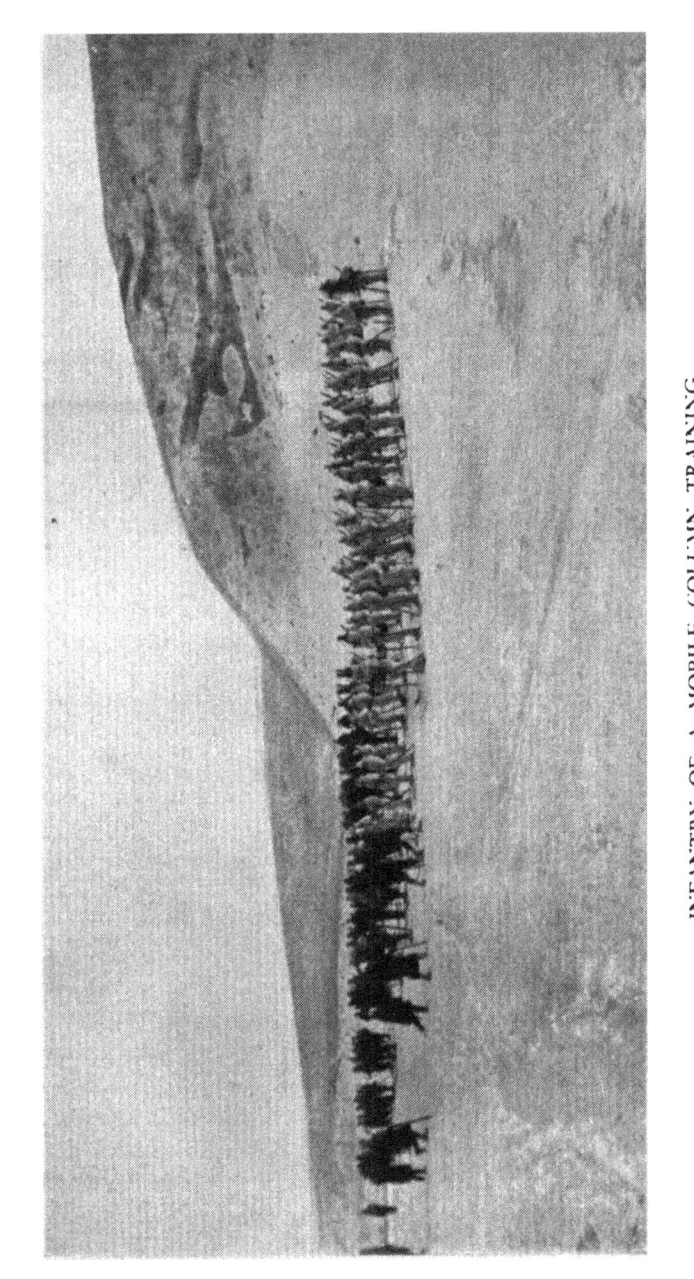

INFANTRY OF A MOBILE COLUMN TRAINING.
The white kit worn by one platoon as an experiment was adopted subsequently.

PREPARING FOR WINTER OPERATIONS 163

Setting aside the Finns, who were all excellent skiers, but whose employment could not be contemplated, I had at present available for cross-country work on snow only Canadian, French, and Italian detachments, with a sprinkling of Serbs and Karelians. No British regular troops had reached the requisite standard of skill, nor could this have been expected of them. More than a few weeks are required to convert the average British foot-soldier into a confident performer on ski or snow-shoe, especially when he is called upon to carry a slung rifle, ammunition, and equipment. Some few showed good promise of mastering with fair rapidity this strange and slithery mode of progression; but it was certain that something approaching a further month's practice would be needed before the remainder could be trusted to cover a dozen miles, even at slow speed, without suffering undue fatigue.

The mass of reindeer transport, too, had not yet been organized efficiently; and our dog-teams (240 animals in all) were not expected to reach us till towards the end of January, and even then would be unfit for immediate work.

If I moved at all, I intended to make an appreciable stride forward, probably one of over 60 miles to Segeja; and I must think of the subsequent establishment of railway communication with my new front. Some of the destroyed bridges south of Soroka had been repaired in the summer, as part of my scheme for bluffing Germans and Bolsheviks into the belief that I contemplated an offensive on a large scale; but the reconstruction of others to as far south as Olimpi, or even beyond, could be taken in hand now with safety, and this must be done before my advance commenced. Another important point was that I wished the new Russian troops to take a share in the operation, and I considered it too early yet to send them into action.

I told Yermoloff, therefore, that I thought it unwise to attempt a forward move until about the middle of February. After hearing my reasons, he agreed; and it was arranged that the next four or five weeks should be devoted to the perfecting of our preparations.

No sooner had we come to this understanding than reports reached me of a minor Bolshevik concentration in southern Karelia. From such information as came to hand, the strength of the force did not exceed a few hundred, and had been collected in the area more with the object of securing adherents and spreading Red propaganda than as a threat against Soroka. This was very likely to be the case; as that portion of Karelia was more thickly populated than the northern and central regions, and from it Yermoloff and myself hoped to secure a good intake of recruits for the Russian army. The most important of its villages were Undozero and Rugozerskaya, and at the latter (which lies 60 miles W.S.W. of Soroka) the Bolsheviks, it appeared, had established an advanced headquarters and recruiting centre.

Even if their only object were to obtain recruits, it would be against our interests to allow them to prosecute it undisturbed, seeing that every enlistment made by them would be one the less for us in the near future. There was the chance, too, that they had shown more energy than the with which I had been accustomed to give them credit, and had equipped a force capable of rapid cross-country movement, and of sufficient size to warrant an attempted dash on Soroka.

If this were so, I could not remain idle. Firstly, I must obtain additional information; and, should this indicate the probability of an advance against me, I must prepare to meet it half-way. Certainly I could not remain on the defensive, and allow Red troops to gain a footing anywhere in the proximity of Soroka.

My determination to postpone all military activity until February must therefore go by the board, and instructions were issued for a mobile force of some 200 drawn from the Canadian contingent and Karelian Regiment, to push forward towards Rugozerskaya. Reconnaissance was to be its chief aim; for my intelligence was sketchy, and the estimate it enabled me to form of enemy strength was little better than guesswork. I wanted trustworthy information as to numbers and dispositions ; and if this could be brought back to me, without serious loss being incurred, the column would have achieved its purpose.

At the same time, I must keep in view my forthcoming advance on Segeja. Rugozerskaya could not be left in Red occupation during my move down the railway ; and, if it were not cleared of the enemy now, must be cleared as part of the Segeja operations—a complication I was anxious to avoid.

The column commander was therefore told that if Rugozerskaya were found to be held lightly, and he considered his chances hopeful, he should not hesitate to make an attempt to capture its garrison or drive it southward. This, however, was a matter which I must perforce leave to his discretion.

The operation was entirely successful. The Bolsheviks seem to have anticipated no danger of attack at a spot so far removed from the railway, for it came upon them as a complete surprise. Information supplied by the natives of a neighbouring hamlet gave the Red strength at Rugozerskaya as about 150. The village was surrounded accordingly and rushed, the whole garrison being accounted for either as killed or prisoners, at a loss to ourselves of less than half a dozen wounded.

This little affair took place on January 16th, and was carried out so neatly and expeditiously that the Bolsheviks found no time to destroy documents or records. Thus all their headquarter papers fell into our hands, and these were found to shed a very considerable light on the situation on our front.

But the most satisfactory result of all was, I think, the confidence with which this small offensive inspired our men. The " Bolshy " was evidently a slack soldier and an indifferent fighter, and we could whip him any time we chose to take the trouble !

Rugozerskaya being in our hands, I decided to retain it ; and a detachment of the Karelian Regiment was detailed as its garrison.

The inclination to push home the success, and endeavour to capture Undozero also, was resisted, as this might precipitate operations for which I was not yet prepared. It was not so remote from the railway as to preclude its being dealt with, when I made my contemplated pounce upon Segeja in a few weeks' time.

CHAPTER XIII

SEGEJA

AFTER the capture of Rugozerskaya, it seemed unlikely that anything would happen to prevent or hamper a February advance. The unexpected, however, occurred; and though it did not actually deter me from putting into execution my original proposals, it altered the whole complexion of affairs on the Murmansk side.

On January 19th the Bolsheviks launched a vigorous attack against Ironside, forcing him to withdraw first from Shenkursk (190 miles south of Archangel) and then from Tarasova, 70 miles farther north.

On January 26th I received a cable from the War Office asking me to prepare a scheme at once for the movement to Archangel via the Soroka—Onega route of one infantry battalion (or 1,000 mobile troops) and one machine-gun company.

Four days later the order came for me to despatch a battalion and half a machine-gun company as soon as possible; and on February 11th this was followed by instructions for the transfer to Archangel of the remainder of the machine-gun company and an additional battalion.

Clearly Ironside's situation was giving cause for anxiety, and, however great the blow to me and my plans, there could be no question of protest or complaint. Infantry and machine gunners must be started off as soon as ever I could make the requisite arrangements.

That I should feel severely the loss of so many British troops needs no emphasizing. Of the reinforcements from home reaching me in the autumn, I had sent to Archangel already one battalion and a battery; and to these were now to be added two more battalions and an invaluable machine-gun company. Out of the 5,000 Britishers shipped to me originally, 1,000 only would now remain in my theatre, half of whom were claimed at the time by Petchenga.

But there was nothing to be gained by dwelling on such thoughts. They must be set aside, and our energies devoted at once to preparations for the march from Soroka. For it was not likely to prove the simple matter that a cursory glance at the map might give reason to suppose.

My responsibility for transport provision was to extend as far as Nukhta (half the distance to be traversed), Ironside arranging for the journey thence to Onega. All initial steps, however, calculated to ensure the success of the undertaking as a whole must devolve necessarily on us on the Murmansk side— and between Soroka and Onega lay 150 miles of wild and desolate waste, yielding no supplies and affording night shelter for small parties only, once Sumski Posad had been left behind.

The route would lie across snow and ice, and though in normal times the track might be well defined, there had been but little traffic this winter along the southern shore of the White Sea, and an hour's snowfall would suffice to obliterate all signs of trail. For those on sledges it would be bitterly cold, and the exercise of the utmost care would be needed to combat the danger of frostbite. The march, moreover, could not be carried out as if under peace conditions. During the first half, the probability of Bolshevik interference would be small; but when nearing Onega it was possible that opposition might be encountered. The usual precautionary measures must therefore be taken, and these would prove exceptionally trying to British soldiers, only a small percentage of whom had received even elementary training fitting them for the work under the conditions prevailing.

It was indeed no light undertaking, either for those responsible for the administrative arrangements or for the troops themselves.

The question of transport came to the forefront immediately. Guided by Shackleton and others of like experience, we had evolved a definite system for the packing of sledges accompanying mobile columns. It had been worked out with scrupulous care to meet the requirements of a fast-moving force undertaking active operations, each sledge carrying every essential, down to the last emergency " Arctic " ration, for a specified number of men. The system, however, could not be made applicable to the complete units now to be moved, except in so far as concerned the few sledges required by covering troops. Fresh calculations were needed before it was possible to estimate the number of sledges required, and these must be based on the type of animal employed.

With a fleet of 600 reindeer sledges at our disposal, and probably another 2,000 at call, it would seem that the working out of loads and the provision of all the transport likely to be required should present no outstanding difficulties. But a reindeer holds strong views on the subject of diet, and his tastes are not to be ignored.

In his own land he shows himself to be the most economical and accommodating of beasts. At the end of a day's march he asks for neither hay nor oats. His only desire is to be free of his trappings and allowed to roam at large. This granted him, he proceeds to nose about in the snow, and with marvellous intuition soon lights upon a patch of his own especial moss. Two or more hours of steady chewing ensue, punctuated by nasal snow-shovelling when appetite demands the opening up of fresh pastures. He is then replete, takes his rest in the open, untethered and ungroomed, and is ready, when morning comes, for his six-hour run.

Could any animal act more praiseworthily, or

make a greater appeal to the heart of a transport officer?

Nevertheless he has his limitations, and the most compelling of these is that he will consent to feed on one type of moss alone. Outside the districts where this grows, he cannot be employed on a journey of any length; for the diet of his choice must be carried for him and, as he is a mighty feeder, the greater part of the load of a reindeer-drawn sledge would consist of food for the team.

In almost every area from the Kola Peninsula to 200 miles southward, reindeer moss abounds; but the White Sea littoral from Soroka to Onega produces none.

The reindeer sledge as a possible means of transport was thus ruled out at once; and though our dog teams were now fit and ready for work, their number was not nearly sufficient for requirements, and they would be needed, moreover, almost at once for our own operations. All that could be done was to provide a few teams for medical and ambulance sledges.

The employment of horse sledges was therefore the only solution. But I imagine that all the horses at that time in the Murman Area fit for the work could have found ample grazing in St. James's Park, and it was only by scouring the country that we were able to collect a sufficient number to meet the transport needs of 500–600 men.

In order to reduce the number proceeding by route-march, the chance was taken of utilizing an ice-breaker then on the point of making what was likely to be her last trip before spring from Murmansk to Archangel. Half a machine-gun company and 300 infantry were put on board, leaving 2,000 to make the overland journey. Owing to the scarcity of accommodation along the route, a system of movement by parties, not exceeding 300, marching fixed stages, was in any case marked out; but, had we been able to provide a sufficiency of transport, the parties might have

A REINDEER SLEDGE CONVOY.

followed each other without check at daily intervals. As it was, much time was lost unavoidably whilst the horses made their return journeys to Soroka.

Detailed instructions for the march were drawn up by Brigadier-General Price, who, I am sure, will be ready to apportion a due share of credit for its success to the officers of the Canadian contingent, on whose store of experience he drew freely.

The units despatched were the 6th and 13th battalions of the Yorkshire Regiment, and the 280th Machine-gun Company; and all arrived safely within Ironside's command, the only casualties being a couple of minor cases of frostbite.

But this weakening of my force necessitated a redistribution of troops and, amongst other changes, called for a further reduction of the Petchenga garrison. Certain of the details brought back from this detached post were conveyed to Murmansk by ice-breaker; but the mobile column of the 11th Royal Sussex Regiment, some 200 strong, made the overland march, employing reindeer transport. The track it followed traversed rough and hilly country, and was at times almost indistinguishable, and the weather was exceptionally cold and unpropitious. Yet the 112 miles from Petchenga to Kola were covered without mishap in $3\frac{1}{2}$ days. The column had earned its name of "mobile," and, while earning it, had gained the best of practical experience.

All these various moves were not, in point of fact, completed until early in March, and it was during their progress that we commenced our first advance down the railway since Soroka had been occupied the previous July.

Yermoloff had set his heart on an early start. In January he had accepted without demur my decision to postpone it for a month; but he had been disappointed, and I saw no sufficient reason for disappointing him again. My two battalions and machine-gun company had gone, or were going, and I was not likely to set eyes on them again. But was I, on that account, to do nothing, and give the new Russian force no chance of expansion? By February my preparations were complete, and I was as well placed to commence my movement then as I should be in March or April. Why then defer it? The Bolsheviks, it was true, had learnt already that I was losing fighting strength, and were proclaiming that they would drive us shortly into the sea. But this served only as an additional incentive to attack. I might have lost a few troops, but I would show at once that I was still strong enough to take the initiative.

The original plan to capture Segeja therefore held good. But before putting it into operation, there was one preliminary to be fulfilled.

I had been instructed recently to confine myself to the defensive, so far as it was compatible with the task of setting the loyal Russian army upon its feet. Thus I felt it incumbent on me to lay the proposition before the War Office. For it was useless to pretend that I regarded the operation as a purely defensive measure, seeing that I purposed an advance of nearly 70 miles, and intended to hold any ground I might gain. I received a prompt reply to my cable, authorizing the attack, and leaving it to my discretion whether I should remain in occupation of any positions captured.

The conduct of the affair was entrusted to Brigadier-General Price. The formation both of his brigade and that of Brigadier-General Turner had been broken up badly by the despatch of so many reinforcements to Archangel; and to meet the changed conditions a scheme of Area Commands had been put in force. Under this Turner assumed command of all troops from Murmansk to Kandalaksha (both inclusive), whilst Price's responsibilities extended from Kandalaksha (exclusive) southwards.

Undozero had been cleared by the Karelian Regiment a short time back, and the enemy's main forward garrison was known now to be at Segeja, covered by detachments at Nadvoitskaya and Onda, the latter (about 50 miles distant from Soroka) being the more northerly.

The Bolshevik strength at and around Segeja was estimated at 400, but strong supporting bodies were reported at Maselga and other points on the railway north of Lake Onega. These could be brought up rapidly by train, whereas we could make no use of the line south of Olimpi. For our success, therefore, we must depend largely on the element of surprise, and Price's plans were conceived with this as a main consideration.

The total force made available for the operations did not exceed 600, whilst, irrespective of reserves, the troops detailed to carry out the initial attacks numbered less than 400. The only British regulars were some 50 machine gunners and trench-mortar personnel. The remainder were Canadians, French, Russians, Karelians and Serbians, the last named being in the majority.

It may seem perhaps that the actions of so diminutive a force are scarcely worth the chronicling; but if the value of a military undertaking is to be measured by the standard of the strength of the force employed, then it may be urged with equal show of reason that no single enterprise of ours in the Murman Area is deserving of mention, except, it may be, the final offensive launched just prior to our withdrawal in September. From the point of view of numbers engaged, our operations, one and all, were, when compared with even the smallest of set-pieces on the Western front, of infinitesimal import—mere reconnaissances, skirmishes, or affairs of outposts.

But considerations other than numbers must be taken into account.

It was the first occasion on which our preparations and training for winter mobile work were to be put to the test in the field, and we were backing the mobility of our men and transport to outwit the Bolshevik in his own country. In a direct line, the distance to be traversed was equal to that between Dover and London, and half as great again by the routes selected for the flanking columns. Save for the railway, there were no defined tracks; and the approaches must be made through unmapped forests, over frozen lakes and snow-covered tundra. Even the railway route presented its especial difficulties, since many bridges between Olimpi and Onda were still unrepaired, and the fast-running streams they spanned originally, though covered probably with ice of sufficient thickness to bear men and sledges, would, with their precipitous banks, constitute serious obstacles to rapid movement. Yet the march of each column must be timed with the nicest accuracy, if surprise were to afford us its full measure of advantage. It was, too, our first attempt to drive the Bolsheviks from positions occupied by them since the previous summer, and the first engagement in which the new Russian army was to be called upon to play a part.

There were, then, many circumstances tending to lift the small operation out of the common rut of military endeavour. But, even if these are set aside completely, the results achieved were such as to justify somewhat more than a passing reference to the fact that we succeeded in driving the enemy from a few advanced positions.

In accordance with the scheme drawn up, Segeja was to be attacked by two columns, one (drawn from the Karelian Regiment) operating from the western flank; the other, with Sumski Posad as its jumping-off place, moving on its objective from the east. Separate columns were detailed for the capture of Nadvoitskaya and Onda respectively.

On February 15th the first move was made, when the column (150 strong) destined to make its final bound from Sumski Posad left Soroka. The remaining columns started from their rendezvous at prearranged

DOG TEAMS EMPLOYED WITH MOBILE COLUMNS.

intervals, timing their movements so that the various attacks should be carried out simultaneously.

On the 17th and 18th the weather was pitilessly cold, the temperature dropping to over 40 degrees below zero, with a biting wind and heavy snow-squalls. These terrible conditions delayed the Karelians, who did not arrive at Segeja till after its capture, though they would have been near enough at hand to give support had the attack from Sumski Posad met with more protracted resistance. The Onda party fared even worse, and, despite heroic efforts, never reached its objective. With skis deep-sunk in newly fallen snow, and in face of the tearing blizzard, the Serbians composing it struggled gamely on, but were forced to abandon the attempt when still some miles from their goal.

Notwithstanding all difficulties, however, the sledges of the Sumski Posad column contrived to cover over 100 miles in 16 hours, and both it and the Nadvoitskaya column, adhering accurately to their appointed time-tables, moved to the attack early on the morning of the 19th.

Nadvoitskaya was captured after a brisk encounter, in which the enemy suffered heavily, and the column established itself astride the railway.

Meantime, the Bolshevik garrison at Onda, hearing firing to its rear, commenced a hurried withdrawal down the line and, an hour or so later, walked into the arms of our men at Nadvoitskaya. Placed at a hopeless disadvantage, it surrendered; and thus nothing had been lost by the inability of the Serbians of the Onda column to fulfil their allotted task.

At Segeja, the Sumski Posad Column, deprived of Karelian co-operation, met at first with stout opposition; but the well-directed fire of our trench mortars and machine guns soon put the issue beyond doubt. Half the garrison was accounted for in killed and prisoners, and the remainder fled, leaving Segeja in our hands.

Previous to the attack, a Russian patrol had been

despatched south to make a break in the railway, and this it succeeded in doing by displacing several rails at a point three versts distant. Near the break, troops and machine guns were now posted in concealed positions, as it was known that reinforcements were being pushed up from Maselga—a fact given away unwittingly over the telephone by a Red commissar to one of our Russian subalterns masquerading as a Bolshevik officer at the Segeja end of the line.

The commissar's information proved reliable. A little later a train packed with troops crept slowly into view. The troop carriages were in front, with the engine pushing behind, and, as no proper outlook was kept, this resulted in the wheels of the leading coach leaving the rails at the break, and bringing the train to a standstill.

Then our machine guns spoke.

It is not pleasant to dwell, even in imagination, on the scene within that train. Cooped up in their narrow compartments, and raked at point-blank range from both flanks by a pitiless stream of bullets, the ill-fated troops must have paid a fearful toll for their leader's lack of caution. Doors were thrust open, and a few—the bravest perhaps, or it may be the most panic-stricken—flung themselves from the accursed death-trap. But it availed them nothing. The death that had sought them within, sought and found them none the less surely in the open.

A dozen jets of hissing steam spouted from the riddled engine, and it seemed a certainty that the whole train, with all its surviving occupants, must fall into our hands. But the driver, better sheltered than his comrades, stuck to his post; and after some long seconds of spluttering remonstrance, he got his locomotive under way, and the train commenced to draw off slowly towards the south, with the derailed coach—one pair of wheels still off the line—swaying perilously in rear. In less than five minutes from the first withering outbreak of fire, nothing was left to indicate the advent of the would-be reinforcements but a few crumpled forms lying silent and motionless on an otherwise deserted track.

But the Bolsheviks evidently set great store on Segeja, or else were bent on wiping out their late defeat; for, on the following day, they delivered a determined counter-attack, their infantry pushing forward boldly, supported by gun fire from an armoured train. But their tactical leading was bad, and their fire wild and ineffective—handicaps too heavy to give courage alone a chance of competing successfully with accurate rifle and machine-gun fire from positions even hastily prepared. The attack broke down, and heavy punishment was once again inflicted.

No further effort was made to dislodge us. The enemy had had their fill of fighting for the time being, and carried out a general withdrawal of 15 or 20 miles to the neighbourhood of Urosozero.

I heard with some surprise the tale of the counter-attack; for such dash and enterprise on the part of Red troops were contrary to my past experience. But my surprise was lessened when I learnt that it had been led by Spiridornoff, the truculent opponent of my earliest days, over whom I had gained a bloodless victory at Kandalaksha, resulting in a long return journey southward for himself and his men. He had shown himself then as not devoid of pluck; and doubtless he hoped to repay with interest his outstanding score against us. He was severely wounded, but carried back to safety. Perhaps he still lives. If so, I imagine he now holds high rank, and devotes himself, in his more sober moments, to preparations for war against those phantom armies which Russian politicians proclaim to their dupes to be threatening the existence of their communistic paradise.

What the Bolshevik losses totalled during this short series of engagements it is impossible to say. Killed and prisoners numbered nearly 200; in that crowded train, few could have escaped unscathed; and many of those wounded in the several encounters must have been carried, or found their own way back, to the shelter of their lines.

Our casualties were surprisingly slight. Of the Britishers, one N.C.O. was killed, and three other ranks wounded; whilst amongst French, Serbians, and Russians the losses did not run into double figures, and none were killed.

This happy result was due largely to the careful arrangements made by General Price and Colonel Leckie (commanding at Soroka) and to the plucky and skilful leadership of the column commanders, two of whom, Majors Mackenzie and Eastham, were Canadian officers. To the troops also belongs a full share of praise, for they had been subjected to no light trial of courage and endurance, and all, including the newly enlisted Russians, had emerged from it with high credit.

I had, in truth, every reason to be satisfied with the outcome. Yermoloff's recruiting area had been extended by 3,000 square miles; the Reds had been taught a most salutary lesson; the feasibility of winter operations had been demonstrated amply; and Price had earned my full confidence. We had gained, moreover, another marked advantage. The Segeja River is spanned by a 400-foot bridge, the last of any magnitude between Segeja and Petrozavodsk; and this we had captured intact. Also, the opportunity was now open for rebuilding the bridge over the Onda, which was of equal span, and had been destroyed by the Bolsheviks in July. Both these were matters of great importance, in view of the possibility of a continuance of our advance at a later date.

At Segeja things had gone well with us. Unfortunately, however, the law of compensation seemed bent on asserting its claim to recognition; for, at about this time, I was faced with a succession of disconcerting incidents within our lines. Two of them were in their nature political, but for all that had a direct and adverse bearing on the military situation. For one the Karelians were accountable; and for the other the Finn Legion.

As has been mentioned already, the people of Karelia, so far as lay in their power, endeavoured to hold themselves aloof from all things Russian. It was not that they felt actual antipathy to Russia (as did the Lapps), but rather that they considered they had met with extreme bad fortune in becoming somehow incorporated in the Russian Empire.[1] At one time they had been an independent race, and the longing for independence was in their blood. Exclusiveness was well enough in its way; but, situated as they were, they found it a one-sided business. However assiduously they might seek to practise it, there was no excluding such unwelcome symbols of their subservience as the Russian administrator and Russian tax-gatherer. And it was subservience against which they kicked.

The past six months had been much to their liking, for during them there had been no interference with their affairs by Russian officials. Commissars had vanished from the picture; the Murmansk Soviet, so long as it existed, had left them discreetly alone; and the new Government of the Northern Province had shown so far no interest in their doings. Thus they had tasted something nearly akin to independence. The taste had been good, and they would gladly enjoy it longer. Why not indeed for always? Everywhere there was talk of the right of small nations to "self-determination," and surely this must mean that Karelia could set claim to an independent status, should such be her choice. She had worked for it too. For had not she provided a force of 4,000 fighting men for the Allies, and won a dozen victories on their behalf, before the Russians had even started to bestir

---

[1] Karelia had formed a portion of Finland prior to 1721, in which year it was annexed to Russia by Peter the Great.

themselves ? The representatives of the Great Powers assembled in Paris could not fail to see the strength of their case, were it put before them ; and the best way to ensure this was to submit it to the Allied Commander-in-Chief at Murmansk.

Such was the line of reasoning of the leading spirits of the Karelian Regiment, and, as its result, a lengthy document reached my hands through the medium of their commanding officer. It was signed by several of the senior Karelian officers as " representatives of the people of Karelia," and amounted to a demand, rather than a plea, that Karelia should be recognized by the Powers as an independent nation. Karelia, in fact, was suffering from a bad attack of the malady known as swelled head.

Now, I was quite certain that Yermoloff would regard the whole affair as nothing but a piece of rank effrontery. He might perhaps see its comic side, but his sense of humour would be swamped by his indignation at the bare thought of his being asked to bargain away so much as a yard of Russian soil. Sooner or later the incident must be brought to his notice ; but, for the sake of future relations between Russians and Karelians, it seemed best that I should use my own influence to put a stop to the business at once, and let him know about it later, as a portion of back history, should I prove successful.

I therefore informed " the representatives of the people of Karelia " that I would take no steps to further their demands. I pointed out that, in the present state of Russia, there would be no chance whatever of their claim being considered, even if backed by their present Government, and that of this there was not the least prospect. I tried, too, to impress on them the absurdity of their ambitions. How were they going to exist as a separate nation ? They had no industries, no seaport, no railway of their own, and no internal communications. Was it possible for a tiny people, penniless and without resources of any kind, to survive as an independent entity? If they wished to better their political status, it would be far better to work in harmony with the loyal Russians who were seeking to establish a sane and stable Government.

My arguments, however, did not serve to convince them, and they asked that their petition might be passed to the Deputy-Governor. Though they did not give expression to it in words, they implied by veiled hints that if their claim were not entertained, they could at least proclaim themselves as independent, and that, in this event, the Provisional Government would not find it an easy matter to coerce them.

There was nothing for it, therefore, but to lay the whole matter before Yermoloff. He, as I had anticipated, showed not the smallest sympathy with Karelian aspirations. Karelia was an integral part of Russia, and such it must remain. The petition, to his mind, amounted to an open defiance of his authority, and he favoured my taking disciplinary measures against the Karelian officers who had identified themselves with it. To this I was opposed, as I felt sure it would lead to serious trouble, culminating perhaps in actual mutiny. I suggested accordingly that we should summon before us the authors of the petition, and that he should explain to them the impossibility of complying with their request.

The resultant confabulation was long, and though its outcome was satisfactory on the whole, there were moments when I looked to the future with considerable misgiving. Yermoloff, of course, was bound to set himself steadfastly against any idea of submitting an official claim for Karelian independence; but, in view of the importance to him of securing the willing services of a force already 4,000 strong, his attitude was, I thought, too frankly unpropitiatory. The Karelians were forced to accept his decision; but they accepted it sullenly, and intimated that they would do all in their power to dissuade their compatriots in the southern portion of Karelia (now being opened up) from enrolling in Russian units under the mobilization scheme. Karelians would enlist of their own free will to serve under Britishers, but would leave no stone unturned to avoid service under Russian officers.

This led to a prolongation of the discussion. I put it to Yermoloff that it would certainly be better for him that such recruits as the extension of our influence over southern Karelia might make available should enlist willingly into the Karelian Regiment, than that he should be put to the necessity of searching them out and compelling them to join a Russian unit. And with this he agreed. But there still remained the question of unreadiness to serve under Russian officers, since it was my aim so to arrange matters that all local forces could be administered by the Russians, when the time for our withdrawal should arrive; and, to this end, I had always intended that Russian officers, as they became available, should be drafted into the Karelian Regiment.

After consultation with Yermoloff, I therefore gave out that, whilst I dissociated myself entirely from their contemplated refusal to serve under any but British officers, their Governor had given his consent to Karelians enlisting in their own regiment instead of into Russian formations. This, however, did not mean that Russians would never be placed in command of them, for the gradual introduction of Russian officers into the regiment would certainly be called for. But I would give a guarantee that the regiment as a whole should remain under my direct control, and that each of the battalions into which it was now subdivided should have a Britisher as its commanding officer.

This compromise was accepted, though grudgingly. A southern boundary was fixed as the limit of the recruiting area for the regiment, and its " Olonetz " battalion (then being raised in southern Karelia) was made into a composite regiment by drafting into it all

Slavo-British Legion detachments then in the southern districts, thus introducing at once the Russian element amongst the rank and file. A start, too, was made of posting Russian officers to this regiment, one of the first being Count Bennigsen, employed up to this time on Yermoloff's staff.

I mention this officer by name, because his influence was largely responsible for the smooth working of the new system. He had been a Captain in the Russian Guards, spoke English fluently, and was well known to all of us at headquarters. A capable and gallant soldier, I was privileged to confer upon him our Military Cross ; and I am glad to be able to record that he contrived to find a safe harbourage in England, after the disasters which befell the loyal Russian forces subsequent to our withdrawal.

The Karelian controversy thus reached a temporary settlement. But it left a feeling of discontent in the hearts of many of the leading Karelians, which was never eradicated, and was answerable, in all probability, for much of the disaffection displayed by the regiment at Kem a few months later.

The second political complication coming to the fore at about the time of the capture of Segeja was, as I have said, connected with the Finn Legion.

For months past there had been an unmistakable spirit of restlessness in its ranks, and I had been watching developments with much anxiety ever since my return from England. Except for helping to keep in check marauding bands of White Finns, the Legion had been useless to me since the Armistice. Composed as it was itself of revolutionary " Reds," I could not employ it against the Bolsheviks, nor could I utilize it even to guard stores at Petchenga or elsewhere, as Poole had given an undertaking that it would not be called upon to serve outside northern Karelia. Thus, since December, it had done little or nothing to earn its keep. This was unsatisfactory enough ;

but I should not have been unduly disturbed had the men shown themselves content to rusticate at Kandalaksha in idle prosperity. Such a programme, attractive though it might seem, did not, however, appeal to them. Finland was calling them, and to Finland they meant to return. If others could not contrive this for them, they would take the matter into their own hands. Twice recently, in direct contravention of my orders, their leaders (Tokoi and Lehtimaki) had attempted to enter into negotiations with Finns across the border, on one occasion crossing the frontier with 200 of the Legion, and consequently endangering the issue of our appeal to the Finnish Government. Unfortunately my position was such that I could do no more than heap my wrath upon them, and threaten to cease my efforts for their repatriation. I was powerless to compel them to walk the path of wisdom.

This inability on my part to take compulsory measures needs, I think, especial emphasis.

The only satisfactory step I could have taken would have been to disarm the entire Legion; but I had not sufficient trustworthy troops to make sure of carrying this through successfully—and failure would have proved calamitous. It was, moreover, certain that many lives would have been lost, even if fortune had gone with us.

The whole situation as affected by the attitude of the Legion, was explained by me to General Radcliffe just previous to our move on Segeja. My letter was written immediately after an inspection of the unit, and discussions with Tokoi, when the impressions these had formed on my mind were still fresh. Thus, if a description of the state of affairs is to be given at all (and given it must be, if events are to be viewed in their true light), nothing can be gained by clothing it in other words.

"*February 10th*, 1919.

" . . . I hope and believe that my efforts as regards the Finn Legion have met with some measure of success. I spent a long time at their headquarters, entering into every detail of their activities and organization, addressing the men both at their headquarters and main detachments, and having lengthy interviews with their leaders.

" I think they trust me ; but they are a pig-headed lot of revolutionaries, and the question of their future remains very crucial.

" One thing is quite certain, namely, that they will refuse to submit much longer to being pariahs and outcasts from their country. They assert—and I think with reason—that the British public and politicians hear one side only of the conditions that obtained during the revolutionary period, and of the deeds committed by either side. According to them, they are the true patriots who tried to save their country, and they swear that such excesses as may have been committed by irresponsible bands of ' Reds ' were as nothing compared with those carried out under the direct orders of responsible ' White ' leaders, of whom Mannerheim was about the worst ! I've cabled and written so much officially about this question that I won't do more now than state the salient points, indicating how they affect my position.

" (a) The Legion comprises about 1,200 fighting men, with a well-trained mountain battery. They will not fight the Bolsheviks, especially as many Finns holding identical political views are now enrolled in the Bolshevik ranks, being forced to this, as starvation was the only other alternative. The Legion, therefore, is not only useless to me as a fighting force, but may at any time constitute a real danger.

" (b) I do not think they are likely to take the law into their own hands till after the announcement of the results of the election which is to take place in Finland early next month, as they live in hope that their own party may get a bigger finger in the government pie. Should they be disappointed, however, and should I not be in a position to tell them that their repatriation is more or less a certainty, there is at least a chance that they will decide to see what can be done by force of arms.

" (c) In the above event, I admit frankly that, though I may threaten and exhort, I shall not be in a position to prevent them from carrying out their decision.

" The reasons are very obvious. They have detachments numbering about 400–500 thrown out towards the Finnish frontier. These I could not touch, and they might be over the border before I could even get to hear of it. I cannot withdraw these detachments, for several reasons, amongst others being a promise by Poole that they should not be employed except in that locality; lack of accommodation elsewhere; necessity for retaining some troops as a frontier guard; and lastly, the fact that whilst the Legion is split up, any concerted action on its part against our interests is rendered more difficult.

" At Kandalaksha there are about 500 (including the battery), and guarding important bridges in the neighbourhood are about 200 more.

" All these could be off towards Finland in a few hours, provided they made arrangements beforehand. The sprinkling of Allied troops in the vicinity would be powerless to prevent them, and they would be away long before my miserable railway could transport other troops—even if I could spare them—from Kem or Murmansk.

" Besides, what troops could I send? It would be almost impossible to send sufficient Britishers as it is, and quite out of the question to do so if, as seems probable, I have to despatch another British battalion to Archangel.[1]

" Certainly I cannot spare any Serbians from the south; the Karelians, even if I could collect enough of them in time, would not oppose the Finns; and I grieve to say that I would lay more than even money on

[1] Orders to send this battalion were cabled from London on the very day I wrote.

the Finns knocking the stuffing out of . . . in half an hour.

"No : if the Finn Legion determines to ignore my orders, it can march into Finland without my being able to prevent it—and it's no use blinking the fact.

"(d) My recommendations and plans are therefore as follows :

"(i) Every effort must be made to compel the Finnish Government to allow my Finn warriors to return to their country as peaceful citizens. I've already cabled my recommendations for bringing pressure to bear.

"(ii) The leaders must be allowed to proceed to England to put forward their case. They must be treated sympathetically, but they must not be allowed to return here until I cable the ' all clear.'

"(iii) If the Finnish Government, despite our efforts, refuses to allow them back, my second string will be an attempt to turn the Legion into a civilian colony here. I have approached the Governor-General already on this point, and he is willing to make the experiment. I doubt much, however, whether the Finns would agree to this, and in any case I am sure it would prove a very complicated business.

"(iv) Failing the colonization scheme, I should try to persuade the Legion to cross the frontier in small parties (unarmed), and take their chance of returning to their own homes.

"(v) As a last resort, and if they said they were determined to enter their country as an armed force, I should say, ' Go, and be damned to you. You go contrary to my orders and to the wish of my Government. Your rations will be stopped, and I shall inform the Finnish Government at once. On no account, however, will I countenance you taking the battery with you. If you attempt this, I will send troops to oppose you. Otherwise you can go your own way, on the distinct understanding that you do so without my sanction, and that you cease forthwith to form part of my forces.'

"I am sure that if things get thus far, this is the only course to follow. If I try to oppose them, it's odds on my being unsuccessful, and not only should I start a sort of civil war, but the Finns would certainly seize the opportunity to destroy railway bridges and generally play the devil. Whereas, if I allow them to go, it will be a good riddance, so far as I am concerned ; and I can swear truly that it was contrary to my orders, and that I did my best to prevent it. You people at home could always make me an official scapegoat, if the Finnish Government got nasty."

It will be seen from the above that my chief concern was lest the Finns should break away from my control, and carry out a small-scale invasion of Finland, thus straining the already delicate relations between ourselves and the Finnish Government. Up to February, though I knew of course that many of the Legion were imbued with Bolshevik tendencies, there had been no reason to anticipate, on this account, any display of active hostility to the Allies. Now, however, the position had changed. Instigated by Lehtimaki, the men commenced to evince open signs of insubordination, refusing to furnish working parties, or to provide train-guards within their own section of the line. Not only this, but there were mutterings to the effect that the railway would be broken if any attempt were made to force them to carry out these duties.

Fortunately, Tokoi was more temperate in his views than the hot-headed Lehtimaki. He was induced, after long argument, to see that his interests lay in working for the maintenance of order and discipline within the Legion, and that the men, whose leader he was, had little to gain and much to lose by defying Allied authority. He therefore gave his promise that he would use his influence to secure compliance with any orders issued. Lehtimaki declined to go so far as this; but he undertook to cease lending encouragement to those who wished to set our authority at defiance.

Thus a peace of sorts was patched up. Unsatisfactory and eminently unstable I knew it to be; but I could aim at nothing beyond preventing mischief until such time as an agreement should be reached, for the repatriation of all who were desirous of returning to Finland.

Meantime, additional British troops must be sent to Kandalaksha; and the mobile column of the Sussex Regiment from Petchenga was ordered thither, though I could spare it ill for such a purpose as acting watchdog over disaffected Finns.

Right up to the last day of August, when it was shipped at length to Helsingfors, the Finn Legion caused me ever-increasing trouble and anxiety; and its example was followed all too closely by the Karelian Regiment. But I have said enough to show how factors outside those of a purely military nature obtruded themselves at this period and added to my cares.

Other untoward incidents must also join the list drawn up by Fate as a set-off to our military success.

On January 22nd a fire at Kandalaksha station resulted in the destruction of five engines and much railway material—most serious losses, in view of our 70-mile extension of rail communication; and on February 1st our largest barrack at Murmansk was burnt to the ground, two non-commissioned officers losing their lives.

In January two British officers were murdered at Murmansk; and accidents deprived me of the services of my A.D.C. and my chief administrative staff officer,[1] both of whom were invalided home.

[1] Lieutenant-Colonel Michael Spencer-Smith, well known as a financial expert and a director of the Bank of England, the news of whose untimely death, as the result of a motoring accident, I have just (January 1928) received.

Most disquietening of all, however, was a flagrant case of indiscipline on the part of a unit on which I had placed hitherto implicit reliance.

A section of French *skieurs* had been employed at Segeja and, after the engagement, instructions for its relief were issued to the headquarters of the company at Soroka. But the section detailed for this purpose refused point-blank to obey the order, the men stating that they had it on M. Clemenceau's authority that they had not been sent out to Russia to fight !

Colonel Begou, Chief of the French Mission, was sent down at once to investigate the matter, and took drastic disciplinary action. His report, however, convinced me that the company could not be trusted to take its place again in the fighting line, and over 200 expert *skieurs* were lost to me.

This is the first case of gross insubordination amongst Allied troops to which I have called attention, and I have mentioned it specifically, solely because, coming at that particular moment, the blow it struck me was exceptionally heavy. Mobile troops were my chief need in the south, and the only substitute for the French company was the mobile column of the Sussex Regiment—and this was required at Kandalaksha as an antidote to disaffection in the Finn Legion.

But I regret to say that it was not, in fact, the first incident of this kind to occur, neither was it the last. I have, however, little desire to wash soiled linen before even a limited public, and still less to furnish it with a detailed laundry list ; and I will therefore confine myself to the general statement that, before the undertaking reached its close, there were units of nearly every nationality upon which I could not rely with absolute confidence.

For this unhappy state of affairs there were many contributory causes. Our own men were not drawn from the fittest and youngest, and it could hardly be expected that foreign Powers should send picked troops to such a theatre. The Great War was over, and others were being demobilized, and according to the men's views, snapping up the best civil billets, whilst they, banished in a forsaken wilderness, were risking their lives for a cause not directly concerned, so far as they could see, with the welfare of their country. Added to this, a misguided Labour press was doing its best to incite discontent, by pouring abuse on the campaign, vilifying politicians and magnifying grievances.

Before writing my despatch of March 1st, 1919, the effect on the *moral* of my troops of the many adverse influences at work had been forced upon my notice on more than one occasion. I did not wish then to particularize, or to lay too great stress on any manifestation of indiscipline, nor am I desirous now of so doing. But I felt constrained to point out some of the causes militating against the preservation of discipline in general, and how they could not fail to reflect unfavourably on the well-being of my force. The following paragraph was embodied accordingly in the despatch:

" Owing to the extreme shortage of civilian labour, I have been compelled to employ a great proportion of them [my troops] on permanent working and building parties, and on similar tasks of an uncongenial nature ; their accommodation has not always been as suitable as I could have wished ; the climate is severe, and trying even to the most healthy ; leave to England is necessarily rare ; local amusements are confined entirely to such as we are able to provide ; any movement of troops by rail is attended by great discomfort, owing to the shortage of suitable rolling stock ; and, during the winter, transport by sea and road entails unusual hardships. Moreover, my men have been surrounded for many months by an atmosphere of disorder, dissatisfaction, and lawlessness, which cannot but affect adversely even the best-disciplined troops."

This statement furnished at least an indication that Murmansk and its surroundings were exercising a contaminating influence on my forces. It sufficed then for a document open to public perusal and, with such amplification as I have given already, must suffice now also.

CHAPTER XIV

THE IDES OF MARCH

BEYOND cursory allusions to the difficulties and hardships attending all winter movements, whether by sea, road, or rail, I have made no attempt to enlarge upon the climatic conditions ruling in the Murman Area between the months of December and March. These, it is true, could be made to furnish an abundance of descriptive material, some at least of which would be likely to stir the imagination of those whose acquaintance with snow and ice is limited perhaps to an unwonted spell of cold in England, or to an occasional winter-sports holiday at some Alpine resort.

But such material has been utilized already by a multitude of writers; some in epics chanting gallant deeds amidst Arctic or Antarctic ice-fields; others in more homely tales, depicting life maybe in the wild spaces of Canada, or perchance—nearer to the scene of our Venture—in " the land of the midnight sun." In both types of work are to be found pictures of Arctic surroundings akin to those that encompassed us in North Russia; and as these are painted for the most part with a vividness and skill I cannot hope to rival, I do not purpose entering the field of description purely for description's sake.

All I wish to ensure is realization of the fact that Murmansk lies 200 miles within the Arctic Circle, and that throughout the winter of 1918–19 we were not hibernating, but prosecuting a military campaign which, small though it might be, demanded nevertheless a strenuous activity.

Naturally the cold was intense, our records showing a lowest temperature of 75 degrees of frost, whilst 64 degrees were registered as late as March 24th.

As a rule, however, the air was still and the atmosphere dry.[1] Thus, as the special clothing issued to all ranks was excellent, no great inconvenience was experienced during the ordinary round of daily routine. Indeed, for my part, I have felt the numbing miseries of cold far more acutely on many a winter's evening at home, with the thermometer close on 40 and puddles innocent of ice, than ever I did at Murmansk on a day of average calm. But at night, or when travelling by sledge, and, above all, when the prevailing wind from the south, sweeping for perhaps a thousand versts across snow-covered expanses, whistled towards Spitsbergen, it was a different matter. Then indeed would the man be foolish who uncovered his hands even momentarily, or failed to draw his wind-proof hood closely around face and ears. He would be inviting frostbite to claim him as a not undeserving victim.

On such occasions, however, the desire to allay physical discomfort was usually sufficient to ensure the taking of all possible precautions. It was when spring was at hand, and the sun, aroused once more from winter sloth, shed its rays on a landscape of dazzling white, that carelessness was engendered.

In the sunlight, and warmly clad, it seemed to the men ridiculous to give a thought to such a thing as frostbite. It could not, they would argue, be really cold, and it was a fumbling business lighting pipe or cigarette with hands encased in fingerless contraptions much like under-padded boxing gloves. So, off would come their gloves and, unless checked, as likely as not, off they would remain.

How near one could go to a touch of frostbite by such inconsequence was brought home to me one bright day in early March.

[1] To those with a scientific turn of mind, it may prove of interest to know that a " pilot " balloon, sent up by our Meteorological Section on March 29th, was kept under observation from 2.20 p.m. to 6.40 p.m. During this time it reached a calculated vertical height of 136,000 feet, at which altitude its height appeared to remain constant. At the time I was informed that this constituted a record.

CROSS-COUNTRY TRANSPORT.
A HORSE SLEDGE SUPPLY CONVOY.

HEADQUARTER REINDEER SLEDGE.
(The animal in rear is trained to act as a brake).

I was presenting decorations after an inspection parade at Soroka, and found it impossible to affix them to the tunics of recipients without removing my thick gloves. These I was careful to discard only for the few moments required for pinning on the insignia, replacing them during the narration of the circumstances in which the various awards had been earned.

It happened, however, that three men were to be decorated in connection with a gallant little affair in which they played a joint part, and one narrative giving the ground for award sufficed for all three. It fell to me, therefore, to affix three insignia in succession without my gloves. When decorating the third man, I found it exceedingly difficult to push the safety-pin through—as I thought—the cloth of his tunic. I pressed harder still, but the tip of the pin would not appear; and it was only when I looked more closely to ascertain the cause that I saw blood oozing from my left hand. I had driven the pin deep into a half-frozen finger, without being in any way aware of it.

Cases of frostbite were, as a matter of fact, remarkably few; and this spoke well for the careful supervision exercised by officers and non-commissioned officers, and for the common sense of the men, taken as a whole.

One of the saddest cases coming under my notice was that of an ex-colonel of the Norwegian army, who had joined the French Ski Company as a volunteer. He was a hard-bitten old warrior, and, though well on in life, could cover his fifty miles a day on ski, and no undertaking was too risky or hazardous for his liking. Unfortunately he met with an accident when on reconnaissance duty, and was unable to reach shelter before night fell. The poor fellow was badly frostbitten, and when I visited him in hospital, I learnt that it had been found necessary to amputate portions of both feet and also several fingers. Though he could never hope to walk again without crutches and both his hands were badly maimed, he bore the blow with most splendid fortitude, telling me with a smile that, after all, it was about time for an old campaigner such as he to take his place upon the shelf.

It might perhaps be expected that, with a temperature ranging during five months from freezing-point to over 40 degrees below zero, our snowfall would be heavy. But this was not the case. Near Murmansk the ground apart from drifts was seldom covered to a greater depth than a foot; and though the fall was heavier in the south, there were few localities in which it lay deeper than 18 inches.

Engines, of course, were furnished with snow-ploughs, and " hold-ups " on the railway were not to be feared, except where drifting snow blocked a cutting on some section of the line over which traffic was intermittent. One such occurred as late as March 16th during a journey to Segeja, when our train ran into a drift near Onda, and it was only after many hours of digging and shovelling that we were able at length to force our way through.

Although therefore frost and snow added greatly to the hardships of even the smallest of military operations, they cannot be said to have exercised otherwise any strikingly deleterious effect on the health and comfort of the troops.

Of far greater moment was the long-continued absence of daylight. Existence for several months in semi-darkness must, I should imagine, prove sufficiently depressing even to those provided with every amenity of life. Situated as we were, amidst highly uncongenial surroundings, with indifferent lighting and the scantiest of facilities for recreation and amusement, it was doubly dispiriting, and led, without doubt, to the lassitude, inertia, and loss of nerve evidenced by many of all ranks and nationalities before winter drew to its close.

From March onwards the period of daylight extended with extraordinary rapidity, and by the end of that month the hours of darkness did not exceed those of a midsummer's night at home. The snow, however, continued to lie till early May, at which time lakes and even fast-running rivers were still covered with unbroken ice.

The effect of the thaw on the larger rivers was almost magical. On the Kem, for example, the ice was sufficiently strong to admit of the passage of carts and sledges on a Monday. The following day a few cracks appeared; and on Wednesday the river was a roaring torrent, sweeping down the ice that had bound it fast a few short hours back, in a seemingly unending swirl of mighty blocks and tangled masses. By the week-end it wore its summer garb; and our dinner table had been graced by more than one fine trout, lured from its waters by an artificial fly.[1]

In connexion with the seasonal changes, there was one seeming phenomenon that aroused our curiosity. Though, in winter, all but the deepest ponds and streams were frozen solid, and the ground was rock-hard for several feet below the surface, yet summer's advent ushered in at once a plague of mosquitoes more maddening than any from which I have been compelled to suffer, even by the jungle-covered banks of the Irawaddy or on the marshy flats of the Struma Valley.

The explanation is doubtless simple; but to us it appeared either that our tormentors were unsurpassed as long-distance flyers, or that the hardiness and longevity of their larvæ were beyond belief. At that we left it, thankful, as we flapped and cursed, that at least they were not of the genus *anopheles*; since, in such a case, malaria would have been likely to prove a far more devastating foe than either German or Bolshevik.

With the coming of March we began to feel that the trials of an Arctic winter were nearly passed. On the 6th, the temperature, for the first time in three

[1] General headquarters were moved from Murmansk to Kem on May 1st.

months, rose above freezing-point; and though the rise was short-lived, it pleased us to regard it as a harbinger of spring. The days, too, were lengthening out rapidly, and there was good hope that the increasing hours of sunlight would charm away the lassitude from which, as I have mentioned, so many had suffered during the preceding period of gloom.

All of us, indeed, viewed the world with a more cheerful gaze. Troubles we had in many, and that others were ahead of us there could not be the smallest doubt; but we had managed so far to compete successfully with those confronting us, even under the unsettling influences of a dreary and demoralizing winter. So why should we be pessimistic as regards the future, now that spring was near at hand, and we should be campaigning soon under conditions likely to be far more inspiriting, and certainly less grievously abnormal?

It was all to the good that we should replenish our store of optimism; for, upon it, the events of the latter half of March and of early April were destined to make a heavy drain.

From the commencement of our operations, one of my difficulties had been to prevent Red agitators from entering the zone nominally under our control. Even in those early days the Bolsheviks realized to the full the value of well-organized propaganda, and it was then, as it has remained ever since, the most efficient weapon of their armoury. Aware of this, they had never spared their efforts to introduce trained propagandists into the Murman Area, and many such were undoubtedly within our lines, even before winter had set in. Now their number showed a marked increase; for not only had the paucity of daylight facilitated their entry, but, at about this time, there was an increasing influx of prisoners of war returning to their homes, and it was an easy matter to include amongst these a sprinkling of specially qualified agents. The detection of these chosen emissaries was baffling, and they did their work well. Circumstances, too, favoured them, at the moment.

In view of the disappointing outcome of partial mobilization, the Governor had announced his intention of enforcing universal conscription and of extending the age-limit of those compelled to serve. This step failed to meet with popular approval, and was employed by the professional agitators as a powerful inducement to disaffection. Added to this, the ground was well prepared for the seeds of disorder both in the Finn Legion and Karelian Regiment.

It would appear therefore that Lenin's tools had good cause for judging the time propitious for a general rising against us. In any case they reported to Moscow to that effect, and it was arranged that the revolt should coincide with the second anniversary of the revolution which, in the March of 1917, had put an end to Czardom, and installed in its stead a Russian Republic. It was planned further that, simultaneously with risings at Murmansk and other centres, my Finns and Karelians should mutiny, and the Bolsheviks launch an attack against us from the south.

The scheme was well conceived and far-reaching, and had it been carried out according to plan, and had I remained in ignorance of it, our position might well have become critical. By this time, however, my intelligence system was working efficiently, and furnished me with reports leaving little doubt as to what was afoot. Moreover, the Bolshevik efforts were unconcerted and, apart from failing in their endeavour to bring my local troops to the point of open mutiny, their preparations for an offensive against my southern posts were not completed until many weeks too late.

On March 17th I received a cable from the War Office to the effect that Trotsky was concentrating against me two fresh divisions. This news served to corroborate my own information regarding the impending attack which was to synchronize with the rising within my lines, and I reinforced my southern garrisons at once by all such troops as I estimated could be spared, without endangering too seriously my hold upon Murmansk.

On the 19th one of my agents, who as an avowed " conspirator " had gained the confidence of many of the plotters, brought me additional details. The rising at Murmansk was to take place on Sunday, 23rd, and, if successful, was to be the signal for similar outbreaks throughout the whole Area. The first step in the Murmansk plan was to raid the Russian barracks for arms. This was expected to prove an easy job, and the leaders were confident not only of securing an adequate supply of weapons, but of being joined by large numbers of recruits recently enlisted in the new Russian army. The prisoners confined on board the old battleship *Chesma*, and numbering several hundred, were then to be released ; and after that the real business was to commence with an attack upon general headquarters. According to my agent, the insurgents calculated on finding many sympathizers amongst Allied troops, including British, and they thought that some of these would even go so far as to side with them openly, if not at first, then at any rate after the headquarter staff had been accounted for. Most flattering prices, he added, had been placed on the heads of Yermoloff and myself.

Further evidence of the plot was forthcoming on the 20th, and I was provided with the names and meeting-places of many of the conspirators. On the morning of this day posters were found affixed to various buildings in the town, notifying the Russian proletariat that the day of the *bourgeois* was nearly over, and that all of them, foreign and Russian alike, were to be " finished off " on Sunday, 23rd.

On the 21st, chiefly on account of what my agent had told me regarding reliance placed by the agitators on Allied sympathy, I called a meeting of all British officers at Murmansk, and gave them a brief address on the subject of the plot that was being hatched. Every unit had, of course, been made aware of the general situation long before this; but many officers were fresh arrivals, and some of these had been doing harm by loose talk regarding conditions in England, and by speaking, in the presence of foreigners, of discontent among their men, in terms of thoughtless exaggeration. To such folly it was necessary to put a stop, and I wished, besides this, to impress on every officer the need for doing all in his power to counter communistic influences. Before we dispersed, a request was made that a précis of what I had said should be drafted and issued to commanding officers; and this was done. For a number of minor reasons I reproduce it now as an Appendix. It gives, I think, a fairly accurate idea of the mentality of our men at the time, and backs up the view that the winter months had exercised a somewhat unhealthy influence on officers and men alike. I wish, however, that I could still adhere to the opinions I then expressed, relative to Bolshevik tendencies in our Labour party.

It is, perhaps, needless to say that precautions were taken to guard the Cinema Hall in which we met. A basket containing so many British eggs might have proved an irresistible temptation to those who had planned to " finish off " the whole officer class in two days' time.

On the 22nd I had my final consultation with Yermoloff, and we perfected our plans for the following day. These were simple, and aimed chiefly at enhancing the power and authority of Yermoloff as civil Governor.

All guards were to be strengthened that night, and special pickets posted in the neighbourhood of the Russian barracks. We were acquainted with the whereabouts of some ten to fifteen of the leading firebrands, and Yermoloff's myrmidons, aided by such Russian troops as he could trust, were to effect the arrest of these before daybreak, together with all in their company. Allied troops were not to lend active assistance, unless serious opposition were encountered. All, however, were to be under arms, with detachments in evidence wherever arrests were to be carried out. If Yermoloff secured the " bag " he expected, no other repressive measures were to be taken; but, later in the day, the Allied troops were to parade in strength, as a reminder that a disciplined force was available to assist the Governor in suppressing disturbance or riot.

Commanders of other garrisons had already made their preparations, and were, of necessity, to be left to deal on their own initiative with any situation that might arise.

Yermoloff's men netted a highly satisfactory catch in the early hours of the 23rd. Our sudden action came as a rude and surprising shock to the leaders of the enterprise, and most of them, together with a score of their more enthusiastic followers, were safely under lock and key before the remainder of Murmansk's riff-raff realized that the day of the great anniversary had broken. When, at length, they tumbled into the streets, they were greeted by proclamations informing them that the authorities were fully conversant with the contemplated rising; that those responsible for its conception were prisoners and awaiting trial; and that neither procession nor demonstration of any kind would be permitted that day.

Deprived of leadership, and with Allied troops most clearly prepared for any emergency, those who had been ready to join in the rising were careful not to commit themselves to open acts of violence during daylight. After nightfall, noisy crowds collected here and there, and shots were fired in various portions of the town. But our guards and patrols sufficed to keep the demonstrators within reasonable bounds and, so far as I could gather, the only casualty was one Russian officer wounded.

The next day Yermoloff was again busy. Mixing with the previous night's crowd, our agents had learnt

DEMONSTRATION PARADE AT MURMANSK.
ARTILLERY AND MACHINE GUNS MARCHING PAST.

that an old repair ship in the inlet (the *Xenia*) harboured a nest of malcontents who had escaped the first round-up. These were swept promptly into Yermoloff's net, and seven or eight of them joined their fellow-plotters in charge of prison guards. These last arrests were, as events turned out, the cause of further trouble. The Murmansk workmen seemingly cared little for the fate of those originally incarcerated, most of whom were found to be Lenin's men sent especially to Murmansk, and not natives of the place. But it was a different pair of shoes now that fellow-employees had been imprisoned, and were to be put on their trial on a charge of abetting insurrection.

A petition was first sent to Yermoloff asking for their release, and asserting that none were implicated in the attempted rising. On this being turned down, a workers' committee was formed, including among its members many higher-grade operatives who had considerable influence over railwaymen and dockers. This committee notified Yermoloff that a general strike would be proclaimed unless the *Xenia* prisoners were liberated pending an enquiry into the recent disturbances; also that the strike would come into force automatically if they themselves were arrested.

Now, at any moment it might be imperative to hurry troops down the line, and thus the risk of the train service being thrown out of gear must, if possible, be avoided. It looked, besides, as if Yermoloff had in his hand an opportunity for placating public opinion, and he was strong enough, it seemed, to hold out the olive branch, without fear of it being regarded as a sign of weakness, now that the real ringleaders were in gaol and deprived of power for mischief. Yermoloff saw this as clearly as I did; but he insisted that he must have some hold on these self-constituted spokesmen, of whose political leanings he was none too sure.

He therefore drew up a form of undertaking, promising that if this were signed by each member of the committee, the *Xenia* prisoners should be released at once on bail. This undertaking was shrewdly worded, and, as its length is not great, its translation is worth giving verbatim:

"We, the representatives of the working classes of Murmansk, accept responsibility for the workmen of the repair ship *Xenia*, who were arrested on suspicion of participating in Bolshevik movements, and we guarantee that, until the enquiry now being held is over, they will neither disappear nor indulge in Bolshevik propaganda.

"We raised the question of their release solely owing to the conviction that the authorities had been misled, and had detained innocent men.

"We recognize the seriousness of the occasion, and realize the criminality of the policy of Lenin and Trotsky. We condemn all those who called for a Bolshevik *coup d'état*, and appeal to the workers to keep calm and trust the authorities.

"In view of Bolshevik propaganda now being carried out, we intend to refrain from all street demonstrations, and appeal to all sober-minded workmen to follow our example."

Somewhat to my surprise, the undertaking was agreed to and signed. Copies of it were then posted up, and the *Xenia* suspects released.

Yermoloff had got the better of the deal. Having given out publicly that they intended to support the local government, the signatories could expect but short shrift if they failed to abide by their word; and, by damning Bolshevism in no uncertain terms, they had placed themselves at the mercy of the Reds, should the latter succeed in regaining power in the district. Anxiety regarding the fate of the document must have caused some sleepless nights for those who signed it, when Bolshevik misrule was re-established at Murmansk.

THE IDES OF MARCH 205

At our Base, therefore, the projected plot had ended in the discomfiture of its backers and, so far from damaging our cause, had, to all appearance, strengthened Yermoloff's hand. For all that, agents on whom I could rely assured me that we were not yet out of the wood. Other agitators, they affirmed, were still at large, and busy amongst the foreign rabble; the copies of the undertaking signed by the workers' committee had been torn down, on the grounds that the signatures upon it had been obtained by compulsion, and were worthless; and rumours were already abroad that the day of reckoning with the *bourgeois* was only postponed.

Our action had secured, nevertheless, its main object: for it had undoubtedly checked an organized rising in the town of Murmansk, the success of which was to have heralded similar outbreaks from the sea to Soroka.

At Alexandrovsk, though there were rowdy demonstrations, and a liberal display of flags bearing inscriptions of "Long live Lenin and Trotsky," our local detachment proved fully capable of dealing with the situation.

At Kandalaksha minor disturbances occurred, necessitating the arrest of half a dozen agitators. But failure at Murmansk had evidently cooled the ardour of would-be revolutionaries. The attitude of the Finn Legion, however, gave increasing cause for anxiety, and it had been ascertained that Lehtimaki had been in communication with the commander of the Finn regiment which was serving with the Bolsheviks, and which had been pushed up recently into the front line.

From Kem and Soroka the tales were much the same—disorderly and threatening crowds, but no attempt at a rising worthy of the name.

At these two centres there was a strong suspicion that guile was to have played a more important part than mob violence.

A certain lady, who held a position of some standing,

issued to all Allied officers at Kem and Soroka invitations to a grand-scale reception and dance to be held on the night appointed for the rising. Reports received by me as to the procedure it was proposed to adopt when these officers should have put in their appearance showed considerable variety. Some went so far as to hint that an attempt would be made to imitate the well-known methods of the Borgias, and all pointed to a determination to denude units of their officers at a time when their presence would be most required. It is possible of course that none had a solid foundation, and that the intentions of the would-be hostess were purely amicable. Whatever they may have been, they were not put to the test, every officer finding, with wonderful unanimity, that his military duties precluded him from accepting her kind invitation. For want of any proof to the contrary, it must be held therefore that Madame's suggested function was nothing but a good-hearted effort to enliven the monotony of garrison life, and condolences are due to her for the lack of appreciation shown in monotonous succession by all invited.

I have told how the situation in the Finn Legion was showing increasing tenseness, but that no insubordinate outbreak occurred on the day fixed for the general rising. On March 30th, however, one of its trusted officers informed General Turner's staff that the Legion, under the leadership of Lehtimaki, was to mutiny on April 6th. The following day I received a report from another source confirming this, and adding details. The mutineers were to destroy two large bridges near Kandalaksha (over which they furnished guards), and then move south to join the Bolsheviks, picking up *en route* sympathizers from the Karelian Regiment.

It looked most certainly as if matters were coming to a head at last; and so serious did I regard the whole affair, that I cabled home asking that naval reinforcements should be sent me, sufficient to furnish a landing party of 400. I should thus be enabled to replace the troops I proposed to despatch from Murmansk, and have in hand a small reserve, in case additional support were needed later at, or south of, Kandalaksha. My request, however, might not be granted, and, at the best, nearly a week must elapse before the reinforcements asked for could reach me. And by then the greater part of the mischief might be done.

It was evident that Lehtimaki had not abided by his word to abstain from revolutionary tactics, and that he was determined to throw off allegiance to the Allies and give his aid to Bolshevism. It may be that the results of the Finnish elections, which the Legion had been awaiting with mingled hope and trepidation, decided him to take the extreme measures he now contemplated, since they made it clear that the Red cause in Finland was utterly discredited. But the forces influencing him were of little concern to me. Whatever they might be, the action he and his followers had in view must be frustrated, lest a situation should arise in the south with which I might find it almost impossible to cope.

The surest way to restore order was to arrest Lehtimaki and his disciples, and it was decided that an attempt must be made to carry this out.

But the Finns in and around Kandalaksha, with a strength of 700–800, and a mountain battery at their disposal, far outnumbered the remainder of the garrison and, for all I knew, Lehtimaki might have made secret arrangements for drawing in the Legion's frontier detachments, 500 strong in all. Every Finn, moreover, was an experienced skier, and they would thus hold a very palpable advantage over my men.

As, therefore, it was unlikely that the ringleaders would submit tamely to arrest, additional troops must be sent, and these it was not easy to find. Admiral Green helped to solve the problem by placing 120 of *Glory's* marines under my orders, and to these were added two platoons of the Sussex Regiment (all I felt justified in sparing from Murmansk), making a total of about 200.

It was arranged that I should go down with these reinforcements; and Lieutenant-Colonel Burton, commanding the Legion, was informed that I wished all his senior officers, both British and Finn, to meet me at garrison headquarters.

There was a special reason why I should go; for I had great doubts of Lehtimaki and others obeying a summons to meet any officer other than myself, and with this view the garrison commander concurred. At the last moment, however, I gleaned news of further trouble brewing at Murmansk, and reached the conclusion that it would be highly unwise for me to be absent from the place for several days. It was settled, therefore, that General Turner and Lewin should act as my emissaries, instead of my companions, as was intended originally.

I felt rather as if I were foisting an exceptionally unpleasant job upon the shoulders of these two; but I found I had little need for worry on this score, Lewin informing me that he welcomed my decision not to accompany them with profound relief.

But, although I was to stay behind, the Finn Legion must not be disabused of the impression that I was going to Kandalaksha. An extract from a letter I wrote to General Radcliffe at the War Office on April 5th shows how we contrived to work this little deception:

" The situation is not without its comic side. I had every intention of going down myself to attempt the arrest of the anti-Allied Finn leaders, and had made all arrangements accordingly. Just before starting, however, I got reliable information that the brutes here were on the war-path again; and this, coupled with Turner's and Lewin's protestations, determined me not to accompany them down the line. I knew, though, that the Finn leaders would refuse to come in to meet anyone but myself, and I had to make them think that I was really coming.

"Every movement or possible movement of mine is watched and reported on ; so much so, that Bolshevik agents at Kandalaksha knew I proposed going there, before I sent my wire announcing my intention of doing so—probably owing to my special railway-carriage having been ordered. Thus I had to resort to stratagem. I had my own railway-carriage got ready and drove down in state to the train, conversed with the railway officials and was as much *en évidence* as possible. Then, just before the train started, I nipped into my compartment ; put on one of the men's long coats instead of my British warm ; substituted a balaclava cap for my ostentatious headgear ; fixed a pair of gold-rimmed spectacles on my nose ; slipped out of the train ; and followed a devious route homewards.

"The cruel part was that the spectacles were meant for reading, and as it was dark, I couldn't see in the least where I was going. I had to wear them for about half an hour, and strained my eyes so badly that for two days afterwards I was weeping continuously.

"Queer things a C.-in-C. has to do in this weird country ! However, the ruse was successful, which is the chief thing."

Turner and Lewin, with their two hundred, reached Kandalaksha on the evening of April 2nd, and learnt at once that the delegates from Knyaja Guba (a near-by detachment of the Legion, with which Lehtimaki and most of his brother hot-heads were serving) had failed to put in an appearance. As it transpired later, they had come to Kandalaksha, but, hearing news of the arrival of a large armed escort—and their consciences being none too clear—had fled back to Knyaja Guba precipitously.

Burton (O.C. Legion) was taken aside first, and told that I had given instructions for Lehtimaki's arrest. Against this Burton protested, asserting that he had given a personal guarantee for Lehtimaki's safety. That he had been altogether unjustified in giving any such guarantee did not lessen the awkwardness of Turner's position; for he must either fail to carry out what he knew to be my wishes, or must allow the word of a British commanding officer to be stultified. He decided finally that Burton's guarantee must hold good, and a fresh summons was sent to the Knyaja Guba representatives instructing them to attend at Kandalaksha the next morning. As this was obeyed by one delegate only—and he not Lehtimaki—it was evident that a visit must be paid to Knyaja Guba.

Before taking this step, however, the air must be cleared at Kandalaksha, especially as Turner had learnt that, at a meeting held during the previous night, the younger bloods had pressed for an immediate rising, and for joining forces with Lehtimaki at Knyaja Guba. The presence of strong guards found by his escort had, it would seem, been the determining factor in securing the rejection of this proposition.

It was therefore broken to the Legion's representatives at headquarters that all details of the intended mutiny were known to us, and that we had made every preparation to crush it ruthlessly. They were also informed that the negotiations for their return to Finland were proceeding far more smoothly, but that every man who failed to stand by us now unreservedly would forfeit at once all claim to be included amongst those to be repatriated. These were the facts, and it only remained for them to settle at once on which side their influence was to be exerted.

The officers present made no attempt to deny that a mutiny was in contemplation, but all asserted that their hands had been forced by Lehtimaki, who had undermined Tokoi's influence and authority. They were now ready to trust Tokoi and to support him, if he considered their interests would be served best by awaiting with patience the outcome of Allied conversations with their Government. Nevertheless it was, they considered, far from certain that the peace could be kept unless Lehtimaki could be won over or removed, as nearly all the men at Knyaja Guba and some at least of those at headquarters were under his thumb.

Whether it was because he considered we now held the whip hand or because his loyalty was something more than makebelief, I do not know; but Tokoi played up to us well. He gave an unqualified vote in favour of peace, and followed this by an impassioned harangue to all such of the Legion as were at Kandalaksha, impressing on them the folly of their meditated action (more especially as it had been found out), and exhorting them to place their confidence in the Allies. He reported afterwards to Turner that he was satisfied that those now opposed to violence were in a sufficient majority to curb the extremists, and that the danger of any mutinous outbreak would be negligible, provided we found means to deal with Lehtimaki and the Knyaja Guba malcontents.

It was then suggested that, as Lehtimaki could not be arrested in view of Burton's guarantee, a free and unimpeded passage to the Bolshevik lines should be afforded him; and Tokoi jumped at once at this solution.

It remained, however, to get hold of Lehtimaki; so Turner and his party proceeded to Knyaja Guba, Burton having been ordered previously to collect together all officers of the detachment. And this time, all were forthcoming.

Lehtimaki was interviewed first and alone; and Turner did not mince matters. He told him that we knew all about his plans and intentions, and that the only reason why he had not been arrested, and probably shot by now, was because the word of a British officer must be held sacred. He (Lehtimaki), on the other hand, had violated grossly his own promise to the C.-in-C., and thus deserved in reality no clemency whatever. He must choose now, once and for all, between Bolshevism and us, and must do so openly. If he selected the former, we were fully prepared; if the latter, then we would continue our good offices with their Government on behalf of the Legion; but, as it was doubtful whether he personally would ever be admitted again to Finland, we were ready to allow him, together with not more than a couple of his comrades, to join the Bolsheviks in the south, under arrangements to be made by us.

The other officers were then brought in, and spoken to with equal candour. Once again the intention of mutinying was not denied, nor apparently was mutiny regarded at Knyaja Guba as a very heinous offence. The line they took was rather that, having been caught out, they must reconsider the whole aspect of affairs. Lehtimaki, for one, gave no sign of repentance; but the prospect of safe conduct to his friends made a greater appeal to him than embarking on a mutiny which, as we were forewarned, might result in failure. After long argumentation, therefore, he announced that he would undertake to work in harmony with the Allies, so long as he was associated with the Legion; and the remaining officers followed suit. All signed an agreement under oath to this effect, and we, as a counterpoise, added a promise that we would do our utmost to send two British and two Finn officers as a delegation to Helsingfors. This promise found fulfilment in May.

Lehtimaki elected to accept Turner's offer, and he, together with one other irreconcilable, were sent down the line, and conducted beyond our outposts. Though he had been one of my chief curses, I could not help feeling a certain admiration for his courage and rigid adhesion to his principles, despite the buffetings of an unpropitious fate. He was, too, not without humour; for his last request to me was that I should furnish him with a testimonial setting forth his excellent qualities and good services to the Allies!

Turner and Lewin had accomplished their mission. Though the means adopted were not those intended originally, and might possibly appear derogatory to our prestige, they were certainly the best of which altered conditions permitted. Their result, in any case, was highly satisfactory, and from that time onward the Legion caused me no serious disquietude. I have perhaps devoted over-much space to its affairs; but for nearly ten months its attitude was for me a matter of very grave concern. Its history can be completed now in few words.

In May, Lewin, Burton, and two Finn representatives left for Helsingfors to discuss the question of repatriation. My first report from Lewin after his arrival was not encouraging; for it told me that the Finnish Government had gained the impression from our Foreign Office that I had no real desire that my legionaries should return to their country, but that my object was solely to gain time for the advent of reinforcements sufficient to carry out their disarmament. All Lewin's persuasive powers were needed to disabuse the authorities of this idea, but he succeeded at length in so doing, and after several weeks the negotiations were brought to a satisfactory end.

On August 31st the Legion (minus a few deserters, and others whose misdeeds during the revolution were probably unforgivable) embarked for Finland, Lieutenant-Colonel W. R. Warren being detailed to accompany it, and act as my representative in the final settlement. His rôle, I gathered subsequently, was neither easy nor pleasant; and when the time came for him to relinquish his work, he was no less delighted to bid farewell to the Finn Legion than I had been when the s.s. *Kursk* bore it, 1,100 strong, down the Kola Inlet, and beyond the sphere of my control.

Whilst Turner was wrestling with the Finn problem, disturbance of the peace, as had been foretold by my agents, was once more threatened at Murmansk. This time, efforts were to be centred in an attack on general headquarters.

A description of the counter-steps we took would be as wearisome to the reader as were these continual alarms to us. I content myself therefore with saying that the main results were that accommodation in the *Chesma* (our prison-ship) was taxed to its utmost, and that many of the inhabitants of the backwaters of the town now found themselves without the weapons which they had contrived hitherto to conceal.

It cannot be pretended that life during these few weeks from mid-March to early April was altogether a thing of joy; for we lived practically in a state of siege. The more important buildings were surrounded by wire and miniature fortifications, and stored with reserves of food and water; windows were loopholed, and made bullet-proof by heaping firewood logs against them; every officer and man slept with a loaded rifle at his side, with bayonet ready fixed; and individual movement after dark was always fraught with risk. Such inconveniences were, however, of small account compared with the measure of success achieved. Moscow had hoped to stage against us, behind our fighting line, so great a number of concerted movements as to shake our hold on the occupied area and paralyse military effort at the front. But, thanks chiefly to accurate information, we had been able to anticipate each attempt, and each, in consequence, had been dealt with without undue difficulty and with little loss of life. Although, too, all reports had led me to believe that the Bolshevik army would play its appointed part in the scheme, and add to my hoped-for discomfiture by a sudden and vigorous attack, its only contribution was a half-hearted endeavour to drive us from Segeja, made on April 7th, and frustrated with ease. That troops were available for far more determined action is certain; and I can only assume that their non-employment was due to the total failure of Bolshevik plans elsewhere, or that, yet once again, I had benefited by the slothful incompetence of Red commanders and staff.

The scurry and anxiety of the past few weeks saw therefore our position in the south unaltered, and our hold throughout the 400 miles of our communications unimpaired and even strengthened.

The Ides of March had come and gone, the ill-omens presaged at their entry unfulfilled.

CHAPTER XV

WE REACH LAKE ONEGA

DESPITE the fact that the Bolshevik forces opposed to me had not profited by the late disorders along my line of communication, and had done no more than deliver one weak and tentative attack on my southernmost garrison, there could be little doubt that they had received recently considerable reinforcements.

On April 10th the O.C. Segeja (Major Anderson) ascertained that some of these were commencing already to concentrate at Urosozero, and that plans were being drawn up for another and more powerful bid to recapture his post.

Faced with this threat, he decided on a bold course. Rather than await the impending onslaught, he would himself attack. Judging that every hour was of importance, he did not ask for sanction, but moved out on the 11th with his armoured train and a total force of less than one hundred, including men of the new Russian army and of the Slavo-British Legion.

His choice of action undoubtedly was right. Hitherto the initiative had been ours, and if the Reds now preened themselves on the idea that it was about to pass from us to them, it was well that this impression should be corrected. Moreover, nothing was more likely to upset their calculations than being attacked at a time when they must have expected that the strain on our resources was unusually great.

Nor could I attribute blame for the launching of the enterprise without my consent. Though the home authorities were averse in principle from further offensive undertakings on my part, this attack was essentially a defensive measure, and it was for the man on the spot to judge whether the safety of his command would be risked by even a short delay.

His decision for prompt attack proved well justified. The Bolsheviks, engrossed in preparations for their own advance, had taken little precaution to guard against a blow that seemed to them so far removed from probability. Though they outnumbered greatly the men of Segeja, their defeat was decisive, and their losses exceedingly heavy in proportion to their strength. Fifty dead were left for burial by us, and forty prisoners taken. In addition, many wounded were seen to be removed on sledges, and a train in which the final retreat was effected was damaged severely by our shell fire.

The booty captured included two field guns with 7,000 shell, one machine gun, over 100 rifles and carbines with many thousand rounds of ammunition, 100 pairs of ski, 22 box cars, points and switches ready packed on trucks, light railway material, explosives, forage, saddlery, and much other material such as would be collected naturally at a forward base, were an advance in contemplation.

The price paid for this success—due largely to the gallantry of the French crew of the armoured train—was one killed and five wounded. Its effect, too, could not be measured solely by tactical results; for it served to discredit anti-Allied agitators by falsifying their prophecies of our imminent collapse, and persuaded many waverers to cast off their allegiance to the Bolshevik cause.

The enemy having been driven from Urosozero, immediate steps were taken to consolidate our hold on the village; this being in accordance with our fixed policy of never withdrawing from any territory, once it had been won.

But its occupation made necessary a further small operation. The road leading north from Povynetz to Sumski Posad runs roughly parallel with the railway, and passes through Vojmosalmi, which, together with neighbouring hamlets, was occupied by Red troops. Now that our spear-head had been thrust forward another 20 miles, these enemy detachments were placed favourably to threaten our communications as well as our flank, and must therefore be evicted.

A battalion of the North Russian Rifle Regiment (the first fully constituted unit of the new army) was training at Soroka, and the time appeared opportune for it to commence its active career. It was ordered accordingly to move down the Povynetz road, and clear the Reds from Vojmosalmi and its vicinity.

Captain Daidoff, a most enterprising and resourceful officer, was in command, and wasted no time. Urosozero had been captured on April 11th, and by the 16th Daidoff had completed his task. He had driven the Bolsheviks helter-skelter southwards; had inflicted ascertained losses of 40 killed and 50 prisoners; and had captured 4 machine guns and many rifles—a fighting début of much promise, up to which I could only hope that the Russian forces would continue to live.

These little victories filled Yermoloff with delight, and his one desire was that we should continue to press forward. As illustrating the feasibility of this, he laid stress on the satisfactory outcome of Daidoff's efforts, secured as this had been without Allied aid, and urged that Russian troops should be permitted to advance at once, even if the Allies should not be in position to co-operate with them.

His wish was very natural. It was, for one thing, perfectly true that, having got the Bolsheviks on the run, it would be sound tactics to keep them running; for their army was notoriously indisciplined, and it was quite possible that an immediate pursuit, besides adding greatly to its demoralization, would result in our gaining many additional miles of territory—and to Yermoloff fresh territory was synonymous with fresh recruits.

But at present I was bound by a policy of non-offence, and must be able to put up a good case before I could hope to obtain sanction for a large-scale advance. For, if I made any forward move at all, I had decided long since that the northern shore of Lake Onega must be my objective.

Neither could I countenance the Russians pushing on alone. They were not yet sufficiently strong to follow more than the single line of advance along which they were now operating (the Povynetz road); and it was quite certain to my mind that an advance by this route must be accompanied by a move down the railway, and probably also by one on its west through Karelia.

Yermoloff, too, underestimated the limitations of the Russian troops. Because a portion of one battalion had done well in a series of rough-and-tumble fights, he assumed that the Russian army as a whole would give an equally good account of itself in future operations, overlooking the fact that the few who had shared in the small successes already won had not encountered organized resistance, nor been subjected to the ordeal of hostile shell-fire. As each mile southward would be likely to see our hitherto guerrilla-like mêlées approximate more closely to the conditions of modern warfare, I felt that the Russians had not been tried sufficiently high as yet to warrant an advance on their part, unsupported by the Allies.

Although, however, I considered myself bound to throw cold water on Yermoloff's suggestion of a purely Russian offensive, there was no denying that an attempt to drive the Reds from Povynetz and Medvyejya Gora, and thus gain access to Lake Onega, offered many inducements.

Amongst these was, of course, included the augmentation of the loyal Russian army; and the type of recruit likely to be obtained would be precisely that most needed. For we were leaving behind us gradually the land of tundra, and nearing a region of which considerable tracts were under cultivation. The inhabitants were almost wholly of the peasant class, and entertained no affection for Bolshevism and its practices, the fruits of which, as discernible by them, were ill-treatment, robbery, and starvation. It was held therefore—and, as events showed, held truly—that they would welcome the chance of turning against their oppressors.

Thus, an advance of a further 50 miles might well lead to the ranks of Yermoloff's army being swelled by several thousand willing recruits of the most promising stamp.

But, if the sketch-map be turned to, it will be seen at once that, in addition to this, certain distinct strategic advantages would be secured :

(*a*) The occupation of Medvyejya Gora and Povynetz would block the only main avenues of approach to the north, whilst, at the same time, my front would be shortened considerably.

(*b*) The extent of country to be watched to the west would be much reduced, owing to the proximity of the Finnish frontier at this point.

It was also possible that my offensive might serve to relieve enemy pressure at Archangel, where the Bolsheviks were giving signs of greatly increased activity.

There would seem small doubt therefore of the soundness of the move, provided always that I could make reasonably certain of success, and quite certain of retaining my hold on the position won, so far as this might depend on my ability to maintain my lengthened communications, and on my administrative services being capable of responding to the additional call made upon them.

The first point to be determined was whether my strength was sufficient to warrant my banking on a successful issue. Towards the close of April the internal situation throughout the whole Murman Area could be regarded with more than average satisfaction. So far as could be judged, the probabilities of another rising were remote ; the Finn Legion was unlikely to give further trouble ; and, though the people of Karelia (as explained later in Chapter XVII) were aspiring once again to cut themselves adrift from Russia, and needed careful watching, I had reasonable grounds for believing that they would refrain from extreme measures.

It would thus be possible, I hoped, to make at least a small reduction in up-country garrisons, and increase proportionately my forces in the south.

But, besides the few hundred additional men I might be able to collect for the offensive in this manner, I had now another source on which to draw.

The Admiralty had not seen its way to comply with my request for naval reinforcements (admitting of a landing party of 400) made at the time when the whole of the occupied territory was seething with unrest, and a mutiny of the Finn Legion appeared inevitable. The War Office, however, had exerted itself at once to respond to my appeal, and had prepared for despatch to me two infantry companies, one of the King's Royal Rifles and one of the Middlesex Regiment. These reached Murmansk on April 17th, and I could reckon therefore on 500 extra Britishers being available for the push to Lake Onega, should it materialize. In artillery, too, I was relatively strong ; and, as we advanced, the ground would become more suitable for the employment of this arm. Though the Bolsheviks would reap a similar advantage, I was ready to back our own gunners every time against such as the Red army could produce.

So far as concerned British troops, I calculated that it should be possible for nearly 1,000 to take the field ; and French, Serbians, and Italians could be spared to the number of about 700.

The Russian army should be able to furnish 1,000, inclusive of a couple of hundred " partisans," a band of free-lances under a Colonel Krugliakoff, whose movements it was not always easy to control. The Olonetz Regiment (a composite unit of Karelians and

Russians) would provide an additional 500 local troops.

With the above heterogeneous array of some 3,000 as my instrument, was I justified in informing the War Office that I could break through Bolshevik opposition, and establish myself on the Povynetz—Medvyejya Gora line?

To start with, the undertaking would be out of harmony with the policy our Government held to be desirable, and approval for it would be given, if given at all, solely on the grounds that I regarded success as almost certain, and that highly beneficial results would be achieved. Regarded therefore from the personal point of view, my load of responsibility would be heavy. Again, if the move were once commenced, it must be pushed through. Half-measures would be useless; for unless I could gain possession of Medvyejya Gora with its lake-side quays and shipping facilities, I should be less secure at 10 miles distance from it than at 50. But the possibility of the Bolsheviks bringing up powerful reinforcements could not be dismissed, and, in this case, the fighting might be heavy and, even were my object gained, it might prove a Pyrrhic victory, leaving me dangerously weak, and with the added burden of 50 more miles of road and railway communication.

The decision I reached finally was that, so far as concerned the actual winning of the new line, the chances were sufficiently promising to warrant the attempt.

The first point being thus determined, the second remained for consideration.

Would my administrative services stand the further strain? For the railway I could answer at once, and in the affirmative. About the middle of April two companies of American railway troops had landed, and I could have wished for no more pleasing gift. Every man of their 600 was a volunteer, full of enthusiasm and the love of adventure; and I pay ungrudging tribute now to the excellent service they rendered subsequently. These two companies could (and did) take over the entire running and repairing of the portion of the line south of Kem, working it as a military section. I should thus be relieved of all anxiety for the maintenance of the railway system. Not only this, but the men, although I was prohibited from employing them in the fighting line, were armed soldiers, and would contribute largely towards the protection of that stretch of the railway operated by them.

On the question of other administrative branches I could not speak with equal confidence. Their personnel, never too large for the work involved, had been weakened recently by the posting of officers and other ranks to Russian formations for purposes of instruction and guidance ; and it might be that the new dispositions (when effected), coupled with the continued growth of the Russian forces, would prove too great a tax upon their efficiency.

Thanks, however, in large measure to the good work of Lieutenant-Colonel Schuster,[1] my chief administrative staff officer, of Lieutenant-Colonel Moore,[2] who was responsible for supplies and transport, and of my other heads of corps and departments, we could say, without undue arrogance, that our administrative machinery was working with marvellous smoothness, under conditions none too favourable.

There was still, we calculated, a margin that would admit of safety, even if it should not admit of perfection, in the continuance of essential services under the new conditions contemplated—and an assurance of safety was sufficient. Perfection, if attainable, must

[1] Now Sir George Schuster, K.C.M.G., C.B.E., M.C., Financial Member (designate) in the Government of India. He relieved Michael Spencer-Smith when the latter was invalided home in January.
[2] Lieutenant-Colonel T. C. P. Moore, C.B.E., now Member of Parliament for Ayr Burghs.

be left till later, when the additional administrative personnel, which the War Office had undertaken to do its utmost to provide, should be forthcoming.

Whilst speaking on this subject, I must admit at once that we were to find our "margin of safety" much too narrow for our liking. Difficulties were experienced at home in furnishing the extra men I had asked for; and all those engaged in administrative work had to put their shoulders to the wheel unremittingly.

Of my own staff, I wrote on a later date to Radcliffe:

"Though my staff are playing up splendidly, they are absolutely beat to the world. Several officers are sick, and over half my clerks are in hospital—simply as the result of overwork. Three days ago I had not a single clerk available for A. or Q. duties. Schuster especially is a shadow of his former self. He, of course, is one of my chief stays at present, and as he has been working about sixteen hours a day for months, I dread his breakdown."

At the time, however, our conclusion was that administrative difficulties need not stand in the way of the proposed enterprise; and as I had made up my mind that our fighting strength was adequate for its task, I cabled to the War Office explaining the advantages likely to be derived, and requesting sanction for an immediate advance.

On April 29th I received a commendably early reply. It struck a note of friendly warning, in that it informed me that I must rely wholly on the troops now at my disposal; but the scheme was approved in its entirety.

There were few last-minute preparations needed; for we had taken already such steps as were possible to ensure a speedy move, should permission be granted. Amongst these were the provision of motor-boats for employment on Lake Onega; the shipment of a field battery from Petchenga; the mounting on railway-trucks of a couple of 4·5 howitzers; the creation of a second armoured train; repairing of the railway; further evacuation of undesirables; and the preparation of an advanced aerodrome.

One submarine-chaser (christened the *Jolly Roger*) and several smaller motor-boats had been found at Murmansk in various stages of decrepitude. With naval help their engines had been tinkered up, and other repairs effected, with a view to their employment on the lakes around Segeja, as soon as these should be free of ice. They had been armed recently with 37-mm. guns, and placed on wagons ready to be railed south. Their crews were to be furnished by the artillery.

Admiral McCully, of the U.S. navy, had added to the fleet by lending me two of his motor-launches, manned by American sailors; and I had also cabled to England for larger boats of the chaser class, with Inland Water Transport crews.

The battery had been brought from Petchenga by trawlers, for which an icebreaker had broken a passage. It had been an awkward job, but accomplished successfully.

The mounting on trucks of the 4·5 howitzers, and the new armoured train, were pieces of work which we regarded with some pride. Experimental firing had been carried out with the howitzers with satisfactory results, and the train, though a lumbering monstrosity in appearance, could be guaranteed to afford good protection against rifle bullets and shrapnel.

The 400-foot span bridge over the Onda had been reconstructed by the end of March, and we could count on the whole length of line as far as Urosozero being restored before the opening of May.

During the fortnight preceding our advance, 350 undesirables were rounded up and dropped beyond our lines, and 300 Letts and Lithuanians shipped to Libau.

Of the new aerodrome I must speak somewhat more fully, as I have not touched as yet upon the work of the R.A.F.

Our first aerodrome had been at Kem ; but in spite of the labour spent upon it, taking-off and landing had always been extremely risky operations with the machines supplied to me originally. These were six R.E. 8's, sent out in November with a personnel of 14 officers and 57 other ranks. Besides being of an unsuitable type for the work, the condition of their engines was so indifferent that only three of the six were ever made serviceable. The officers, too, though they worked desperately hard at their machines and flying-ground, and showed magnificent pluck, were mostly inexperienced, only one of them having done as much as eighty hours' flying prior to his arrival.

When at home in December I had begged for some Avros, but had been informed by the Air Ministry that one of their staff had reported the Murman Area as totally unfit for planes of any sort. I had pointed out that the officer mentioned had never been a mile inland, and could therefore have had no opportunity of judging ; but my pleading was in vain, and I had to wait until the beginning of June before I could rely on any efficient help from the R.A.F. I am quite convinced that, had machines of a suitable type been sent me, we could have fashioned an aerodrome with a level surface of hardened snow, sufficiently large to be utilized by them from December to April.

To get back to facts, however, we had at this time only three patched-up R.E. 8's ; and the thaw might deprive us any day of the use of even these, unless we could find another aerodrome with a firmer surface under the snow than that of the tundra-covered ground at Kem.

After much search, the only alternative site discovered was at a spot close to the railway midway between Segeja and Urosozero, alongside what was known as Siding 19. It was a caricature of an aerodrome, being in reality nothing but a glorified sandpit. But the surface was hard and fairly level ; and, as there was no other choice, my R.A.F. officers decided to try it. And try it the splendid fellows did, making several flights of much value. It took its toll of aircraft, however—as was perhaps to be expected—and at the final stage of our advance, one semi-crippled machine was all that was left of the original six.

All the above preparations had, as I have said, been put in hand, in anticipation of sanction being given for the proposed offensive ; and, having obtained that sanction, little remained to be done but to shift general headquarters to Kem, assemble the troops at their jumping-off places, and give to Price the word to go.

The advance was to be made in three columns moving on an initial front of 60 miles, and was to be carried out in two bounds : the first from Urosozero to Maselga ; the second from Maselga to Medvyejya Gora.

The right column, consisting of the Olonetz Regiment, was directed to clear the western and southern shores of Lake Segozero, and act as a flanking guard. The centre column, composed mainly of British troops, was ordered to advance rapidly down the railway ; whilst the left column, which consisted almost entirely of Russians, was to follow the Vojmosalmi—Povynetz road.

The movement commenced on May 1st, and the centre column occupied Maselga on May 3rd, after forty-eight hours' continuous fighting. The capture of the village was a serious threat to the communications of the enemy on the west of Lake Segozero, and they withdrew rapidly to the south, closely pressed by our right column.

The left column had encountered some stiff opposition, but had driven the Reds from Tolekina, and established itself 20 miles east of Maselga.

Krugliakoff's " partisans " on the extreme east had, in the meantime, pushed on to Danilova.

Our first objective had thus been gained, and the enemy forced back along the whole front, with considerable losses in men and material.

A pause of some days now ensued in order to accumulate supplies and ammunition, and to repair the damage done to the railway by the enemy during his retreat.

On May 11th the right column was attacked at Karelska Maselga, the Bolsheviks making a determined effort to recapture the village. The Olonetz Regiment repulsed them, with losses amounting to 40 killed and 20 prisoners, together with three machine guns captured. But two of their British officers (including a gallant battalion commander, Major L. A. Drake-Brockman, of the Royal Marines) were killed, and another British officer was wounded.

On the 15th the advance was resumed, the three columns now operating on a reduced frontage of 35 miles.

The centre column came into action at once, encountering a strong covering party, which it dislodged, after inflicting upon it appreciable losses, including 30 killed. Unfortunately we lost another commanding officer in this small affair, Lieutenant Muir, commanding a trench-mortar battery, being killed.

On the 16th the Reds were found to be holding a series of entrenched lines, and, as the ground was too marshy to admit of turning movements, a frontal attack was necessitated. This was carried out in dashing style by the Middlesex and K.R.R. companies, supported by gun fire from railway trucks. It met with complete success, and many prisoners and machine guns were taken.

On the 17th and 18th further progress was made, the proximity of the railway becoming more favourable for cross-country movement, and the enemy being manœuvred out of a number of prepared positions.

By the night of the 18th/19th the column was within 5 miles of Medvyejya Gora, but here the resistance stiffened to a very marked degree. On this, a captured order shed some light; for in it, Trotsky abused wholeheartedly the Red commander opposed to us, informing him that his was the only front on which the Red army had sustained an unbroken series of reverses; that there must be no more retirements; and that Medvyejya Gora, at any rate, must be held " to the last gasp."

Certainly the Bolsheviks at this stage showed greater tenacity than ever they had done before, and it was evident they had the help of a much-increased artillery. Their gun fire, including that from 6-inch howitzers, was at times really heavy, but, luckily for us, was never concentrated and seldom accurate. Our guns, now able to come into action away from the railway, proved far more efficacious, and enabled us, little by little, to win forward.

On May 21st Medvyejya Gora was captured by a combined assault of British, French, Italian, Serbian, and Russian troops. The flanking columns had assisted materially in the victory. On the west the Olonetz Regiment had pressed on slowly but consistently, and by routing a strong flank guard (of whom they accounted for over 60 in killed and prisoners) on the morning of the 21st, had placed the Red lines of communication in jeopardy. This, without doubt, had helped to convince the Bolshevik commander that he had gone near enough to compliance with his orders to hold on " to the last gasp."

The Russian column to the east had captured Povynetz on the 18th, after several days' desultory fighting, and Daidoff, ever impetuous, had already sent strong patrols 30 miles down the eastern shore of Lake Onega, whilst, 40 miles ahead of these, Krugliakoff and his " partisans " ranged the country in search of recruits—and, it may be, plunder.

Around Medvyejya Gora, measures were taken at once to make our grip secure. But the Reds had been trounced too thoroughly to permit of their rallying for counter-attack, and we were left in undisturbed possession of the line, on whose capture we had set such store.

This is not a military text-book, and the drawing of lessons and deductions is outside my aim. But, in justice to all who played leading rôles in this three-week push from Urosozero, there are certain aspects of the operation on which I feel impelled to comment.

When the movement commenced, the thaw had just set in; and unless the import of this is realized, full value cannot be accorded to the work accomplished by the three columns.

Of roads, such as we know them, there were none; and the few tracks existing were, with the exception of the immediate approaches to Lake Onega, all but impassable for wheeled traffic even under the most favourable conditions—and these did not embrace the period of thaw.

The Russians were best placed; for the Povynetz road was regarded as a main thoroughfare, and though its surface was certainly no better than that of an unmetalled country lane, it was direct and well-defined.

A single-track railway, with many embankments and little ballast, does not lend itself well to the passage of guns and transport; and the progress of the centre column was hampered still further by the fact that nearly every bridge had been destroyed.

But the trials besetting these two columns were as nothing compared with those encountered by the men of the Olonetz Regiment on the right. They were moving through country which, for the most part, was low-lying and marshy, and traversed only by foot- and bridle-paths. As these crossed many streams, bridges over which were either non-existent or broken down, neither the hundred-mile march accomplished by the column itself nor its provisioning could be classed as simple undertakings.

There was, too, the question of communication. We had no portable sets of wireless; the only per-

A TEMPORARY HINDRANCE TO OUR ADVANCE. (*From a photograph by J. Sewell*)

manent telegraph or telephone lines were those along the railway and the Soroka–Povynetz track—the last named being so inefficient as to be practically useless; no roads ran from east to west; and our signal personnel was exceedingly small. With parallel columns moving on a front ranging from 60 to 20 miles, little military knowledge is needed to grasp the difficulty of disseminating intelligence or issuing orders, in circumstances such as these.

A further handicap imposed upon the directing staff was the unreliability of our maps, which were inaccurate as well as incomplete. Thus, not only were calculations of time and distance frequently upset, but it was found impossible to include in instructions such topographical details as were needed to ensure complete co-ordination of effort.

It may perhaps be wondered why our advance was not postponed for a short period, since conditions for the movement of troops were at their worst during the first few weeks of thaw. Apart, however, from various other considerations discountenancing delay, there was one of special importance.

A naval flotilla had always been maintained on Lake Onega, and would now be at the disposal of the Bolsheviks. If I failed to reach the lake before the ice broke, and it was once again open to navigation, I should incur the risk of the flotilla co-operating with the enemy's land forces; and, even if I defeated the latter, I should find it hard to cope at once with the former, especially if I were still deficient of aircraft.

If, on the other hand, I could arrive at Medvyejya Gora while the lake was still ice-bound, I should have time to organize an artillery defence, and also to bring down, launch, and test our own boats; for the inshore ice was always the earliest to melt. Further, I could start on the construction of bases both for motor-boats and seaplanes (expected to reach me by the end of May) without fear of disturbance from enemy craft; and, should luck favour us, we might even capture some shipping frozen in at the northern angle of the lake.

The earliest date on which it would be possible for Bolshevik ships to operate could not, of course, be foretold with certainty; but I gathered it was likely to be between mid-May and early June. If, therefore, I intended to dispute Red naval supremacy, I could not afford to delay my attack on Medvyejya Gora.

Although our advance had been held up for somewhat longer than I had counted on, our luck, as things turned out, did not fail us.

When the Russians entered Povynetz, they found several steam-launches fast in the ice at some distance from the shore, an unsuccessful attempt having been made evidently to remove them. These were salved within a few days and annexed by us. At Medvyejya Gora, too, we made a small but useful haul of lighters.

Close inshore was clear water, and though the ice farther out was still some inches thick, it was disappearing rapidly, and we were faced with the practical certainty that the lake would be open sufficiently by the end of the month to allow of the Bolshevik flotilla steaming northward.

Our preparations must accordingly be pushed forward with all speed.

Our Murmansk motor-boats had commenced their rail journey towards the south, even before the enemy had been cleared from their final positions, and were now brought up to within two miles of the lake. It was thanks to the speedy repair work of the American railway troops that they were able to get thus far; but farther they could not go until the reconstruction of a 60-foot bridge had been completed. Fir trees were felled promptly; rough rollers fashioned; and the boats dragged overland to the shore by hand. Two of them were afloat, and had carried out their trials, before the first truck had passed over the repaired bridge.

The *Jolly Roger*[1] was launched on June 4th, and became the "flagship" of our then existing fleet of 6 motor-boats and 2 steam-launches.

These few boats, slow as most of them were, and with engines on which continued reliance could not be placed, were better than nothing, and could be employed usefully for patrol work. But I awaited anxiously the arrival of the speedier boats from home, and also of the two flights of seaplanes, which I had been told were on their way to me on board H.M.S. *Nairana*.[2] I had cabled on April 26th asking for three seaplanes to be despatched forthwith by some other ship, if *Nairana* were not ready to sail at that time, as it appeared to me of the utmost importance that planes should be available for use immediately we reached Lake Onega. It would seem, however, that it was found impossible to comply with this request, and I could only wait until *Nairana* drew in at Murmansk.

Meantime, my artillery must be given its best chance of supporting the flotilla. This meant posting guns about six miles south-east of Medvyejya Gora, where the channel approaches its narrowest; and, as a preliminary to this, the Bolsheviks must be driven from their holding on the railway eight miles distant.

On May 29th a limited advance was therefore ordered, and the following day the Reds were dislodged, and the ground they had held was occupied permanently by us. Localities suitable for bringing artillery fire to bear on the navigable passage were then selected, and field guns brought into position. I had hoped to guard the entrance to our bay yet more securely by laying a small mine-field across it; but my efforts to obtain mines were unsuccessful, as none

---

[1] This old chaser proved an ill-fated vessel. Her engines gave constant trouble, and on July 8th she caught fire, blew up, and sank, with the loss of five lives.

[2] A seaplane carrier, which had been with us in North Russian waters the previous summer.

were procurable either from the navy or from Archangel.

On June 3rd two enemy vessels appeared at the northern end of the lake, and though they withdrew without showing any inclination to fight, their advent proved that the ice was no longer a bar to navigation, and that any day might see the appearance of a stronger force, bent on something more than reconnaissance.

The early arrival of my seaplanes became therefore a matter of great urgency; for, without their co-operation, the lake flotilla, as then constituted, would be likely to fare badly in any serious naval encounter.

Nairana had reached Murmansk at the end of May, and as ice prevented her from getting through to Kem, arrangements had been made immediately for railing down to Medvyejya Gora her precious freight of one flight Fairey III C's and one flight Shorts. Unloading and erection commenced on June 4th, and on the 6th the first machine was in the air.

And it was none too soon.

Two days later, four armed Bolshevik vessels rounded Shunga Peninsula, steaming north-west towards Medvyejya Gora. Our flotilla accepted the challenge at once, and our first naval action ensued.

The bold attack of our little craft might or might not have met with success had they been operating alone, but the issue would certainly have been in doubt. Fortunately for them, however, they could now rely on seaplane assistance, and it was this assistance that made victory quick and sure.

The enemy were seemingly wholly unprepared for attack from the air, and no sooner was the first bomb dropped than they turned about, dispersed, and steamed off at full speed. A running fight resulted, in which the Bolshevik ships suffered considerable damage. For the zigzag course they followed in order to evade the falling bombs, and the panic with which their crews were seized, rendered their fire wild and inaccurate. Thus our own boats got off unscathed,

INSPECTION OF THE R.A.F. AT MEDVYEJYA GORA. *(From a photograph by J. Sewell)*

whilst their guns secured many direct hits. No bomb, however, found its target, and all four enemy ships made good their escape.

Later on, with a flotilla of much increased power, and with additional planes at disposal, we fought and won other naval actions; but in none was success more urgently needed than in this our first encounter. Had we been worsted, not only would the blow to our prestige have been enormous, but we might have found it a matter of extreme difficulty to maintain our shore positions.

Long-delayed help from the Air Force had come just, and only just, in time to turn a possible reverse into a victory, the moral effect of which alone had a value almost immeasurable.

CHAPTER XVI

RELIEF FORCES FOR ARCHANGEL

LEAVING my force established now in fair security on the northern bounds of Lake Onega, I must turn to matters that exerted a far more definite influence on the destinies of our Venture than did the successful series of operations recently concluded.

It will be remembered that enemy pressure had compelled Ironside to evacuate certain of his more southerly posts towards the close of January, and that, in consequence of this, I had been ordered to send him some 2,500 British reinforcements by the overland route from Soroka. In spite, however, of this addition to the strength of the Archangel force, the Bolsheviks in that area continued to push forward; and during February and March the situation on the River Dwina, and also along the Vologda railway, remained critical.

Though both these fronts were stabilized later, Ironside's position must still give cause for considerable anxiety. The Bolsheviks had shown themselves capable of a determined effort to recapture Archangel, and had met with a sufficient measure of success to raise the *moral* of their troops, and to encourage them to a renewal of their offensive when conditions should be more favourable—and these would materialize at the end of April or in early May. For by then the thaw would have set in on the middle reaches of the Dwina, whilst the ice would still be thick enough to preclude the movement of river-craft near its mouth. The Bolsheviks, therefore, would be able to employ the waterway as a line of advance, with freedom to utilize their armed monitors a week, or it might be a fortnight, before our own flotilla could proceed upstream to oppose them. By then, too, the enemy could concentrate large reinforcements, whereas no reinforcing troops could hope to reach Archangel till at least a month later.

So far as I myself was able to gather, I do not think that Ironside contemplated for one moment anything approaching disaster. But there could be no obscuring the fact that he would be ill-placed to meet a determined onslaught, should such be made at the opening of spring.

On his side, as on mine, the results of the Russian scheme of mobilization had fallen short of expectations; and of such few units as had been raised and trained, though some had fought well, there were several regarding whose loyalty and staunchness he held grave misgivings. His British and Allied troops too had, like mine, been subjected to the many demoralizing influences attendant on their political environment and an Arctic winter's will-sapping gloom; and I could appreciate fully his apprehension lest the time of trial should find that they too had lost more than a little of their fighting efficiency.

Despite, however, the natural anxiety bred by these considerations, I am confident that he never mistrusted his ability to prevent the Bolsheviks setting foot in Archangel, and that the possibility of an Allied *débâcle* was, in consequence, far removed from his mind.

Be this as it may, it is certain that the partial successes gained by the Reds raised at home disquietening fears for the safety of the Archangel force, and brought to the fore once more the need for a decision as to future Allied policy in Russia.

As has been pointed out already, our own Government had made repeated efforts to induce the Allies to determine definitely what should be their joint line of action; but, so far, these had been unavailing. At the beginning of March it brought the question forward yet again, and pressed for a decision that all

Allied troops should be withdrawn from Russia as early as climatic conditions should render it practicable. Our Cabinet even went so far as to authorize the War Office to make preparations with this in view, and both Ironside and myself were informed accordingly that, in all probability, Archangel and Murmansk would be evacuated during the coming summer.[1]

But evacuation might not prove so easy a matter. On the Murmansk side the Bolsheviks had been driven 400 miles from our sea base and, though there would be danger of our communications being cut by anti-Allied elements within our lines, it was unlikely that actual embarkation would be hampered by enemy action.

At Archangel conditions were otherwise. Bolshevik pressure was severe already, and it was at least conceivable that Ironside, unless his force were strengthened, might be faced with the problem of embarking his men with an undefeated enemy close upon him. Prudence therefore dictated clearly that he should be furnished with reinforcements adequate to ensure his safe withdrawal.

Although, however, the despatch of reinforcements to Archangel was so manifestly desirable, their provision presented very especial difficulties.

Even had it been possible for me to transfer troops, the number I could have spared would have fallen far short of that required; but, in point of fact, any transference of troops from Murmansk to Archangel was practically out of the question. I could not send them by sea, as even ice-breakers could not force a passage before May; and the overland route through Onega could be regarded no longer as safe for small detachments (and parties must be limited to 300, for reasons already given) since the Bolsheviks had made their recent advance. All that lay in my power was to

[1] It was not, however, until July that I received definite orders for the evacuation of all Allied troops from Murmansk before the following winter should set in.

endeavour to draw away a portion of the enemy forces from around Archangel, and this, as I have stated, was one of the considerations influencing me, when deciding on my forward move to Lake Onega. Reinforcements, therefore, could not reach Archangel until the ice commenced to break, and they must be composed of fresh contingents found by one or more of the Allied Powers. As had ever been the case in time of need, Great Britain consented to shoulder the burden.

Now, it must be remembered that our Russian policy had always met with the strong disapproval of the Labour Party, which had protested with exceptional vehemence against our North Russian undertaking from its very outset. Though this obstructionist attitude was just as short-sighted and misguided as was Labour opposition to the action taken early in 1927 in order to safeguard British lives at Shanghai, it was nevertheless a factor to be taken into account. For, apart from the few who grasped the importance of Allied intervention in Russia, and thus followed with intelligence our efforts to aid in the reconstitution of a stable government in that country, the population of England could be divided roughly into two classes: those who had been led astray by the explosive clap-trap of Labour extremists, and those who had not troubled themselves to acquire any real knowledge of the Russian situation, and regarded it therefore with indifference. The former class was but a fraction of the latter, but it was exceedingly noisy; and if additional troops were to be sent to Russia, its clamour must first be drowned with music more harmonious and more in consonance with the nation's true spirit—the music of many million tongues, which, though dumb now from ignorance or apathy, would voice unhesitating approval of the Government's proposals were the existing facts made known honestly and clearly.

The aid of the reputable Press was therefore enlisted, and the issue placed before the public in its naked truth. British troops were in danger and in need of help; they had served their country well under conditions such as our soldiers had seldom been called upon to face; now, worn by months of hardship, they were sorely pressed by a relentless foe. Were we to leave them to struggle on as best they might, with disaster perhaps in store for them, or send the succour needed to extricate them safely? Those whose memory carries them back to the early days of April 1919 will recollect the prominence given to Russian affairs at that period. Full accounts were published of operations in all theatres; special paragraphs appeared describing the life and activities of our men in the northern zone; and leading articles were written, dealing with the strategic and political aspects of the situation. One of the last mentioned (a *Times* " leader " of April 5th) is at my hand now, and I quote a few extracts from it, not only because it is indicative of the tone adopted by all our foremost journals, but because it shows also that our decision to evacuate North Russia was not as yet to be made public. The necessity for sending reinforcements must be emphasized, without disclosing our intention to withdraw.[1]

" The cold facts about our military position in Northern Russia will, we hope, put an end to this cry

[1] Unfortunately the Bolsheviks were given ample warning of our contemplated evacuation, which was announced officially in our Press many months before it commenced. Both Ironside and myself pointed out the handicap imposed upon us by thus advertising our line of action, but we were told that " a growing feeling of alarm and distrust, created by ignorance and fomented by organized mischief-makers," had made it necessary to issue a definite statement of the Government's intentions; and that, otherwise, we should be faced with a situation in the home country that would react inevitably even more unfavourably on our position than the publication of the facts. A glowing tribute this to the patriotism and brotherly feeling of our communist " mischief-makers," who were more ready to imperil the lives of hundreds of their own countrymen than to still their own revolutionary cries.

about withdrawing from Russia. We could not withdraw if we would, for our army at Archangel is frozen in, and has been since the beginning of last winter. Whether we would not withdraw if we could is less certain ; but at any rate, if we meant to withdraw, the last thing we should think of doing is to announce our intention beforehand. What is more, whether we had made up our minds to go or to stay, we should have to begin by sending more troops. An embarkation in face of the enemy is the most perilous operation in war, and to carry it out successfully it is usually necessary to begin some sort of offensive movement, even if it is only a feint. We shall, therefore, want more men for Northern Russia, and regrettable though this need of reinforcement is, we hope that it will be accepted without opposition."

Again :

" Our Army, most of it, went there [to North Russia] during the crisis on the Western front to prevent Northern Russian ports from being used as a base for German submarines, and to prevent the enemy from enlisting on his side the potential strength of Russia, as he would have done had the war been prolonged. By the time the armistice was concluded they were frozen in. Now they are in danger and in need of help, and the alternatives are leaving them without reinforcements and consoling ourselves for a military disaster by some resounding generality, or assisting the men first and talking about our principles afterwards. Between such alternatives there can only be one choice, whatever our political views may be."

In a land such as ours, sound at core despite the rotting influence of Bolshevik teachings, there could be but one outcome of this publicity. The position once realized by the people at large, the Government's task was half accomplished ; and when it was made known that the formation of an Archangel relief force was in contemplation, the step was hailed with enthusiasm. Volunteers were forthcoming in plenty, and two strong contingents, each numbering some 4,000, were soon in readiness for embarkation. The first was sent in vessels specially strengthened to withstand the buffeting of ice-floes in the White Sea, and succeeded in entering Archangel port as early as May 26th. The second arrived on June 10th.

Whether Ironside would have contrived to pull through without this addition to his strength can only be conjectured; but most assuredly he would have experienced many moments of deep anxiety, and it is at least doubtful whether he could have emerged with success from the critical period in July, when serious mutinies occurred in many of his Russian units, and he found it imperative to stabilize every front with British troops.

But the arrival of the relief force at Archangel, though it meant much to Ironside, was of course of no direct benefit to me. I might even say that such effect as it produced on the Murmansk side was unfavourable to my interests, in that it aroused for a time a feeling of discontent amongst my men.

When the relief-force ships touched at Murmansk, those on board announced that, according to officials at home, they had come to replace all troops in North Russia, and that these were to be sent back at once in the very ships in which they themselves had voyaged out. Now, my own men were quite aware that there was no intention of relieving them as yet, and they jumped to the conclusion that the three battalions, the gunners, and the machine-gun company which had formed originally a part of my force and had been sent as reinforcements to Archangel, were to be given preferential treatment, and would soon be on their way to England, whilst those at Murmansk were doomed to stay on for a period of unknown duration.

As my headquarters were at Kem, it was some time before this misrepresentation reached my ears, and by then it had gained so strong a hold that I considered it necessary to make an official explanation to the effect that the only British unit at Archangel to be relieved immediately was one battalion (Royal Scots) which had been in Russia almost from the date of our original landing, and had been through exceptionally trying experiences ; and that the remaining British units at Archangel would be treated on exactly the same lines as those at Murmansk.

There were other small matters too, in connexion with the relief force, which it pleased my troops to regard as grievances.

It would appear that those in the relief force were to be granted Arctic pay, whereas we had ceased to draw it since the end of April ; and, unmindful perhaps of the parable of the vineyard, my men failed to see the justice of this ruling. A more trivial point still was that every newcomer was adorned with the ribbon of the General Service medal, though the men of Murmansk had been prohibited so far from wearing it—and this differentiation was resented.

Unjustified as was one of these complaints, and slight as were the grounds for the remainder, their result in the aggregate was sufficient to give rise in my mind to that undefinable feeling of things being not quite as they should be amongst my Britishers, for some time after the passing through of the relief force.

These little heart-burnings were, however, temporary maladies only ; and, except for them, the measures taken to ensure safety at Archangel affected me neither for good nor ill. But the warning of withdrawal most certainly did.

Coming in March, and with the date of probable evacuation given as some time during the summer, I might find myself left with but three months in which to place the Russian army in a position to fend for itself in the Murman Area—and nearly everything remained yet to be done, before I could be satisfied that this goal had been reached.

Russian fighting strength must be trebled at least, and for this reason, as I have emphasized more than once, every promising opportunity must be seized of opening up fresh areas for recruitment. But this was not all. Should Yermoloff, as I hoped, succeed in raising a field army of 6,000–7,000, very large increases in officers and non-commissioned officers would be demanded, and these it would be impossible to obtain locally. Archangel might be able to furnish a few, but other sources must be tapped. In England, France, Germany, and Finland many Russian officers were congregated, those in Germany being for the most part prisoners of war; and every endeavour must be made at once to get as many as possible shipped to Russia, together with any trained non-commissioned officers whose whereabouts could be ascertained.

Institutes, too, must be established forthwith for the instruction of Russian officers and other ranks; and long before we left, flying, artillery, signal, machine-gun, mechanical-transport, and horse-transport schools had been inaugurated. Besides this, the Russian administrative services must receive early and much-needed attention, and this necessitated the immediate attachment of qualified Allied officers to the various Russian departments.

If withdrawal were to take place at the earliest practicable date, thus allowing a bare three months for these preparatory measures, I could not look for more than a partial success. Certainly there would be no opportunity of creating a Russian Air Force, and little hope of Russian gunners attaining a satisfactory standard of proficiency. But I could do no more than utilize to the full such time as might be available, and each measure was initiated as speedily as occasion offered.

Although I myself knew that evacuation was intended in the comparatively near future, this was a piece of knowledge I kept to myself; and all I felt it wise to impart to Yermoloff was that the Allies could not be expected to remain for ever, and that he should take every advantage of their assistance, whilst still at his disposal, to advance his own state of readiness.

That the decision to withdraw came to me as a disappointment I make no pretence to disguise. I was as heartily tired of war and its concomitants as any officer or man in or out of the fighting services; my task could not be regarded as either easy or congenial; and my health was not so good as I could have wished. Thus my inclinations, as an individual, went all in favour of quitting Russia as soon as I could get on board a ship to carry me off. But my experiences, circumscribed to some extent as I admit them to have been, led me to believe that our own interests lay in prolonging our assistance to the anti-Bolshevik movement and, in addition to this, I felt most strongly that we were bound in honour not to abandon the loyal Russians until their chances of holding their own were less problematical than they would be, even after a lapse of several months.

I, however, was but a pawn on the board, and could have no determining voice in the fixing of policy. For all that, politics could not be dissociated entirely from a command such as mine; and as long back as November I had compiled a memorandum on "The Future Policy of the Murmansk Force," and had submitted it to the War Office when in England. Also, in looking through old papers, I see that I mentioned the same subject to General Radcliffe when writing on March 7th. This letter must have been penned and despatched only a few hours previous to my receipt of the withdrawal warning, and when I was still in doubt whether we intended to put an end to our commitments or to make a more powerful bid to overthrow Bolshevism; and in it I discussed both courses, with especial reference to my own sphere of operations. Sent as this was, uninfluenced by home instructions, and on so early a date, I have perused it myself with some interest in view of subsequent happenings, and venture therefore to give the following extracts, paraphrased here and there, so as to read more as a sequential whole :

" There are a good few out here anxious to see this job through ; and I am one of them, simply because my knowledge is sufficient to assure me that any evacuation would be against our interests, and utterly opposed to our code of honour. But I quite realize the difficulties which the home authorities will have to face, if a definite decision to remain out here till the Bolsheviks are hammered is arrived at.

" In these days of Peace Conferences and Leagues of Nations, the poor old War Office will, I am afraid, have even less voice than before in formulating our policy. All the same, you are bound to be called upon to put forward the military aspect, and therefore it is up to Ironside and myself not only to keep you in really close touch with events, but also to submit to you suggestions and recommendations based on our first-hand knowledge.

" I would like first of all to call attention to my ' Future Policy ' memorandum of November 22nd, 1918. I still adhere to the principle that, if we are not going to withdraw altogether, we ought to make a real effort *at once* to smash the Bolshevik power at Petrograd. If successful, this would have an enormous effect, and it seems to me still that the method I suggested is the best. I say ' at once ' because, as I pointed out, the Bolshevik organization is undoubtedly improving rapidly. Moreover, if we do not give them a bad knock before July, it will be years before we can hope to get the better of them. After June they will be getting in their harvest, and there will be no lack of food in central Russia. Besides this, the territory in their power contains practically everything wanted to make them self-supporting, and they will soon have sufficient organization to exploit these resources successfully. Thus, if they can now hold their own, though extremely short of food and lacking in other requirements, they should be able to more than hold their own after June, unless we can inflict a telling blow before then.

" Assuming, however, that any action on a large scale is ruled out of court, as I fear the situation at home will necessitate, what then is the best course to follow? The simplest solution, from a political point of view, would be to withdraw both from Archangel and here about July or August. Those who are keen on thus following the line of least resistance can certainly make out a very plausible case, besides being assured that they are engineering an excellent bid for popularity. They can adduce all the old arguments about ' brother Bolshevik,' the expenditure of money, the desire for peace, and discontent amongst the troops, etc., etc., and can urge also that by then we shall have given the Russians every chance to mobilize their resources and to stand by themselves ; and that, as we cannot stay for ever, we might just as well go then.

" There are, however, other points of view. To begin with, a withdrawal from either here or Archangel will not prove an easy operation, especially in the case of Archangel : for, apart from the Bolshevik army, we shall have to reckon with a tremendous revulsion of feeling against us, coupled with a natural inclination to curry favour with the Bolsheviks (so soon to return) by a display of ill-disposition towards us.

" Moreover, what is to happen to those, notably the men of standing, who have sided with us ? We shall be in duty bound to remove all who wish to get out of the country, and between Murmansk and Archangel they are likely to run into thousands. How do we propose to deal with them ?

" Suppose, too, that we clear out successfully, and manage to take away the bulk of those who wish to be removed, what will happen in these localities ? Either those who remain will chuck in their lot with the Bolsheviks, or they will endeavour to keep them out.

In the former event, except for denying this place to the Boches during the war period, all our efforts here will have been in vain ; in the latter, no resistance can be kept up unless we continue to supply money, food, and material, and even then the outcome will be exceedingly doubtful.

"And what of our political integrity? If we leave these people in the lurch, we have got to be prepared for our good name being spattered with mud ; and leave them in the lurch we certainly shall, if we clear out before giving them a much better chance of standing on their own. As things are now, the departure of the Allies would mean the collapse of the whole anti-Bolshevik movement in the north, and this would prove a nasty jar to Denikin and Co. Quite possibly it might mean that Bolshevism had come to stay—which heaven forbid.

"Thus, taking it for granted that we cannot hope to send to Russia a force big enough to administer a really heavy blow within the next four or five months, there is no doubt whatever in my mind that we ought to maintain here and at Archangel sufficient troops to prevent a Bolshevik return. And, apart from upholding our national honour, it would pay us hand over fist.

"On this side I should need only a small force—say 5,000 Britishers. This would be sufficient to safeguard most of the area I now hold, and to induce the Russians to continue their efforts ; and given it, every foreign soldier in the land can return to his ancestral hearth for all I care.

"My own opinion, too, is that, even if Archangel is abandoned, we ought to hang on here. Strategically it would be sound for the Russians to operate from this side, for the several reasons I gave in my memorandum ; but there are other considerations as well. This is the coming place, as being an ice-free port, and we shall score a hundred-fold if, at the end of all this pother, we are in a leading position to influence its future. If the foreigner thinks it is not worth the candle and wants to go, so much the better for us. This, of course, is outside the purely military standpoint, and I only put it forward as an additional inducement for us to stand by our guns. Quite apart from it, I hold that we should be committing a grave error by withdrawing altogether.

"Needless to say, I have no personal desire to remain in this forsaken spot a moment longer than necessary. It has caused me already to lose much of my hair and more of my temper. But, after eight months, I have got a fair grip of the situation, and I am quite sure, firstly as a soldier, and secondly as a Britisher, that our duty and interest lie in our retaining a footing here, even if all the other Allies rat."

The views to which the above letter gave expression I saw no reason to alter at any time up to our withdrawal seven months later; nor, indeed, have the events of the last nine years led me to believe that they were unsound in principle.

For the sake of future peace and prosperity throughout the world, it appeared to me that the overthrow of the Bolshevik régime was a prime essential, and the surest and most expeditious way of achieving this would be an immediate and much-increased effort on the part of the Allies. Should the situation not admit of such an effort, then the next best thing would be to continue to lend such backing to the anti-Bolshevik elements as would suffice at least to hold them together and encourage them to prolong their endeavour. According to my thinking, much would not be needed, as the influence for stability of Allied (and especially British) help was immeasurably greater than could be gauged by the percentage of troops employed.

On the other hand, a complete evacuation, besides depriving the Russians of the additional material assistance required temporarily, would rob them of that feeling of moral support which went so far towards sustaining their hopes of ultimate victory.

So convinced was I of the disastrous moral effect likely to be produced by a total withdrawal that, when this course was decided upon definitely in July, I asked for sanction to remain behind with a Mission of 300 volunteers drawn from my own troops. Even this small party could have done much towards ensuring efficient organization and, what was of greater value still, would have afforded a tangible proof of our continued goodwill.

My proposal, however, was not entertained, and I must acknowledge that, in the circumstances then existing, there were many good reasons for its refusal. But when the sad news reached me of the defeat and disintegration of the Russian army of Murmansk which I had helped to raise and train, I could not altogether set at rest the feeling that this catastrophe might perchance have been averted, had it been found possible to accede to my request.

CHAPTER XVII

FINLAND COMPLICATES OUR TASK

BEFORE returning to the final stages of our operations by land, air, and water, conducted from our advanced base on the shores of Lake Onega, I must revert once more to affairs connected with local politics. In these both Karelians and Finns figured yet again, but this time the Finns were not the recalcitrant Reds of my Legion, but the Whites of a now officially friendly Finland.

The special political phase with which I now deal will be the more clear if it is borne in mind, first, that Karelia had belonged to Finland until annexed by Peter the Great 200 years back, and, second, that the Karelians of 1919 were clamouring for independence, or, at the least, for freedom from what they regarded as the yoke of Russia.

On March 29th I received a telegram notifying me that Finnish troops were being brought back hurriedly from Reval to Helsingfors. Though the ostensible reason for the move was entirely pacific, a suspicion existed that it was closely related to a rising due seemingly to take place in Karelia on April 10th, when the Karelians were to proclaim separation from Russia and demand incorporation with Finland.

Not to put too fine a point upon it, the wire hinted strongly that Finland saw what she considered a splendid opportunity of regaining her lost territory, and was preparing to lend active assistance to the Karelians in ridding themselves of Russian control.

Should this prove a true prognostication, it would add yet another and a most untimely complication to a situation already far too involved for my liking.

My chapter entitled "The Ides of March" shows how, at this period, our security was threatened throughout the length and breadth of the occupied area, and how, amongst other anxieties, I was confronted with the possibility of mutiny in the Karelian Regiment. This possibility, if the inference drawn by the author of the telegram should prove correct, looked like becoming a certainty; and not only this, but I should be called upon to reopen operations against the White Finns, with the Karelians now their allies instead of their opponents. For as Yermoloff's interests must be paramount, it was obviously out of the question for me to countenance this Finnish project of annexation.

The whole position was kaleidoscopic. Six months previously my Karelians had opposed the White Finns strenuously and had served me well, though knowing that I was at war with the Bolsheviks no less than with White Finns and Germans. Subsequently they had demanded complete national independence; and now it would appear that they were undecided as to whether they wished to espouse the Red Bolshevik cause or become part of a White-governed Finland. Such small indication of loyalty to the Allies as they evinced could be set down as little more than a desire to serve their own temporary interests; whilst of loyalty to Russia they had none.

It was this last factor, I think, which counted more with them than any other. Subservience to Russian authority was repellent to them. They would have preferred to rid themselves of it by establishing Karelia as a free and independent State; but this they now knew could be accomplished only by force, and they doubted their chances of success, if working single-handed. Incorporation with Finland was a second choice; but it offered a better prospect of fulfilment, as it coincided with Finnish ambitions and would meet with Finnish support. That, at least, was how I appreciated the situation—on the

FINLAND COMPLICATES OUR TASK

assumption that the deductions drawn by those in touch with Finnish affairs were worthy of credence.

Whether this was the case I could not tell for certain; but events pointed most emphatically to some kind of Finnish-Karelian pact, even though the Finnish Government might not be implicated officially.

At about the date given me as that fixed for the rising in Karelia, armed parties of Finns were reported as assembling close to that portion of the frontier lying west of Lake Onega, and these crossed the border a few days later, and marched into southern Karelia.

It seemed to me strange that so southerly a point should have been selected, if the real intention was to encourage revolt in the Karelian Regiment; and, granted this intention, I could only presume that the Finns hesitated to advance by a more northerly line for fear of encountering Allied troops, and that they hoped to gain the adherence of the Karelians of the south before coming into conflict with us.

A somewhat disturbing feature was that this Finnish incursion synchronized with an epidemic of desertions from the Karelian Regiment, many of the men contriving to get away with their arms, and making invariably for the Finnish frontier.

But, for the time being at any rate, I could take no military steps to check these enterprising bands of Finnish soldiery, and I could only await developments, hoping that theirs was merely a spasmodic movement to which the Government of Finland gave no encouragement, or that their aim was not that which I had been led to suppose.

Additional light was thrown on the situation on April 26th, when I learnt that 5,000 White Finns were moving on Olonetz and Petrozavodsk, and that, in co-operation with local Karelians, they were endeavouring to clear the Bolsheviks from that area. This was by no means the same thing as a Karelian-cum-Finn rising against Yermoloff's authority, and therefore against the Allies; indeed, it even looked as if I had acquired an unexpected ally in my fight against the forces of Bolshevism.

But there remained nevertheless a decided element of danger; since Finnish motives were hardly likely to be disinterested, and the probability was that, should her efforts be rewarded with victory, she would claim suzerainty over such Karelian territory as she might wrest from the Reds.

I cabled home therefore at once, requesting that Finland should be asked to give a guarantee that her military operations were directed solely with a view to assist in overthrowing the Bolsheviks, and that she would hand over to the Government of the Northern Province any territory she might gain.

Whether our Foreign Office took the line suggested by me, I am not sure; but information reached both Yermoloff and myself shortly afterwards to the effect that the Finnish force in Karelia was composed entirely of volunteers; and that the Government, though supplying them with arms and other necessaries, had given no official authority to the War Ministry for the direction of their movements. We learnt at the same time that the " volunteers " had occupied Olonetz, and had issued a proclamation announcing the deliverance of Karelia from the Bolsheviks, and the right of Karelians to self-determination. This news was followed in early May by a statement made by the Finnish Prime Minister in the Diet, in which he asserted that his Government, although not pursuing a policy of annexation, would not hinder Finnish nationals from rendering assistance to their Karelian kinsmen in their struggle against Bolshevism. These were excellent sentiments; but it struck me that if Karelian aspirations were confined to ousting the Bolsheviks, it was hard to understand why their efforts to pull with the Allies—whose one aim this was—should show so sad a lack of enthusiasm.

To Yermoloff it was altogether a most disconcerting business. He mistrusted both General Mannerheim and the Karelians; and was convinced that the greater the success of these so-named volunteers, the greater the future trouble in store for us. It behoved me therefore to walk warily, although my advance towards Lake Onega was then in progress, and it would have meant much to me, had I been able to count on working in conjunction with a force which had, apparently, an exceedingly hopeful chance of cutting the line of communication of my opponents.

As we pushed our way forward, we learnt that the White Finn advance on Petrozavodsk had been checked by the Bolsheviks; and their doings were brought directly to our notice ten days after the capture of Medvyejya Gora, when two messengers arrived at Price's headquarters with letters purporting to be from the commander of the " 9th Finn Army Corps " and his chief intelligence officer. These gave us to understand that splendid successes had been won by the " Finnish National Army," and that it needed only our immediate co-operation to bring about the complete overthrow of the Reds from Petrograd northwards. We were asked to furnish our strength and dispositions, and to enter into an agreement to prosecute the campaign in accordance with a common plan.

I had, however, no inclination either to make an agreement of this nature or to supply the emissaries with information regarding my troops. To begin with, all I knew about them for certain was that they were Finns; and many such were fighting in the Bolshevik ranks. They might be, and probably were, " White," but even so I was not prepared to give away to them any details of my force.

I instructed Price therefore to send one of them back with a letter, in which I made it clear that I could come to no arrangement with them until I received a written guarantee that the annexation of Karelia formed no part of the Finnish programme. The second messenger was to be detained on the plea that his services would be of great value as a liaison officer!

A week later I found that there had been no cause to doubt their *bona fides*, for two more messengers put in their appearance, one being an agent attached to my intelligence service. They admitted that the White Finns had come off second best in recent encounters with the Bolsheviks, but asserted that 3,000 of them were only awaiting my instructions to renew their advance. Their forces, according to the dispositions they gave, were scattered over a front of nearly 100 miles, with the nearest detachment 50 miles from me. Co-operation, in these circumstances, would be hard of attainment and unlikely to bear satisfactory fruit, even had it been a wise political move, of which both Yermoloff and myself still entertained doubts. The messengers therefore departed, taking with them my regrets that the time for combined operations had not yet arrived.

The whole matter continued to hinge on Finnish designs regarding Karelia, and nothing had transpired as yet to lull my suspicions that annexation was contemplated. This was now spoken of openly by the men of the Karelian Regiment as the object which they and all Karelians had in view, and desertions became so commonplace and the attitude of the regiment so doubtful that I felt compelled to disband it as a unit, and to reorganize its personnel on an entirely fresh basis.[1]

[1] For many months past it had been clear that any hope of employing the regiment as a whole against the Bolsheviks must be abandoned. Those Karelians in the Olonetz Regiment (part Russian and part Karelian) had done well; but most of them had been enlisted south of Kem, and were of a different stamp from the men recruited originally.

The bulk of the regiment had no fighting value, and its *moral* had been further undermined by this latest idea of Karelia's incorporation with Finland. As constituted at present, it was not worth its keep.

Possibly a few might be ready to oppose the Reds, and, if so, these must be formed into a separate unit. The remainder, if their services were retained at all, might be used as pioneers, local guards, or labourers.

On May 20th, therefore, the Karelian Regiment was disbanded,

Nevertheless, as an aid to smashing up the Bolshevik army between Petrograd and Lake Onega, I should welcome the help offered by the White Finns, provided my mind were set at rest concerning Karelia's future.

I wired to the War Office, therefore, emphasizing this point, and explaining also that combined action could not be secured if the Finns remained scattered over so wide a front, along which they were weak everywhere. The best hope was, in my opinion, for them to continue to threaten Petrozavodsk with (say) half their force, whilst the remainder concentrated at a named point to the north, where I would undertake to get in touch with them.

The result of this suggestion was a message from the White Finn commander received by me on June 26th. In this he expressed his willingness to co-operate with me in accordance with the scheme I had put forward; but he stipulated that all Russian and Red Finn troops under my orders should be withdrawn sufficiently far to ensure that they should not come in contact with his White Finns.

If the cat had been halfway out of the bag before, it was out completely now.

and the men were offered the choice of enrolling in any of the following :

(*a*) Volunteer Battalion—of picked men, ready to fight against the enemies of Russia anywhere on the northern front.

(*b*) Pioneer Company—for road and bridge construction in the forward area.

(*c*) Garrison Guard Company—for guarding railway-bridges and other important points.

(*d*) Frontier Guard—to act as outposts on the approaches from Finland.

(*e*) Labour Battalion—unarmed, and not to be employed in the battle area.

Those declining to enrol in any of the above were to be liable for mobilization in the Russian army.

It is scarcely necessary to say that, in spite of the pay comparing unfavourably with that in the other units, the Labour Battalion and the Frontier Guard were well to the front in popularity.

The desire to allow my Red Finns no opportunity of pursuing their family quarrel with the Whites was understandable ; but a proviso that Russians should be barred from sharing in the operations could have but one interpretation. If Karelia was to come under Finnish sway, Russians must have no part in freeing her from Bolshevik domination.

We were still walking round the old circle, our steps leading ever to our point of starting ; and once again I was forced to reply that I could not discuss co-operation. Red Finns I could promise not to employ, and they would remain where they were, 300 miles from the scene of contemplated action ; but my task was to assist the Government of the Northern Province in ejecting the Reds, and, were I to make a further advance, Russian troops would certainly be called upon to play a leading part. I expressed the hope, however, that our respective forces would work in friendly conjunction.

The hope for harmonious working to which I gave expression was to prove vain ; for after our first forward move from Medvyejya Gora, White Finn troops were found in some of the outlying villages, and these caused me unending trouble until Bolshevik successes drove the whole volunteer rabble back into its own country. Not only did they exert every effort to detach the inhabitants from their loyalty to Yermoloff's Government, but, having failed in this, they signified their displeasure by terrorizing the villagers with threats of torture and massacre. Looting was their favourite pastime, and their other iniquities were many and varied. I was driven at length to organize a small punitive expedition, and arrested 15 of them—a step which resulted, after a few days of increased tension, in a marked improvement of manners. Shortly afterwards, and greatly to my joy, the entire " Volunteer Force " or " Finnish National Army " or " 9th Finn Army Corps," whichever may have been its correct title, faded away. The

FINLAND COMPLICATES OUR TASK

Bolshevik army had shown itself the less inefficient of the two.

The withdrawal of the White Finns was followed almost immediately (July 10th) by a wire from our Military Mission at Helsingfors, stating that, owing to recent reverses, the Finnish Government had decided to send regular troops to assist their volunteers in Karelia, and asking me if I could join hands with them west of Petrozavodsk within a fortnight. It was suggested that co-operation might now be feasible, in view of Finland having waived her claims on Karelia pending settlement of the question by a plébiscite of the Karelian people.

Stress of circumstances had evidently compelled the Finnish Government to declare its hand, and the suspicions to which the movement had given rise from its outset were shown to have been justified abundantly. As, however, the mooted plébiscite would not be likely to take place till long after our departure from Russia, and as I could do nothing to prevent it, whatever my own especial standpoint might be, I should have felt bound to fall in with the proposal had it been within the bounds of practicability. This, however, it was not; for I had received instructions already that any fresh advance made by me must be carried out by Russian troops only, and the Russians were not yet ready for a move on so large a scale.

The Finnish regulars who were to support the Volunteer force, if sent at all, accomplished nothing; and, so far as I was concerned, Finnish Whites ceased to be a factor in the military situation.

The episode, so long as it lasted—and this was for over three months—had, however, occasioned me many unpleasant hours of doubt and anxiety, and had, besides, left an impression for ill upon my old Karelian Regiment that I found it impossible to obliterate during the whole of the remaining period of our occupation.

In the heyday of its activities against Germans and

White Finns during the previous autumn the regiment had numbered nearly 4,000 good fighting men; but before the close of operations it had dwindled to 600 combatants—a result attributable largely to Finnish influences.

My reorganization scheme (see footnote on p. 256) gave promise of better things during its first month's trial; but in June some Russian-speaking American sailors, then at Kem, commenced a secret and intensive anti-British propaganda campaign amongst the rank and file. Conclusive evidence against these American seamen was forthcoming, and they were dealt with appropriately by their own authorities. But the mischief they had wrought had gone too far to be undone; and, in addition to some 300 men of the Olonetz Regiment (who had been at the front for many months, and had given a good account of themselves), I could never collect more than a further 300 Karelians for employment in the fighting line; and the conduct of even these could not be given unqualified approval either in quarters or in action.

It was a sad fall from the great achievements of past days. But, bitterly disappointed as I was at Karelian shortcomings in 1919, these could never efface entirely my feeling of gratitude for what Karelians had accomplished in the crucial months of 1918, when they, together with my backsliding Finns, had stood almost alone between me and the menace of von der Goltz's army, and had not failed me.

Even as I look back now, the recollections of 1918 are more clear-cut than are the unhappier memories of the following year; and as my wild and undisciplined soldiers of Karelia pass finally from my tale, it is, I am glad to think, the remembrance of their onetime greatness that takes the foremost place in my mind.

The history of my local levies, both Karelian and Finn, has now been brought to its close; but that of the new Russian army, upon which was to devolve the task of keeping the Reds at bay after our withdrawal, remains yet to be traced.

A portion of one regiment and a " partisan " detachment had, as I have narrated, played a not unworthy part in the push to Lake Onega; but they formed a fraction only of the 3,500 under arms by the commencement of June. The remainder were undergoing training, and my various inspections showed me that their progress towards efficiency was slow and halting. They needed more instructors; were dispersed overwidely in small detachments; and, above all, required a competent officer in chief command.

Repeated applications to the Russian authorities at Archangel produced a few additional non-commissioned officers capable of recruit training, and my advance enabled me to concentrate complete units at Maselga and Urosozero, where accommodation was ample, and the men were removed from the subversive influences of Kem and Soroka. But both my staff and myself were too fully occupied to admit of our paying close attention to the many details of training and interior economy, upon which so much must depend if preparation to take the field were to move smoothly and rapidly.

It was, therefore, with unbounded satisfaction that I heard that a Russian general was on his way from Archangel to take over command of all Russian troops within my area. He arrived with one staff officer, and reported to me on June 6th.

From the time of our first meeting I entertained for General Skobeltsin a most friendly feeling of appreciation. In its best and widest sense he was a " gentleman " through and through—courteous and morally fearless, and with a standard of rectitude high set. He was, moreover, a well-educated soldier of wide experience. His manner was unassuming and quiet. His quietness indeed was so marked as to lend an impression of habitual sadness—an impression, I think, not far removed from fact, for his country's sorrows were his own.

Though under no delusion as to the difficulties surrounding the work he had undertaken, he never doubted that the cause of loyal Russia would triumph in the end. It was a just cause, and that to him was sufficient guarantee of ultimate success—and who can say, even yet, that his faith was not justified?

As a foreigner, I could not lay claim to any intimate knowledge of his characteristics, but my daily intercourse with him showed me enough to make me certain that he possessed many of the qualities which go to the making of a commander of merit. Whether, however, this would be apparent to others whose contact with him was less close, and especially to the rank and file, I was by no means certain. For he seemed to me wanting in some degree in that forceful personality and energetic zeal usually associated in the soldier's mind with a successful leader of men. It may be that his unobtrusive nature, coupled, as I have said, with a certain austereness and lack of joviality, lent a weight to this impression greater than was warranted. The impression, however, was formed on my mind from the start, and there it has remained ever since. Though he possessed many of the qualities tending to inspire confidence, a great number did not show above the surface, and were discernible only by those who looked deeply. And the gaze of the Russian soldier, so far as my experience taught me, does not penetrate below the outer crust.[1]

General Skobeltsin's advent gave a much-needed fillip to the work of preparing the Russian army to take the field. In many ways it must have been irksome to him to serve under the eye of a chief who was not only a foreigner, but also his junior in age and relative rank;

[1] If, as I hope and believe, General Skobeltsin is still living and in safety, and should these pages meet his eye, I trust he will pardon this expression of opinion, mistaken perhaps but honest, of one who holds him in great regard.

but of this he gave no sign, and I can say with truth that no British subordinate could have given me more loyal and willing service. So far as lay in my power I accorded him every assistance, and, realizing this, he made a ready response to all my demands.

After the capture of Medvyejya Gora, recruiting for his army was brisk, an intake of several hundred recruits from the surrounding district being reported within three days of the Bolshevik rout.

I was able, too, to persuade him that we were likely to gain rather than lose by converting Krugliakoff's scallywag " partisans " into a properly constituted unit. At present it was their wont to disappear into the blue unbidden, making it impossible to rely on orders reaching them, should they be required to co-operate at short notice in any given enterprise, and upsetting all arrangements made for their supply. Moreover, I was unable to exercise effective control over either their movements or actions, and could never be certain they were not up to some devilment calculated to bring discredit on my force. As " partisans " they numbered about 300, but expanded into a full battalion within a few weeks. Krugliakoff, however, was seldom content unless conducting some hare-brained undertaking on his own ; and the training of the newly formed unit had to be turned over to other hands, whilst he continued to range the country with a select band of his most experienced filibusters. I am bound to confess, too, that he did some very excellent and gallant work ; and my regret was almost as great as his own when I felt compelled to order him back to assume command of his battalion, when it was considered ready to take its place as a front-line unit. This was at about the time of our next southward move (early July), when the total strength of the Russian army had reached nearly 5,000, of whom, however, about 1,500 must be regarded still as recruits.

Though the Russian army was thus making satisfactory headway, the increase in my command was not in point of fact appreciable, even numerically; whilst its actual fighting value in July probably compared unfavourably with that of three months earlier. For, as a set-off to the growth of the Russian forces, I lost many Allied units.

Before the end of May I was instructed to concentrate all French troops, in anticipation of their return to France; and they left at the beginning of June. I was thus deprived not only of the company of *Skieurs* (which admittedly had been of little use for some months), but also of a complete Artillery Group which, in addition to carrying out its legitimate rôle, had supplied armoured-train crews.

On June 7th orders were received to hold the whole of my Royal Marine detachment in readiness for embarkation; and, a couple of days later, the Canadian Government called for the immediate return of its contingent.

Before the middle of July both American transportation companies were withdrawn—an unlooked-for and unsettling blow to railway efficiency. And, to cap all this, I was informed that every Britisher who had arrived at Murmansk prior to February 1st must be shipped back to England before the end of August—an order affecting my original infantry and machine-gun companies, and a large portion of the personnel of my administrative services.

It will be seen, therefore, that the withdrawal of Allied troops commenced several months before our final evacuation (October 12th), and consequently I had reason to be glad that sanction for my various advances had not been withheld, since these had opened for recruiting an additional area of at least 12,000 square miles, and had led to the strength of the Russian army being more than doubled.

Though the departure of so many Allied troops naturally weakened my fighting line, it was chiefly along my communications that their loss was felt.

(From a photograph by J. Sewell)

SABOTAGE.
REPAIRING DAMAGE DONE BY MALCONTENTS.
DERAILMENT OF HEADQUARTER TRAIN.

For, although there might be little danger of a recrudescence of internal trouble on a scale equal to that of the early spring, there remained always the possibility of disaffected gangs attempting to stir up local feeling against Yermoloff's authority, and endeavouring to hamper our operations by damaging the railway, or by other acts of sabotage.

The popularity of our undertaking, in fact, was even yet by no means universal, and of this there were ever-recurring proofs. When, for example, we shifted general headquarters from Murmansk to Kem, a bold but clumsy effort was made to wreck our train by placing on the line two boulders each the size of a well-filled coal-sack. The engine was put out of action for a time; but beyond this, and the fact that we were all awakened with unaccustomed suddenness at 3 a.m., no harm resulted. Later on, too, owing to a faulty setting of points (which was almost certainly deliberate), the train in which some of my staff and myself were travelling to Medvyejya Gora was derailed. In this case three coaches were overturned, two of our escort badly cut and bruised, and several horses injured.

These "accidents" and other minor indications of ill-will too numerous to be detailed were in themselves of little account; but they showed that some at least of the population were in love neither with our anti-Bolshevik programme nor with those concerned in its prosecution. Moreover, unless their petty activities could be curbed, they might become emboldened to try their hands at more ambitious schemes of hindrance; and to apply the curb would grow increasingly difficult after I had been deprived of some 1,500 Allied troops.

On the whole, however, I was inclined to the belief that I could maintain intact my communications with Murmansk; but, in order to reduce risks, a forward base was established at Kem port, which could be utilized in emergency throughout the summer.

As regards the fighting front, I was satisfied that we could hold our own on the ground already won. Whether we could do more depended on the extent to which our lake flotilla was reinforced, and on the soldierly qualities of the 5,000 officers and men now composing the new Russian army.

CHAPTER XVIII

KAPASELGA AND AFTER

FEW places could have been found offering greater promise of providing the facilities needed for our varied requirements than did Medvyejya Gora.

Within half a mile of the village lay a small harbour. It was protected by a quay, along which the railway extended, and furnished perfect shelter for our lake flotilla.

Close to the gradually shelving foreshore the ground was firm and open, the establishment of an excellent seaplane base thus presenting few difficulties. And—our greatest stroke of luck—a site was found at Lumbushi (3 miles distant on the Povynetz side) easily convertible into an aerodrome which, though perhaps not perfect, gave on completion sufficiently satisfactory results.

We were well off, too, in the way of accommodation. For though the Bolsheviks had fired some of the buildings before their retreat, enough remained standing to house 2,000 in comfort, and many pleasant spots were available on which tents could be pitched. Povynetz was undamaged, and its whole garrison was billeted in comparative luxury.

Along the northern edge of the lake were scattered a number of fair-sized habitations, now deserted; and these became the headquarters of various schools of instruction—a purpose for which they served well.

Added to all this, railway yards and sidings were spacious and ample, and the ground in their vicinity well adapted for the formation of supply and other depots.

Collected within our twelve-mile frontage we

had, therefore, nearly every convenience we could hope for.

The only real drawback was that no railway ran between Medvyejya Gora and Povynetz; and the connecting road, though better than the marshy tracks to which we had been accustomed hitherto, was without metalling, and liable to be cut up badly by wheeled traffic. But even this handicap was minimized to a large extent by the possibility of employing water transport, so long as our combined fleet and air force retained supremacy over the enemy's flotilla.

Beyond these many military desiderata, the locality had, besides, much else to recommend it.

The deadly monotony of tundra and pine forest gave place at the lakeside to scenery akin to, and as beautiful as, that of many a world-famed Scottish loch; and, on a bright summer's day, I have gazed on few fairer sights than the broad and shimmering expanse of Lake Onega's waters, backed by noble hills clad from base to summit in greenery of every shade, and with its foreground of tree-dotted undulations merging, now by the gentlest of grassy slopes, and now by steeper and rocky declivities, into a sun-kissed beach of pebbles.

To those to whom the beauties of nature brought no message, there was at least the satisfaction of living in a climate that, from June to September, was near perfection; whilst the fisherman, if lucky enough to have his tackle at hand, found almost at his door a well-stocked trout stream wherein to test his skill. Mosquitoes, it is true, were with us still in plenty; but even they, touched perhaps by Medvyejya Gora's soothing influences, seemed less bellicose than their brethren of the north.

From the purely utilitarian point of view the place had, too, one very special advantage over all others occupied by us up to the present; and this was that the land surrounding it was blessed with real soil, such as could be turned to man's uses. At Murmansk, and for

A CORNER OF LAKE ONEGA.

(From a photograph by J. Sewell)

many hundred miles to its south, it was impossible to grow even a turnip. There was no soil, and therefore no cultivation. The only garden I had ever seen before reaching Lake Onega had been at Kem. It was about the size of a billiard-table, and its owner, an enthusiastic horticulturist, had had every pound of his earth shipped across from Archangel.

But Medvyejya Gora was within the fringe of an agricultural district and, in happier times, much of the land stretching east to Povynetz would have been under cultivation. Of this we had been aware before our advance commenced, and, being full of hope, I had asked my Director of Supplies to obtain from home an abundance of green vegetable seeds. This he did, and our first week at Medvyejya Gora saw the preparations for our garden in full swing.

I can take no credit for this modest brain-wave. It was born of a purely selfish craving for green foodstuff, such as is known to all to whom the taste of cabbage, cauliflower, or any green food has been, for months on end, nothing more than a tantalizing dream. Our rations could hardly have been better, but they did not run to fresh green vegetables. As their nearest approach, onions were issued freely; but the onion, though doubtless a first-class anti-scorbutic, is apt to pall when served as an unvarying adjunct to the joint, and, moreover, is not loved by all.

I remember well partaking of *Glory's* hospitality one evening. Our dinner, I feel sure, was excellent; but forgotten long since are all its details save one— an overlarge helping of common but glorious cabbage.

To the memory of that cabbage our vegetable garden owed its origin; for I knew that its products, should our amateur efforts meet with success, would make a tremendous appeal to every Allied soldier.

Cabbages, however, were not likely to come to maturity in time to benefit us; and though we sowed a few seeds on chance, our main crops were lettuces and mustard and cress. These grew fast and well, and enabled an occasional and most welcome all-round issue to be made. Needless to say, neither mustard nor cress was served out as the delicate fronds such as a hostess might hand round in wafer-like sandwiches at afternoon tea. For we could not afford to cut our crop until the cress had the appearance of miniature shrubs, and the mustard was getting distinctly leggy; since it was only by allowing them to reach this stage of luxuriance that they furnished sufficient volume to make an issue worth while. They proved, at any rate, palatable and health-giving, whether boiled as " greens," as was the custom with the more timorous, or eaten boldly, as fashion decrees, uncooked.

Although, however, our new line afforded so many outstanding facilities, much solid work was needed before we could reap their full benefit; and Medvyejya Gora was soon a centre of bustling activity.

The railway once opened up, supplies and stores of all kinds were accumulated as fast as a limited rolling stock would permit; the R.A.F. became busy as beavers laying wooden groundwork for their seaplane base, and also for portions of their aerodrome; motor-boats were brought to the quay and launched; camps were pitched, roads repaired, and defence lines constructed. All worked with a will at their respective jobs, for all knew that our hold on the place must be permanent. With R.A.F. and flotilla bases once established, and instructional schools in being, there could be no question of withdrawal; and, even should a forward move be made, it was certain that we should find no locality so well suited to the requirements of an advanced base before Petrozavodsk were reached—and the capture of Petrozavodsk could, unfortunately, form no part of my programme, since Allied troops were not to be employed for further offensive action.

In view of the above prohibition and of the necessity for intensifying the training of the Russian forces, I was in no hurry to recommence land operations; but circumstances were to arise which made their speedy resumption almost imperative. Encouraged by our late successes and near proximity, the inhabitants of the northern angle of the Shunga Peninsula rose against the Bolsheviks, and sent us an appeal for arms and assistance. This was on June 3rd, when Russian troops (supported by British artillery) had already taken over our forward line astride the railway 8 miles to the south, and all Allied contingents had been drawn back to positions either in support or reserve. Of the remaining Russian units, Daidoff's battalion was at Povynetz, and Krugliakoff's command, now in a period of transition from its " partisan " state, was to the east of the lake.

I could not respond to the Shunga request by sending Allied troops ; the Russians holding our front, even if strong enough, would take a long time to push through ; and Krugliakoff's men were not yet properly organized. There remained only Daidoff, and it was decided that he, with a party of 400, should be despatched by water from Povynetz to the peninsula, with reserves of rifles and ammunition for the arming of the population.

That an undertaking of this nature involved risk could not be disguised Enemy craft might attack the boats and lighters conveying the force and prove too powerful to be beaten off by our meagre naval escort ; Daidoff might find that the rising had been quelled, and himself too weak to retain a footing ashore ; and, however successful he might be, there would always be the difficulty of keeping him supplied, since nothing could reach him except by boat, until such time (if it ever came) as the Reds were driven sufficiently far south to open up road communication with him.

This last consideration was especially serious, as I did not know for certain when I might expect the promised " chasers " as reinforcements for my flotilla, and until their arrival the maintenance of a regular system of water convoys might prove impracticable, should the enemy fleet show even moderate enterprise.

Once again, however, the future interests of the Russian army swung the scale in favour of the enterprise. The Shunga Peninsula promised to be a most fruitful recruiting-ground, likely to produce its hundreds, if not its thousands, of adherents to the anti-Bolshevik cause, and its exploitation was therefore highly to be desired. Risk there might be, but not, it would seem, more than was commensurate with probable rewards.

Daidoff and his men were transported accordingly across the intervening 20 miles of water, and landed at Shunga village on June 4th. He pushed inland at once, and in his first encounter gained a striking little victory, in which 70 of the enemy were accounted for.

To quote the words of my official despatch:

" This proved the commencement of a widespread anti-Bolshevik movement which played an important part in subsequent operations, and yielded eventually a very large number of recruits for the northern Russia army. It is hardly too much to say that the eviction of the Reds from the Shunga Peninsula and its occupation by Allied troops were mainly responsible for raising the loyal Russian forces to a strength sufficient to enable them to undertake singlehanded, with a reasonable prospect of success, the defence of the territory already won by them with Allied assistance."

Though time was to show that failure and not success awaited Skobeltsin's army, the extension of our hold to the Shunga Peninsula resulted in at least 2,000 fighting men being added to its strength.

During its initial stages, however, the occupation of the peninsula was a source of no slight anxiety: for (as told at the close of Chapter XV) the Red flotilla made its appearance in some strength at the head of the lake shortly after Daidoff's successful landing, and it was clear that communication with him might at any moment become precarious.

If, therefore, we were determined on pressing home the advantage gained already, and securing the large influx of recruits hoped for, there appeared only one course to follow—namely, to open up communication with Shunga by land. This would entail an advance of from 10 to 15 miles, which must be carried out by Russians without Allied assistance, except for the backing afforded by some additional artillery, the lake flotilla, and the R.A.F.

The attack on the enemy at Siding 10 (see sketch-map illustrating final operations facing page 304) was to be entrusted to Russians of the new army, whilst the Olonetz Regiment was to advance on their right, and co-operate by a wide turning movement.

The Olonetz Regiment did well, but the new Russian troops along the railway failed miserably. No sooner was fire opened on them than they bolted, and so hurried were their movements that a section of British howitzers supporting them was almost surrounded by the pursuing Bolsheviks, and nothing but the gallantry of their teams enabled the guns to be saved. The Russians were ordered to make a second attempt, but once more they refused to advance under fire, though ready to blaze away every round of ammunition they possessed in any direction that seemed easiest.

It was useless to make further efforts to induce them to push home the attack; and, as the flanking column was not sufficiently strong to press forward alone, the whole movement was held in temporary abeyance. Besides the blow given to my hopes by the behaviour of the Russians, the predicament in which we now found ourselves was not a pleasant one.

Two considerations came to the fore at once. The Bolsheviks must not be allowed to remain in possession of Siding 10, and something must be done to inspire the Russian troops with confidence.

Never before had the Reds been able to pride themselves on getting the better of us, and, as the time when the Russians would have to confront them alone was approaching so near, it was all-important that their pride on this occasion should be short-lived. They must be attacked again therefore, and this time they must be driven from their position. It would mean the employment of Allied infantry, but this could not be helped. I could only trust that my sin would be pardoned when the circumstances were made clear to those at home.

But the Russians too must be made to play their part, and as a means towards ensuring this, a sprinkling of Serbians was allotted to each Russian company detailed for front-line work. They were to be distributed throughout the company and act as "whippers-in"; and I will say at once that this method of persuasion had a most stimulating and successful effect. The Olonetz Regiment on the right was reinforced by artillery, some R.E., a company of Serbs, and my newly raised mounted infantry! This last consisted of 20 volunteers, mounted on mules, and commanded by my A.D.C., who had pleaded so eloquently to be allowed to undertake the job that I had not had the heart to refuse him.

The railway column, which was detailed to capture Siding 10, was to include British infantry and a British machine-gun detachment; the majority of the Russians formerly composing it forming now a left column which was to move by the Fedotova road and endeavour to gain touch with Daidoff.

On June 13th the attack was launched.

The Bolsheviks at Siding 10 appeared to sense that this time they were up against something more businesslike than recent displays by Russian troops; for they did not stay to dispute our advance at close quarters, and their position, though found to have been well fortified, was captured without casualty of any sort, a result for which chief thanks were due to the accuracy of our artillery fire.

The right column, too, working well to the west, made good progress towards Kartashi in face of slight but continuous opposition; and the left column advanced almost unopposed to within a few miles of Fedotova.

The Russian reverses had thus been wiped out, so far as this was possible. But land communication with the Shunga Peninsula was not yet assured; nor could this be looked for until the enemy were driven from Dianova Gora, in the neighbourhood of which his guns were now in action and able to command the coast road leading through Fedotova. We must therefore either continue to press south, or be content to rely solely on communication by water with our forces on the peninsula. As already explained, we could not make certain of continued safe passage for our boats from Medvyejya Gora to Shunga; but this was not the only reason urging me to sustain our effort by land.

The time was proving exceedingly critical for the new Russian army, and its whole future was at stake. Bolshevik propaganda was active in its ranks and sapping its will to fight; the men mistrusted the ability of many of their officers; and even those honestly desirous of seeing an end of Bolshevism were dispirited by the contemptible show put up by Russians at Siding 10 when without Allied aid.

The Russian army must have its confidence in itself restored; and the best way of bringing this about was to follow up our success by further victories, in which Russians should take a gradually increasing share. As we progressed, too, they would come into more direct touch with the strongly anti-Bolshevik peasantry of the south, and this, coupled with unremitting efforts to raise the *moral* of those still undergoing training (taken in conjunction with General Skobeltsin, their new commander), would, I hoped, produce salutary results.

Orders were issued, therefore, for a forward move along the whole line west of the lake.

On June 20th the right column, after a long and circuitous march and daily fighting, captured Kartashi, inflicting on the enemy exceptionally heavy casualties.

The advance of the railway column (now reinforced by further Allied troops) was much delayed by forest fires, but it drove the enemy back steadily, and reached within striking distance of Kapaselga on July 4th.

On the left, the Russians moving on Fedotova gained touch with Daidoff's men on June 25th; and on the 28th, assisted by a few Allied details, attacked Dianova Gora. Not only was this village carried, but Unitsa also was occupied shortly afterwards.

Our crowning success was on the night of July 5th/6th, when the Reds were driven in confusion from Kapaselga by the combined attack of three columns, leaving many prisoners in our hands.

As the Olonetz Regiment had pushed forward already to Svyatnavolok and Tivdiya, we had succeeded by June 6th in establishing ourselves on the line Svyatnavolok—Tivdiya—Kapaselga—Unitsa—Shunga.

Communication by land with Shunga Peninsula was thus established, and our aim had been accomplished in full.

I have refrained purposely from giving more than a bare outline of this small series of operations. It included at least twenty separate engagements, and details of these would be wearisome to any but those having in them a personal interest.

It may be noticed, too, that I have mentioned but few units by name, and for this omission I have a definite reason. At one period or another of the advance from Medvyejya Gora to Kapaselga there had been employed portions of nearly every unit within my command, including British regulars, Royal Marines, Canadians, Americans, Italians, Serbians, Russians, and Karelians; and although a great majority did excellently, it is an unfortunate fact that it was not only with the behaviour of Russian soldiers that I had cause to find fault. To state the unvarnished truth, I was compelled to withdraw from the front more than one small body of troops and relegate it to the lines of communication. To reveal the identity of these would be objectless; but, by a process of elimination, it might prove possible of establishment were I to praise by name those to whom praise is so deservedly due.

I refer to the matter now in substantiation of the closing pages of Chapter XIII, and also because the reader would gain an impression totally at variance with facts were he to conclude that our path was rose-strewn and that everything went with us as joyously and merrily as the proverbial peal of marriage-bells. If the state of the Russian troops is borne in mind, little imagination is needed to judge of the adverse effect produced upon them by the delinquencies of others with whom they were fighting side by side; nor did such untoward incidents help to mitigate the labours and anxieties either of Price or my own staff.

Setting aside unpleasant thoughts, however, the capture of the Kapaselga line gave every satisfaction both to Skobeltsin and myself; and even the light " telling off " which I received from the War Office when I made it known first that I was employing Allied troops did not depress me greatly. It was bound to come, and I had of course deserved it; but I had been allowed a free hand once the movement had been started, and I could give a fairly accurate guess at the working of the unofficial mind behind the official pen. What mattered chiefly was that the operations as a whole had achieved exactly what we wished for. The Medvyejya Gora—Shunga road had been opened up; the aggregate losses of the Bolsheviks had been heavy, and our own exceedingly light; and our position, blocking as it did all main approaches from the south, was one of the best we could have selected. Except for subsequent advances in the Shunga Peninsula itself, the new line remained practically unaltered up to the time of our final thrust just previous to withdrawal.

We were not, however, to be allowed to hold it undisturbed. Previous to our occupation of Kapaselga we had learnt that the Bolsheviks were concentrating a considerable force of Red Finns and organizing for counter-attack on a large scale.

On June 24th these Finns, supported by naval gunfire, commenced an attack on our Shunga forces, and for a time Daidoff was hard pressed. Our success on the mainland then bore fruit, for we were enabled to send guns to his support, and their fire soon dominated that of the enemy ships, one of which was sunk. Fighting continued on the peninsula for many weeks, the brunt of it, on the Bolshevik side, being borne by Finns. Our Russians held their own throughout July, making slow but steady headway southwards; and the situation turned definitely in their favour on August 3rd, when Tolvoya was captured by them in conjunction with the lake flotilla—a brilliant little action to which reference is made later.

On July 14th Tivdiya was attacked heavily by 800 Reds, most of whom were Finns. The garrison, commanded by Captain Cursons, of the Middlesex Regiment, and consisting almost entirely of the Olonetz Regiment, put up a great fight, and finally beat off the assailants with considerable loss.

These attacks, and others less serious delivered against various points of our line, corroborated the report that the Bolsheviks were bent on recovering some of the ground recently lost by them; and this intention was made still clearer to us by the capture of certain documents in which Trotsky laid especial stress on the necessity for retaking Medvyejya Gora. News received by my intelligence branch pointed, too, to large enemy concentrations at and south of Petrozavodsk, irrespective of the Red Finns already pushed forward. Of the authenticity of this news there could be little doubt; for the Bolsheviks must have collected no small force to deal with the White Finn Volunteers, and as these latter had been dispersed and hustled towards their frontier by early July, the whole Bolshevik strength could be turned now with safety against ourselves.

A further Allied offensive being quite unlikely to meet with War Office approval, besides being undesirable even from my own standpoint, it remained to decide what other course of action was best for Russian interests.

Had it been left to them, both Yermoloff and Skobeltsin would have been inclined to risk another effort by Russian troops alone. But to any such scheme I was emphatically opposed.

The Russians at present in the front line had certainly shown signs of improvement during the later stages of the Kapaselga fighting; but they had had Allies around them and, in some cases, even mingled in their ranks. It was by no means certain even yet that they would be anxious to attack without Allied help; and they would not in any case be sufficiently strong to give the project a chance of success, unless reinforced by many of those still undergoing training—to my mind a most mistaken policy. Even assuming that training battalions were incorporated, and that all fought well, victory could not be certain, and it might be that I should be called upon to employ Allied troops to extricate them from some dangerous predicament. And this contingency I was not prepared to face.

I declined therefore to sanction a general Russian advance; but, in order to give every chance of increasing the flow of Daidoff's recruits, I raised no objection to the continuance of his offensive in the Shunga Peninsula, always on the understanding that he must expect no assistance, beyond that of the R.A.F. and flotilla. So long as we held firmly to the Kapaselga front, this could do but little harm, and would almost certainly help to swell the Russian ranks.

Although, however, all offensive action on a (for us) large scale was ruled out for the time being, there could be no thought of sitting tight on our defence line and allowing Bolshevik preparations for a northward move to proceed unimpeded. The enemy could not be sure of our inability for further aggression, and we could at least keep him guessing as to our intentions ; also, we might force him to postpone the strong attack so evidently contemplated by severing his rail communication with Petrozavodsk, and keeping it severed until our Russians could take the field with a stronger and more efficient army.

It was decided, therefore, to carry out frequent raids on a bold and extensive scale by land, air, and water.

The R.A.F. bombing machines were instructed to pay special attention to the docks and railway centre at Petrozavodsk and enemy armed vessels on the lake. They were also to make it their constant endeavour to break the railway-bridge crossing the Suna River near its mouth. This was one of the largest bridges between Petrograd and Murmansk, and the destruction of even one span would render the railway useless for many days. These R.A.F. raids were very effective, and must have proved most demoralizing to the Bolsheviks, who were unable to put in the air any machines wherewith to counter our craft. The destruction of the Suna bridge, however, was no easy matter ; for it provided but the narrowest of targets, and was well defended by machine-gun posts. Success indeed by the R.A.F. was almost more than could be hoped for, and it looked as if nothing could be done to prevent the Reds from making full use of their railway.

For all that we succeeded in burning down the bridge for more than half its length, and, though bordering on the incredible, the work was accomplished by a land party.

During the period of our operations very many acts of individual gallantry came before my notice ; but I doubt if any excelled in pluck and cool resource this feat of destroying a large and vitally important bridge, known to be furnished with a strong guard, and situated fully 30 miles behind the enemy's lines.

Attached to the intelligence staff and stationed at

Tivdiya was an officer by the name of Lieutenant E. A. Small, of the General List. Small had collected round him a band of some forty devoted Russians, with whom he penetrated constantly in rear of the Red defences, picking up much valuable information, and carrying out at times lightning raids utterly bewildering to the Bolsheviks in their rapidity and boldness.

Knowing what store was set on the destruction of Suna bridge, he and his followers volunteered to make an attempt to burn it ; and on July 18th they set out. Their progress was slow, for they were forced continually to lie in hiding, and it took them five days to reach their goal—120 long hours, during each of which the nerve-strain must have been intense. Once arrived, however, they did their work expeditiously and well. The guard was taken so completely by surprise that it fled at once, and Small's men set themselves immediately to firing the bridge's wooden piers. They must have been experts in incendiarism, for the alarm had been raised and time was short, yet they started a fire which blazed merrily and high, and was not extinguished until all that remained of the northern half of the bridge was a gaunt skeleton of charred timber. The whole party made good its escape, taking with it as trophies two captured machine guns.

Whilst speaking of Small, I must mention yet another of his exploits, almost equally brilliant, when with 35 of his band he surprised the headquarters of an enemy brigade, captured its commander, the entire brigade staff and 50 other prisoners, and put out of action a 3-inch gun by carrying away its breech block. Richly deserved was the D.S.O. bestowed upon him as an " immediate award."

Rail communication from Petrozavodsk being thus broken at Suna bridge, it was up to the R.A.F. to see that its repair should be made as difficult and lengthy an undertaking as possible. This they ensured by repeated bombing and machine gunning, on one occasion even adding to the damage by destroying an additional span.

According to refugees who made their way to our lines at the beginning of August, the burning of the bridge upset Bolshevik plans to a very marked degree. When questioned regarding enemy preparations, they affirmed that, since June, a special division had been in process of formation at Moscow for despatch to the Murman front, with the express intention of recapturing Medvyejya Gora; but that, on receipt of news of the destruction of Suna bridge, the project of sending forward this new division had been abandoned.

It is quite possible therefore that, but for Small's exploit, we might have been fated to sustain an exceedingly heavy attack at a time when my Allied contingents were at their weakest; my Russian troops still ill-prepared for combat on the scale which such an attack would have rendered necessary; and (as will be described later) my communications around Soroka threatened by the mutiny of Ironside's Russian regiment garrisoning the town of Onega.

Of the work of the lake flotilla during this period of systematic raiding I have made as yet no mention, and before telling its share I must trace very briefly its growth from a weak and rickety infancy to sturdy adolescence.

The thought of creating a flotilla was first conceived in April, when our forward positions were around Segeja, and the idea of a push to Lake Onega, if entertained at all, was little more than a dim vision.

Our intention was to employ four or five derelict motor-boats found at Murmansk, together with an additional couple provided by the American navy, for patrolling the comparatively small lakes of Vigozero and Segozero, so soon as the melting of the ice should permit of their navigation.

Before the thaw had completed its work, however, we were well on our way to Medvyejya Gora, and a flotilla for the smaller lakes near Segeja was needed no longer. What we required were fast craft, sufficiently seaworthy for use on the more turbulent waters of Onega, and capable of meeting in open fight enemy armed vessels up to some 300 or 400 tons. Submarine chasers with a speed of 30 knots and transportable by rail would be the ideal type; and these I cabled for immediately the project for the Lake Onega advance began to take shape.

Pending their arrival, or the loan from Archangel of vessels of a similar class when their passage across the White Sea could be effected, we must rely on our own craft, though all save one were open boats, small and slow, and built for use in smooth waters only. The one exception was the *Jolly Roger*, an old chaser, triple-engined and triple-screwed, able to make 30 knots at such times as all three engines functioned well. Such occasions, however, were lamentably few, and 18 knots was found to be nearer her average speed. None the less no other boat could approach her in pace or armament, and she was marked out at once as our "flag-ship." She carried wireless, a 3-pounder, and several machine guns.

Of the smaller boats, a couple were armed with 37-mm. guns, and the remainder with machine guns only. Their speed varied from 6 to 8 knots in calm weather.

In command was Lieut. Stenhouse, R.N.R., with Major Mather, R.N.V.R., as chief administrative officer.

Such was the fleet we launched on Onega, and such it was when (as narrated in Chapter XV) it fought and won its first action on June 8th.

Its growth during June was very hesitating, a few small boats acquired from Archangel and Kem adding but little to its fighting strength. The opening of July was an especially anxious time, for the Russian fleet was beginning to act with increasing boldness, and the *Jolly Roger* was still the only boat capable of operating at any distance from our base at Medvyejya Gora—

and on July 8th she caught fire owing to the bursting of a petrol tank, blew up, and sank.

At this crucial juncture, however, the reinforcements asked for from home commenced to arrive at Murmansk. These consisted of six 40-foot chasers and six 35-foot motor-boats, the former armed with one 3-pounder and one machine gun apiece, the latter with one machine gun. The officer in command was Commander Curteis, R.N., and he brought with him 14 officers and 120 ratings.

The boats were rushed down to Kem as fast as special trains could carry them, and all were afloat by July 20th.

With a dozen serviceable craft manned by trained crews, the days of our anxiety could be considered as past. True, the Bolshevik fleet comprised nearly 20 vessels of from 50 to 400 tons, compared with which our boats were but midgets. But six of ours were really fast movers and, whilst armed with a most useful weapon, would offer a small and elusive target. They would have, moreover, the enormous advantage of Air Force co-operation. And better things were still to come. Archangel made a splendid response to our call and sent across four submarine chasers and two fast motor-boats, together with 10 officers and 100 ratings, most of whom were naval cadets. These joined the flotilla within a week of the launching of our new boats.

By the end of July our fleet had been organized as under in three divisions, the whole under the command of Curteis :

(*a*) British flotilla—8 chasers or fast motor-boats, armed with 3-pounders and machine guns.

(*b*) Russian flotilla—4 chasers, armed with 3-pounders ; 2 fast motor-launches with machine guns.

(*c*) Transport division—5 motor-boats and 1 steam-launch.

Here was a fighting machine very different from that provided by the few small and unreliable boats with which we had contrived to secure a temporary naval supremacy when first we reached the lake. From it much might be expected should opportunity offer—and expectations were not falsified. The full tale of the flotilla's activities cannot be told; but it took a praiseworthy share in many combined operations by land and water on both eastern and western shores; in conjunction with our planes it engaged successfully the enemy's fleet on several occasions; and obtained complete mastery in the northern waters of the lake. Its most notable achievement was perhaps in connexion with the attack on Tolvoya (Shunga Peninsula), in which it acted with Daidoff's men and the R.A.F.

Our Russians on the peninsula had been meeting with considerable success, but had found it beyond their power to drive the Reds from Tolvoya, the chief factor in this being the close support received by the enemy from their fleet.

Plans were drawn up, therefore, for a combined undertaking, and put into execution on August 3rd.

Four Fairey seaplanes were the first to arrive in the battle-area, and they found three Bolshevik vessels close in to Tolvoya port. These they attacked with bomb and machine gun, driving two of them southwards in panic, whilst the third was run ashore and abandoned. The flotilla then came up and joined in the fight. It did not last long, for our boats by their superior speed were able to cut off the enemy's retreat, and their gunfire, added to the bombing and machine gunning of the planes, quickly decided the Bolsheviks that the game was no longer worth the playing. Both ships were captured and, together with that which had been run aground, were brought back later to Medvyejya Gora.

The naval action over, our flotilla sent a landing-party ashore, and carried the Tolvoya defences alongside the Russians of the Shunga Column, inflicting a telling defeat on the opposing Red Finns.

In the land engagement 60 prisoners were taken at

Tolvoya itself and many more by the pursuing Russians; whilst 30 fell into our hands as the result of the naval fight.

Our captured prizes were:

(i) The 300-ton twin-screwed steamer *Silni* with an armament of two 3-inch guns, one 3-pounder, and 6 Colts.

(ii) A small armoured destroyer mounting two 3-inch guns and two machine guns in revolving turrets.

(iii) An armed tug and several barges.

After this most satisfactory little affair the Reds fought exceedingly shy of exposing their ships to attack by our flotilla; but further toll was taken of them by the R.A.F., whose attentions the Bolshevik vessels found it hard to escape in any portion of the lake.

In July and August the total enemy losses in ships amounted to four sunk, either by bombs or gunfire, in addition to the three captured at Tolvoya.

It can be gathered from the foregoing that, although we made no attempt to advance on the mainland after the occupation of Kapaselga, fighting came by no means to a standstill. The enemy delivered many minor attacks on our positions, irrespective of those mentioned; and both on the Shunga Peninsula and along the opposite shore Russian troops were continually in action. They were, too, doing better than I had expected, and might have accomplished even more had I not been forced to withdraw Krugliakoff's battalion to meet the possible threat of a Bolshevik irruption on my communications—a tale unfolded in the following chapter.

Besides, however, being a period of continuous fighting, it was also a period of preparation. Recruits for the Russian army were flowing in, and their enrolment, equipment, arming, and training proceeded apace; whilst specialist instruction was intensified, and no effort spared to render the Russians self-supporting in all branches and departments.

SEAPLANE BASE AT MEDVYEJYA GORA. *(From a photograph by J. Sewell)*

My recollection of them now is that the six weeks following the taking of Kapaselga were as crowded and strenuous as any we had passed. To me they were tinged with sadness also. For in July the total evacuation of North Russia by the Allies was decided upon definitely and irrevocably, and I knew we must quit Murmansk with the work to which we had set our hands still uncompleted. The news of our approaching withdrawal could be withheld from Yermoloff no longer, and I informed both him and Skobeltsin. In some measure they were of course prepared for it, since rumour had been busy for weeks past; but they had clung to the hope that withdrawal would not be absolute, and that some kind of mission, however small, would remain behind as proof for all to see of our continued goodwill.

When told that no single officer or man was to stay, their disappointment was acute; but each acknowledged generously and wholeheartedly the debt they owed to the Allies and to Great Britain in particular, admitting that the assistance we had afforded already exceeded by far the obligations imposed by friendship and sympathy. Both had their pride, and both were men of courage. So there was no word of complaint, no hint of dissatisfaction; nothing but the expression of a fixed determination to continue the fight till victory should be assured. But beneath a brave exterior there lurked, I knew, the spectre of doubt—a spectre which I feared greatly that time's passage would fail to exorcise.

And thus it was that sadness laid its hold upon me.

CHAPTER XIX

LORD RAWLINSON ARRIVES

MENTION has been made of a threat to my communications, to guard against which I was compelled to withdraw a portion of my troops from the Lake Onega theatre, and bring them back hastily to the neighbourhood of Sumski Posad. This was brought about by happenings in the Archangel sphere of operations. On July 7th a mutiny occurred in one of Ironside's units on the Dwina, and before it could be quelled five British and four Russian officers were murdered.

This incident had no direct influence on the affairs of the Murmansk side; but it proved the forerunner of a second and far more serious outbreak, which gave rise to a position impossible for me to ignore.

On July 20th the whole of the troops of the Russian army holding the Onega sector of the Archangel front mutinied, and the entire district, which included the town and port of Onega, was handed over to the Bolsheviks.

Ever since I had pushed south from Soroka in the early spring, the possibility of an attack on my communications had always existed.

From the west, after our capture of Rugozerskaya, it had been perhaps hardly probable; for we had cleared Karelia during our advance, and I was able now to keep a fair watch on the comparatively narrow neck of 50 miles between Kapaselga and the Finnish frontier.

From the east, however, the danger was greater, and it is open to doubt whether I should have been justified in placing 140 miles between my front line and the White Sea, had it not been that Ironside's troops held the towns of Onega and Bolshiozerki, and thus debarred the enemy from utilizing the highway debouching at Soroka. Even so, I had always taken the precaution of maintaining an outpost at Sumski Posad; and, as we went forward, intelligence posts had been established at Vojmosalmi and other villages where tracks from the east met the Sumski Posad—Povynetz road.

Had there been any leader amongst the Bolsheviks possessed of enterprise and daring, he would have found many openings for bold strokes against my lines of communication, such as would have caused me to give far closer thought for their safety, and forced me probably to denude my fighting front in order to afford them increased protection.

My twelve months in opposition to the Bolsheviks had, however, convinced me that their commanders were set against incurring avoidable risks, and that few, if any, would be found ready to seize a favourable chance of striking a blow, should it demand initiative and pluck in any way out of the common. I considered therefore that I need entertain no excessive fear for the safety of our vital link, the railway, from the action of enemy forces from without.

But the news from Archangel put the whole question on an entirely different footing. The town of Onega and the surrounding country, instead of being in the hands of our own troops, were now occupied by the enemy. Together with Ironside's Russians who had gone over to them, the Bolsheviks in the district numbered several thousand, and they were within 70 miles of Sumski Posad. Should they conceive the plan of moving on Soroka—and it was one promising great results—three or four days' march would bring them within striking distance; and although the Bolsheviks on my own front might have allowed such an opportunity to pass unheeded, those on the Archangel side had shown signs of greater enterprise, and the possibility of attack could not be overlooked.

Counter-measures on a satisfactory scale were not easy to take at this time. In June I had lost all my

French troops, as well as my Royal Marines and Canadians; and my two American transportation companies had embarked at Murmansk a few days back. My strength in Allied troops was thus at almost its lowest ebb, and there were strong indications of a coming Red offensive, having as its view the recapture of Medvyejya Gora. Railway administration, moreover, was running none too smoothly, as the working of the southern section had only just been handed over to Russian personnel by the departing Americans, and the loss in efficiency was very marked. Traffic from Murmansk also was much dislocated in this month of July by the destruction of more than one of the larger bridges by fire, the result either of accident or malevolent design. It was likely therefore that the transport of troops to Soroka either from south or north—never a speedy matter—would occupy an even longer time than usual, and thus I could not afford to wait until the threat should become more pronounced. At the same time, I had no wish to weaken my front unduly, and perhaps needlessly.

This being so, I decided to assemble at once a small force, which should be based on Sumski Posad, and ordered to move forward in the first place as far as Nukhta, should circumstances permit.

A section of howitzers and a company of Serbians were therefore brought back immediately from the south, together with two chasers from the Lake Onega flotilla. These last were launched at Soroka, and proved a most valuable asset.

Colonel Woods, who had raised the Karelian Regiment in our early days, was placed in command, and authorized to collect a band of partisans from the neighbourhood of Sumski Posad itself, and from the area he should traverse. He was just the man for the job, and in a very few days he had gathered together quite a respectable following. Who they were and how he got them were unknown to me; nor did I make indiscreet enquiries. Some of them perhaps were his old Karelians drawn to him by ties of the past, and others were probably Russians who had either avoided the mobilization order or were outside the limits of age for conscription. Their antecedents in any case were of little importance, so long as they accomplished what was demanded of them ; and this they certainly did. With them in the van, and his " fleet " scouting ahead along the coast, Woods shoved forward, and succeeded eventually in occupying Nukhta after several skirmishes with Red troops detached from Onega, in which his chasers co-operated well.

But there were, as I have mentioned, other tracks by which the Onega Bolsheviks, had they so wished, could have moved against my communications and even endangered Woods's line of retreat.

Krugliakoff and his one-time partisans (now transformed into a regular unit) were concentrated accordingly at Povynetz and Vojmosalmi, whence strong patrols were pushed out north-east and east to distances up to 30–40 miles. These patrols also encountered Red troops, but the probability is that these were nothing more than marauding parties, as they showed small inclination to fight, and were seemingly without supports.

Meanwhile, with a view to securing additional troops for Soroka, the evacuation of Petchenga was expedited. I had felt obliged so far to maintain a garrison at this distant outpost, if only as a guard over prisoners and the mass of stores accumulated there in order that the place should be independent of Murmansk during the previous winter. The work of bringing back these stores had been proceeding gradually as opportunity offered ; but the whole of the remaining food supplies were now disposed of to Petchenga monastery ; other stores, together with prisoners, were shipped to Murmansk ; and the final evacuation completed by July 25th. I was thus able to send south as reinforcements several hundred infantry and other details.

An attempt to recapture the town of Onega was made on August 1st by some of Ironside's Russians, with a backing of British Lewis gunners and supported by a monitor. It was, however, unsuccessful, as the Russian troops declined to go forward to the attack. Onega therefore remained in Red possession, and so remained throughout the whole of August, with Woods's men (now reinforced by a picked company of Russians) close up and on careful watch for any westward move in force. No such move was in fact made, though encounters with small enemy parties were frequent.

On August 30th our navy bombarded heavily the town and port, making at the same time a feint at landing troops. It was hoped that this demonstration would assist the Russian columns which were advancing once again on Onega from the Archangel side. But the Bolsheviks were not to be intimidated, and clung to their ground.

The date fixed for our evacuation was now drawing very close, and General de Millar was exceedingly anxious that Onega should be regained before the departure of the Allies. Lord Rawlinson (who by then had arrived from England to co-ordinate the withdrawal of the Archangel and Murmansk forces) directed me therefore to furnish a force of 400-500, irrespective of Woods's command, to assist in the undertaking. They were to be sent by sea and landed in the vicinity of Onega port.

It was not a project that pleased me greatly. My men had quite sufficient on their own hands, and it would not be a simple matter to find the numbers required; it was likely, too, to prove still less simple to persuade the long-suffering Serbs of the necessity of thus employing them—for circumstances forced me to include a couple of hundred of them amongst the troops earmarked. Their commanding officer did indeed object to his men being taken for what he considered an extraneous job, the more especially as they were envisaging already an early return to their own country, and had done even more than their full share of fighting from the first week of my landing in the country onwards to Kapaselga.

Thus my mind was much relieved when Woods reported on September 8th that Onega was in flames, and that the Reds had abandoned the town. Two days later Russian forces from Archangel marched in unopposed.

So far as the Murmansk theatre had been concerned the yielding up of Onega to the Reds had resulted in nothing more than a few skirmishes. But it had opened the road to possibilities of a highly disconcerting nature, and had exercised a disturbing influence on my plans for a period of some seven weeks, during the earlier portion of which it had been necessary to keep certain units in a state of constant readiness, in case it might be found essential to assist Woods in stemming a Bolshevik attack which, if successful, must be fraught with disastrous consequences for my whole front.

As shown in the preceding chapter, this menace from the east did not put a stop to the pursuance of the policy decided upon when first we occupied the Kapaselga line on July 6th. Long-distance bombing raids were carried out unremittingly by the R.A.F.; the flotilla was employed constantly in supporting the Russian land forces on both shores of the lake; and our mainland garrisons in the neighbourhood of the railway allowed little respite to the enemy troops immediately opposed to them.

Contemporaneously, fresh Russian units were taking their place in the field, and the training of others was nearing completion. So far as could be judged without submitting it to the supreme test of battle, the material of which these new formations were composed appeared excellent; and on this I had many opportunities for forming an opinion, as I made it my custom, whenever feasible, to accompany General Skobeltsin during his inspections. On the parade-ground the men were as smart and soldierly-like as could be expected; their fire discipline seemed satisfactory; and such tactical exercises as I saw them practise were carried through with an admirable blend of dash and intelligence.

Whether their hearts were in the right place, however, it was impossible for me as a foreigner to say. Skobeltsin believed so; and I could only trust his prescience was not at fault, though one incident added to the doubts I could not but entertain after my many disappointments. This was when an infantry battalion that had completed its training at Maselga refused to entrain for the front. The trouble was caused by a score of Murmansk sailors, some of the few who had been enlisted instead of being dumped, as the remainder had been, in No-man's-land, and who were bent still on propagating mischief. Outwardly the bother ended with their arrest, to make sure of which proceeding according to plan an Allied detachment had been drafted in; but it was hard to obliterate the suspicion that men who had been led so easily by a handful of irreconcilables would fail to act staunchly when tried more highly than on the training-ground.

As a set-off to this sign of disaffection there was, however, the undoubted fact that the Russians in the front line were displaying a far more healthy spirit than formerly, and that their fighting qualities were improving appreciably.

As their army now totalled between 6,000 and 7,000 (exclusive of Karelians), with two field batteries and a sufficient proportion of engineer units, it had become a force with which the Bolsheviks would have to reckon seriously. Russians, too, manned already half the boats of the flotilla, and they would experience little difficulty in providing crews for all the fastest and most powerful craft. In the air they were more backward, but the training of several pilots was well advanced.

Such was the situation when Lord Rawlinson arrived in North Russia on August 9th.

His coming had been heralded by a cable from Mr. Winston Churchill, then Secretary of State for War, received by me on July 31st.

In this I was informed that, after very careful consideration, it had been thought essential to appoint Lord Rawlinson commander-in-chief of the forces in North Russia. The reason given was the necessity for the withdrawals from the separated theatres of Archangel and Murmansk being accurately timed and concerted, and it was held that this could be ensured only by the presence of a superior authority on the spot. I was, however, to understand that the appointment did not imply any lack of confidence in myself, nor want of appreciation of my services.

A wire on similar lines was received also by Ironside.

A decision such as this had never entered into my calculations, and I will admit at once that I was not then, not have I ever been, impressed with its necessity. It would be an easy matter to argue out its various pros and cons, but a discussion of this nature would occupy much space, and I doubt its interest to the general reader. I confine myself therefore to giving it as my firm conviction that, had Ironside and myself been left to complete our respective tasks, the evacuation of both theatres would have been effected without hitch of any kind; that, between us, we should have asked for fewer additional troops from home than actually accompanied Lord Rawlinson; that work at my headquarters would have been lightened; and that Yermoloff and Skobeltsin would have trodden their difficult paths more contentedly.

In order that Lord Rawlinson might have at his disposal a body of troops as a general reserve, the following were despatched to North Russia, and arrived on August 27th:

>   Two infantry battalions.
>   Two machine-gun companies.
>   Two field batteries (personnel only).
>   One field company R.E.
>   Tank detachment.

A third infantry battalion and the remainder of the machine-gun battalion were kept in readiness for embarkation, but their employment in Russia was found unnecessary.

Other reinforcements destined for Murmansk arrived earlier, and included a battalion of Royal Marines and a long-promised French contingent of 600 infantry and machine gunners. As, however, my Italians (1,200 strong) and practically the whole of my small original "expeditionary force" sailed for England on August 10th, the month saw no gain to me in numerical strength, despite the coming of Marines and Frenchmen.

Before receiving the news of Lord Rawlinson's appointment, I had visited Archangel in company with Yermoloff for the purpose of consultation with General de Millar and Ironside as to the action to be taken on both sides previous to withdrawal. The whole question had been discussed in all its details, and an understanding reached fully in conformity with de Millar's wishes.

On August 11th, at Lord Rawlinson's request, I crossed again to Archangel, where further conferences were held.

It may perhaps be remembered that when writing to General Radcliffe in the previous March, and referring to a memorandum I had compiled as far back as November 1918 on "the future policy of the Murmansk force," I had emphasized the value of operations against the Bolsheviks from the Murmansk side, and had pointed out that, in my opinion, we ought to maintain our hold on the Murman Area, even if compelled to give up Archangel.

I was interested therefore to note that Lord Rawlinson's efforts at the outset of our talk were centred on endeavouring to persuade de Millar to abandon Archangel and concentrate all his resources on the western shores of the White Sea. This he urged, as he doubted the possibility of the Russians putting up a successful fight on both fronts.

The recommendations he put forward are best given in the words of his own despatch:

" A careful study of the situation as described in the reports and appreciations of Generals Maynard, Ironside, and others, had convinced me that his [General de Millar's] best and safest course of action from the military point of view was to evacuate Archangel, while maintaining his position on the Murmansk front.

" I was anxious, however, before deciding definitely on the nature of the advice which I should tender to the North Russian Government, to make myself acquainted at first hand with General de Millar's political and military views as well as those of the commanders on the spot.

" I, accordingly, not only discussed the situation very fully and in all its aspects with Generals Ironside and Maynard (who had come over from Kem for the purpose), . . . but also took the first opportunity of approaching General de Millar on the question of the defence of both fronts after our departure.

" These conversations only served to strengthen the conclusions I had already formed in my own mind, and I decided to recommend General de Millar to agree to the following proposals:

" (*a*) The abandonment of the defence of Archangel after our departure.

" (*b*) The evacuation to other parts of Russia of those amongst the civil population who might be victims of Bolshevik reprisals.

" (*c*) The transfer of the North Russian Government to Kem or Murmansk.

" (*d*) The concentration of all the best elements among the Russian troops for the defence of the Murmansk front."

These recommendations, as I had reason to anticipate, did not, however, meet with de Millar's acceptance. No less than Lord Rawlinson he was a trained soldier;

and the advantages to be derived from concentrating on the Murmansk side, whence he could threaten Petrograd, and where he would have at his back an ice-free port, were not likely to be overlooked by him. As we knew, indeed, he had given consideration already to this alternative, and had rejected it. For its attendant political drawbacks outweighed in his mind its military gains; and he was convinced that no victories he could hope to win along the Murmansk—Petrograd railway would compensate for the loss of Archangel. On this point he was undoubtedly more fitted to form a judgment than any foreigner, and his determination not to surrender Archangel was, moreover, backed by his supreme commander, Admiral Koltchak.

It is easy now to say that he would have been better advised had he followed the suggestions put forward, seeing that not only was he forced to evacuate Archangel eventually, but his Murmansk army suffered overwhelming defeat. But he played for the greater stake with a full knowledge of the risks, and his decision might well have been justified but for Koltchak's lack of success. Neither can it be said with any certainty that the ultimate issue in the Murman Area would have been affected. The catastrophe might perhaps have been postponed, but not, I fear, averted.

The choice, in any case, lay with him. Having declined to accept the opportunity offered him of quitting Russia, he was now being urged to select a path of comparative safety by shifting his Government to Murmansk. But he elected to remain at his post, though knowing well its perils, in the sure belief that thus he would be acting in the best interests of the cause he had at heart. He chose the man's part, and all honour to him.

General de Millar's decision remaining unshaken, Ironside and myself were called on to explain our plans for evacuation. With Ironside's there is no occasion for me to deal, as I was concerned only with dates, which could not yet be fixed. Mine included an outline of my scheme for a combined Allied and Russian offensive immediately prior to our withdrawal. But as it was unlikely that this could be put into effect before the middle of September, I proposed in the meantime to exploit our recent successes in the Shunga Peninsula. The victory at Tolvoya on August 3rd had put our Russians in a strong position, and the prospects of clearing the whole peninsula appeared bright. If this were achieved, not only would recruiting for the Russian army be given a fresh impetus, but our final advance (the aim of which was to be the line of the River Suna) would be much facilitated, and the front to be held after our departure rendered more secure.

General approval was given to my suggested policy, though Lord Rawlinson expressed a wish to discuss the situation with Skobeltsin before agreeing to so extended an advance as that to the Suna River. He raised no objection, however, to my proposal for a continuance of the Shunga operations.

On August 13th I returned to Kem, where I took the earliest opportunity of enlightening General Skobeltsin regarding the outcome of the Archangel conference. He was delighted that permission had been given for carrying out my project of a forward push from Tolvoya, but not so pleased when informed that the scope of our September advance was still under consideration, and that, for the present, I could give him no guarantee that the limit set for Allied co-operation would not fall short of that I had contemplated originally. To his query as to when a ruling on this point would be given, I could only say that Lord Rawlinson intended visiting Kem shortly, and would then talk the matter over with him.

Skobeltsin's reply might have come from de Millar. " As concerns Allied assistance," he said, " I am of course entirely in Lord Rawlinson's hands. But the responsibility for military affairs will be mine when the

Allies leave, and I must see to it that I win the best position before summer ends. On every ground I must attack, and, if successful, I will not withdraw again. Therefore I aim at holding the Suna, and I must make that line my goal, even if all Allied help is withheld."

To this standpoint he adhered firmly; and the arguments in favour of a retirement to our old Medvyejya Gora line, put before him by Lord Rawlinson when discussing the problem later, left him unmoved.

Any withdrawal would, he declared, be fatal; for it would undermine the *moral* of his men, just at a time when encouragement was needed most.

Who, then, can blame him for his steadfastness?

Was it not better to cling to hopes of victory than to take a half-way step towards defeat?

CHAPTER XX

WITHDRAWAL

OUR continued operations in the Shunga Peninsula gave every satisfaction.

It was a field well suited for the employment of Skobeltsin's new troops, since their opponents were for the most part Finns and not fellow-countrymen, and they were welcomed as deliverers by a peasant population bearing no love for the Bolsheviks and their Government.

Aided by the flotilla, they defeated the Finns in many encounters, and routed them finally on August 21st with a loss of 140 killed and 90 prisoners, many machine guns and large reserves of ammunition falling into our hands.

A few days later the whole peninsula was reported clear of Red forces.

This was excellent hearing, as also was that of the repulse of an attack on Kapaselga, in which Russian troops played a commendable part.

Things were going well; and I made my preparations for our final advance, feeling that, when evacuation came, Skobeltsin would be left in a position of far greater security than I had deemed probable three months previously.

The actual date of launching my offensive must depend on that fixed for the commencement of embarkation; and this, in its turn, must be influenced by the progress of events at Archangel.

Obviously, evacuation from Murmansk could not precede that from Archangel. The ideal arrangement would be for both to be carried out simultaneously, a reserve being retained on my side, ready for shipment across the White Sea, until it was known that all had gone well at Archangel.

This course, however, could not be followed; for the navy required Murmansk as a base at which to refit the river-craft from Archangel before they should start on their ocean voyage to England, and it was judged that this would occupy about a week. Thus evacuation from Murmansk must be delayed until some ten days after Archangel had been cleared.

As it was intended that Ironside's withdrawal should be completed on or about September 25th, my own could be timed with sufficient accuracy for the first week of October. It was settled, therefore, that my attack should commence about the middle of September.

In view of General Skobeltsin's unswerving attitude, Lord Rawlinson consented to the adoption of my original plan for a combined Russian and Allied attempt to gain the line of the River Suna. As this would involve an advance of some 35 miles, he stipulated, however, that no Allied troops should operate south of the Nurmis River (see sketch-map illustrating final operations facing p. 304), so that all risk should be avoided of upsetting rail and shipping arrangements already worked out.

The orders for the operations, though drawn up by me and receiving Lord Rawlinson's concurrence, were issued in the name of General Skobeltsin, under whose command all Allied forces detailed to take part were placed nominally. This was done so that credit for the success we hoped for should go to the Russian commander who would assume subsequent control, and thus increase his prestige and raise the *moral* of his men.

The object I had in view was twofold. First, to strike the Bolsheviks such a blow that they would be unable to interfere with the final handing over of my front to the Russians, or with the withdrawal of my Allied troops immediately to follow. Secondly, to inflict, if possible, such casualties as should spread demoralization in the enemy's ranks, and render them incapable of an early resumption of the offensive. Skobeltsin would thus, I hoped, be afforded time to consolidate his position on his new line or, should he consider it advisable, to resume his advance at the moment of his own selection.

It must be mentioned here that the Soviet Government was fully cognizant of our impending withdrawal. It had been proclaimed in every newspaper in the United Kingdom, and in many on the Continent, some even going so far as to prophesy the approximate date on which our men might be expected back in England.

Even without this detailed assistance, it was not difficult for the Bolsheviks to guess with fair accuracy when the evacuation might be expected ; for we must be out of Archangel by mid-October at latest, if we were to make absolutely sure of a clear passage through the White Sea entrance. As, too, they were not lacking in shrewdness, they would anticipate our endeavouring to strike them a blow on both fronts just prior to the extrication of Allied troops.

At Archangel they had seen the blow fall already, and it had been followed on September 10th by the initial stages of Ironside's withdrawal. The Red commander opposed to me had, accordingly, every reason to assume that he too would be called upon to face attack in the near future.

We could not therefore expect to take the enemy completely by surprise, and it was all the more necessary that, when we struck, we should strike swiftly and with all available strength.

At the same time we must bear in mind that our aim would not be fulfilled if the Reds retired in good order before us, and we did nothing more than advance our front a few dozen miles. We were out to smash their *moral*, and so must do our utmost to contrive that their losses should be heavy.

As I am not writing for the military student, I shall adhere to my usual custom, and confine my account of the operations to essentials. Their course can be traced without difficulty on the sketch-map facing this page.

Broadly speaking, the direct advance was to be made by two columns, one working down the railway, the other moving on its east, and being directed in the first instance on Yamka (6 miles S.E. of Siding 7).

Turning movements were planned to be executed by three columns :

(*a*) Wide on the west, from Svyatnavolok via Koikori and Ussana on Konchozero.

(*b*) Also on the west, but on an interior line, from Tivdiya via Kav Gora on Lijma.

(*c*) From Shunga Peninsula, with Siding 5 as its objective.

It was hoped that (*a*), if it succeeded in reaching Konchozero, would roll up the left flank of the enemy's forces, should they make a stand on the line of the Suna, and convert defeat into rout.

The object of both (*b*) and (*c*) was to get in rear of enemy positions on the railway known to be held by considerable garrisons. These, if all went well, would thus be caught between the flanking and central columns.

The scheme, in effect, amounted to an attempt to " round up " the enemy at each of several successive stages of the advance. The central columns, too, were to make it their constant endeavour to work round the enemy's flanks and rear.

It was evident that much would depend on the movements of the various forces being timed with reasonable accuracy, and calculations were based on the estimated rate of progress of the central columns, presuming they went " all out " and met with the success we anticipated.

One of the main difficulties was to judge how long it would take for the western column from Svyatnavolok to reach Konchozero, as it had been ascertained that both Koikori and Ussuna were held.

A preliminary operation was therefore undertaken

SKETCH MAP ILLUSTRATING FINAL OPERATIONS

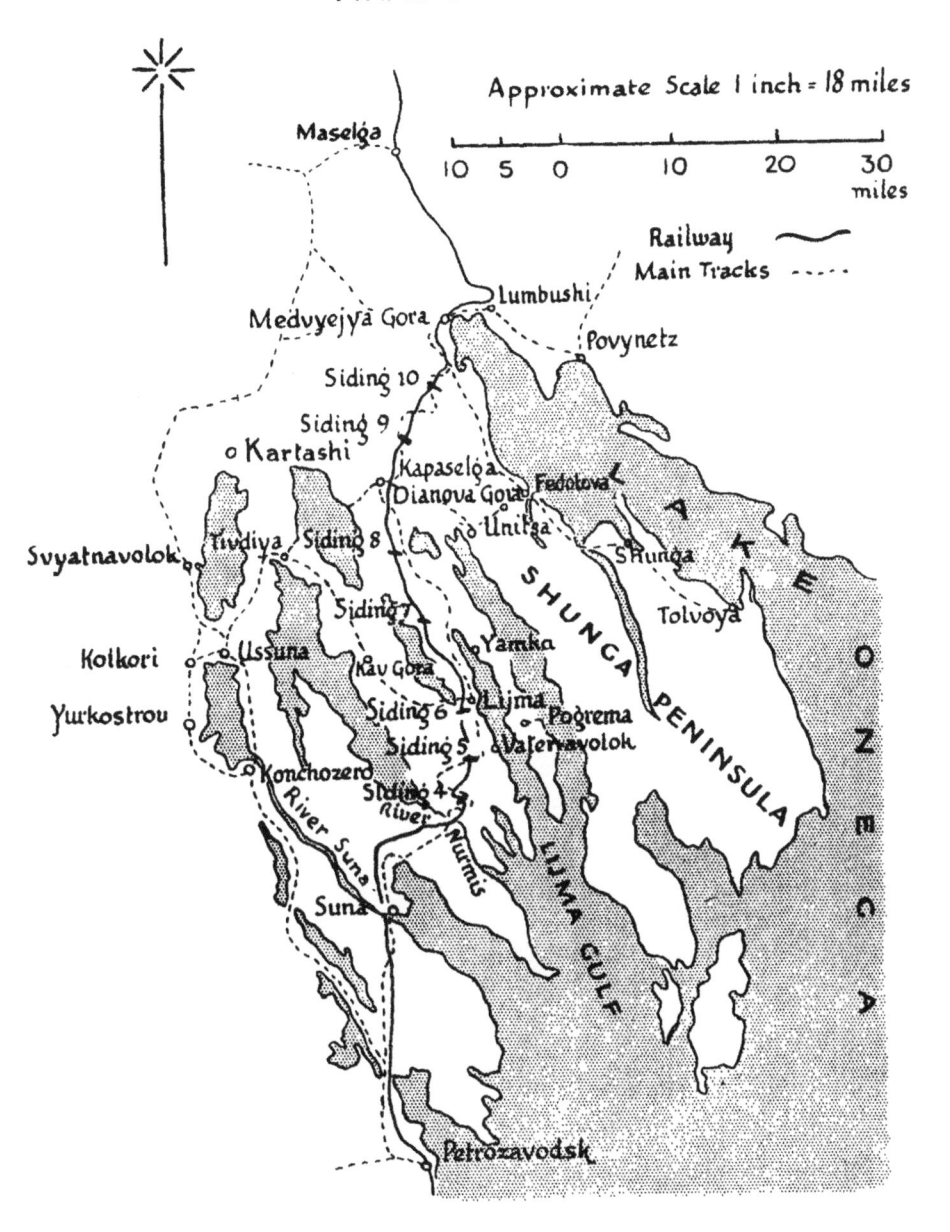

Approximate Scale 1 inch = 18 miles

Railway ~~~
Main Tracks -----

- Maselga
- Medvyejya Gora
- Lumbushi
- Povynetz
- Siding 10
- Siding 9
- Kartashi
- Kapaselga
- Dianova Gora
- Fedotova
- Svyatnavolok
- Tivdiya
- Siding 8
- Unitsa
- Shunga
- Tolvoya
- Kolkori
- Ussuna
- Siding 7
- Yamka
- Yurkostrou
- Kav Gora
- Siding 6
- Lijma
- Pogrema
- Siding 5
- Valenavolok
- Konchozero
- Siding 4
- River Suna
- River Nurmis
- Suna
- Petrozavodsk

SHUNGA PENINSULA
LIJMA GULF
LAKE ONEGA

with the object of capturing these two villages. A force was employed which, judging by our past standards, was far removed from weak. It comprised all arms (if my 20 mule-mounted infantrymen are elevated for the occasion to the status of cavalry), and numbered over 1,000, of whom 700 were British, with 5 guns. In addition, a Russian battalion of 600 was in reserve.

Both attacks failed. The positions held by the enemy (who once again were Finns) were naturally strong, and had been well fortified ; and the Britishers —newcomers from England—were not accustomed to the type of forest fighting. Our troops were withdrawn ; and the Finns, seemingly elated by their victory, promptly attacked Svyatnavolok. They were, however, driven off after a stiff fight.

If we were to secure a really sweeping success in our big offensive, it seemed to me of great importance that co-operation by the western column in its final stages (near, as we hoped, the Suna) should be made as certain as possible. Further attacks on Koikori and Ussuna were made accordingly by Russians and Serbs on September 11th.

But once again we had to admit failure.

This second lack of success was disconcerting ; but there was no time to organize another attempt before the date fixed for our main advance, and I could only trust that both villages would then be carried.

On September 14th the final offensive was launched along the whole front, the total number of troops employed being about 9,000, of whom close on 6,000 were Russians. In order to facilitate their more speedy return to the north on the completion of the operations, nearly all the Allied troops engaged were allocated to the two central columns. Here they led the advance, the Russians accompanying them being retained in support during the first two days.

On the right, progress was held up yet again at Koikori and Ussuna, the Finns once more putting up a most determined resistance. The western column, indeed, never succeeded in breaking its way through, and all idea of its reaching Konchozero had eventually to be abandoned.

Every praise is due to the Finns. They did what no Bolshevik troops have ever done previously, holding their ground stubbornly against three of our attacks, in two of which Allied troops participated. The Bolsheviks owed them a tremendous debt; for they kept the Red left flank inviolate, and put an end to the hope of our Russians gaining an overwhelming victory on the Suna.

It is true that, on the 17th, we got back a little of our own; for a most plucky raid carried out by Lieutenant Small (see p. 281) resulted in the capture at Yurkostrov of an entire brigade staff and 50 other prisoners. But this was a trifling gain in comparison with what might have been achieved, had we not been baulked by Finn doggedness.

On all the remaining fronts, however, the tale was very different.

The central columns drove the Reds back rapidly, capturing many prisoners at Siding 7 and Yamka. The railway column then pushed on, and Lijma was captured in conjunction with the flanking column from Tivdiya, which had taken already heavy toll of the enemy at Kav Gora.

But the crown to our first day's success was set at Siding 5, and for this much credit must be given to the lake flotilla.

Steaming with great audacity round the southern extremity of the Shunga Peninsula, it transferred 150 Russians, under Lieutenant (acting Major) M. B. Burrows, from the peninsula to the mainland, and in conjunction with them ousted the Reds from Vatenavolok. Russians and flotillamen then struck for Siding 5 and, together with the railway column, which was then approaching, accounted for nearly the whole garrison, Burrow's party alone capturing 310 prisoners.

By the night of the 14th/15th our railway front had thus been established at Siding 5.

As the starting-point for the central columns had been in the vicinity of Siding 8, we had covered 20 miles in less than the same number of hours, despite almost continuous fighting.

There could be no complaint that my instructions to go " all out " had not been complied with.

It was found necessary on the 15th to clear the spit of land jutting out into Lijma Gulf, and on which is situated the village of Pogrema ; and this was accomplished before nightfall, the enemy making his chief stand at Pogrema, where 50 prisoners were taken.

Simultaneously the advance on the mainland was continued in the face of fairly stiff opposition, and Siding 4 was captured.

On the following day British troops occupied the line of the Nurmis, and the limit had been reached beyond which no Allied units were permitted to operate.

It was now for Skobeltsin to determine whether or not he should shove forward at once with his Russian army. Had the western column been able to gain its appointed position at Konchozero, doubtless he would have decided to continue the advance with the minimum of delay, and he would have stood every chance of bringing off a really effective *coup* ! But, unfortunately, the Russians of the western column were held up still at Koikori and Ussuna, and its Allied personnel was preparing for the return march to Medvyejya Gora.

Skobeltsin decided therefore to postpone further offensive action until he should have established himself firmly on the Nurmis, and have brought up his reserves.

Except for the disappointment of the western column's failure, he had, I think, no cause to be displeased.

The Bolsheviks had been hustled and hammered without respite for three days, and their casualties had been exceedingly heavy. For, time and again, they had found their retreat cut off, and had been compelled to fight or surrender. In prisoners alone they had lost 1,000, besides large quantities of supplies, rolling stock, and war material.

Incidentally, too, the most powerful of their vessels on the lake, a four-funnelled destroyer, had been put out of action, at least temporarily; for she had been struck repeatedly by Air Force bombs and gunfire, and had been viewed crawling slowly southward, enveloped in flames.

In addition, the Nurmis afforded a satisfactory line of defence; all ground to the east of the railway (including the Shunga Peninsula) was clear of the enemy; and, thanks to our outflanking policy, the Reds had been afforded little opportunity for destroying the railway, which was practically intact.

Koikori and Ussuna provided flies for his ointment. But, situated as he now was, he should find no great difficulty in dealing with their garrisons. Koikori, in fact, was reported already as burning.

His main cause for anxiety would be the enemy's fleet, which must prove a source of serious danger for another month, unless his new-fledged Air Force could continue to give his lake flotilla something approaching the splendid assistance forthcoming, up to the present, from our own airmen.[1] Taking all things into consideration, he was, as he had reason to be, highly pleased with the results achieved. If the Allies had to go, they had at least accomplished much in their final effort to help him.

Preliminary steps for handing over the Nurmis

---

[1] Four days after the withdrawal of Allied troops from the front, Skobeltsin had ample proof of this danger. A Bolshevik fleet of 16 vessels steamed up the Lijma Gulf, and landed troops at Vatenavolok, well in rear of the Nurmis line. Though the advantage thus gained by the enemy was not pushed home, Skobeltsin decided that it would be more prudent to draw back his front to a position farther up the gulf, and established himself on a new line through Kav Gora and Lijma.

defences to the Russians were commenced on September 18th, and by the 22nd all Allied troops which had taken part in the recent operations had either been concentrated at Medvyejya Gora, or were on their way thither from the fighting front.

By the 25th the transfer of the flotilla, of R.A.F. machines, and of all war material in the forward zone had been completed, and Skobeltsin and his army stood alone to champion the cause of loyal Russia.

It was just at this time that a most bitter blow befell me. My health broke down, and the medical authorities insisted that I must give up all idea of continuing to carry on my duties. It was useless to kick, and I could only console myself with the thought that I had seen my labours reach their crowning-point, and that little remained to be done but complete the evacuation in accordance with time-tables already prepared.

Though I was kept in close touch with the progress of events, I was allowed to take no active part, and Brigadier-General H. C. Jackson, of Lord Rawlinson's staff, assumed control in my stead over the further conduct of our withdrawal.

One small *contretemps* marked its final stages.

I had anticipated always the possibility of rail communication being severed north of Kem, and had urged upon Lord Rawlinson the advisability of arranging for the provision of shipping at Kem to meet this eventuality.

He had considered at first that such a step was unnecessary, and Admiral Green was not greatly in its favour, partly because none but transports of light draught could berth alongside the quay of Kem Harbour, and partly because of the risk—infinitesimal though it might be—of vessels being impeded by ice during their subsequent passage to Murmansk.

Later, however, it was decided that the navy must be prepared to convey by sea, either from Kem or Kandalaksha, a small portion of the force, should necessity demand it; and it was well that this precaution was not neglected.

For some time past deserters from my old Finn Legion had been endeavouring to stir up trouble in the Kandalaksha district. They had collected a gang of some 100 miscreants, all of whom were armed; and it was now reported that they were planning to hold up our withdrawal by damaging the railway. Their usual gathering-place was believed to be a village near a creek 15 miles east of the town, and this it was proposed to raid.

A British detachment was detailed for the purpose, and it proceeded to the locality by boat. It was, however, ambushed whilst still afloat, and was forced to beat a retreat, after suffering casualties of 3 killed and 4 wounded, besides 2 officers and 11 other ranks reported missing.

This was a distinct score for the Finns and their Bolshevik friends—and they improved upon it. For, despite the precautions taken, they succeeded in burning down several bridges north of Kandalaksha.

This went close to necessitating the postponement of the date of departure from Murmansk of those units still south of the break; but some were transported by sea, and Russian engineers contrived to patch up the line in sufficient time to admit of the remainder continuing their journey by rail and adhering approximately to their intended programme.

At Murmansk itself both military and naval evacuation proceeded smoothly.

By October 10th the refitting of the Archangel riverboats for their voyage home had been completed; and on the evening of the 12th our last troopship cast off her moorings, and swung into the tide of the Kola Inlet.

The Murmansk Venture had ended.

What I have written in earlier chapters has, I hope, served to convince even the most sceptical that the

WITHDRAWAL

Murmansk Force was sent to Russia to meet an urgent strategic need, and that it fulfilled its allotted task during the closing phases of the Great War with a measure of success fully justifying its despatch.

I trust also that I have satisfied the fair-minded that ample justification existed for continuing our assistance to the anti-Bolshevik elements after we had ceased to be at war with the Central Powers.

Some there will be who dispute this last contention; but few of these are likely to be found outside the class that welcomed the access to power of Russia's disrupters, and welcomes still their maniacal creed. And with this class I differ gladly.

To my mind, our action at Murmansk in common with that in other parts of Russia can give rise to no feeling of self-reproach, and to one only of regret—namely, that the help we gave fell short of that required to throttle in its infancy the noisome beast of Bolshevism.

THE END

APPENDIX

PRÉCIS OF AN ADDRESS TO BRITISH OFFICERS GIVEN AT MURMANSK ON MARCH 21ST, 1919

I HAVE asked you to meet me here this afternoon, gentlemen, because I want to speak to you about a somewhat confidential matter affecting the interests of my whole force.

No officer in chief command, whatever orders he may issue, or however well his immediate staff may serve him, can carry on without placing enormous dependence on his regimental and departmental officers. If they do not back him up to the best of their power, it is quite certain there will be differences, and probably confusion, within his force, even under the most favourable conditions—and we all know that conditions out here are very far from being favourable. Thus I want to tell you of one or two ways in which you can help me more fully to carry out my somewhat thankless task in this country.

To make what I mean clear I must, however, say a few words first about our position out here.

As you know, I came to Murmansk nine months ago with a very small force, my main object being to prevent the Germans taking this port and converting it into a submarine base. Incidentally, I had to deal with large bodies of White Guard Finns from across the Finnish frontier, and a very considerable Bolshevik force.

Now there is a vast change in the situation; for the German menace is passed; the White Finns can be practically disregarded; and the Bolshevik armed forces have been driven well south. It would seem, therefore, that most of my difficulties have been removed

APPENDIX 313

and that all is plain sailing. I can assure you, however, that this is very far from being the case. Difficulties of the most complex political nature are constantly cropping up, and unfortunately the time occupied in dealing with them prevents me from seeing as much of the officers and men serving under me as I could wish. However, the majority of those difficulties affect only myself and the home Government, and there is no need to speak of them now. There is one, however, which touches us all very closely, and it is one which each of you can assist me to overcome.

As you are aware, the few better-minded and more highly educated Russians in these parts are determined not to allow the Bolsheviks to regain their hold here. They knew that the Allies could not stay on for ever, and they determined therefore to raise a military force of their own. They commenced with conscription on a very limited scale, but this did not bring in nearly the number of men they needed, and they decided consequently on universal mobilization throughout the district.

Now before there was any talk of a Russian mobilization, there were malcontents here, and down the railway, imbued with Bolshevik views, and always ready to stir up ill-feeling against the Allies; and this plan for a full mobilization has given them an opportunity which they have not been slow in taking. The result of their efforts is a widespread feeling of unrest amongst a fair proportion of the inhabitants of this place in particular, and I know from information I have received from many sources that a plot is on foot for a rising in Murmansk, with the object of seizing arms and ammunition, exterminating British and Russian leaders, overthrowing Allied control, and taking on the running of Murmansk themselves.

This is not the first or second time that I have received intimation that I and others who were supposed to have a certain amount of power here were " for it "; so, ordinarily, I should not take much notice of the warning, despite the fact that I received it first just previous to the Ides of March. But on this occasion there is one circumstance that makes it advisable to take more than usual notice of the threat, and one circumstance that has led me to call you together here to-day.

The first is that Sunday next is the anniversary of the massacres by Bolsheviks at Petrograd, and we are bound to have Bolshevik demonstrations, if not active trouble. The second is that the Bolshevik element here undoubtedly relies not only on the sympathy of some of the Allies, but even on their open assistance—and British are said to be included. That is the point to which I have been leading up, by what may perhaps seem to you rather a roundabout route ; but I wanted to show clearly that I had grounds for considering that the attitude of some of our troops was not without its adverse effect. As regards the contemplated rising itself, I do not want to say much now ; for forewarned is forearmed, and I hope that the precautions I am taking will prevent it altogether or, if it comes, put a stop to it quickly.

Now to return to my main point.

I do not for one instant imagine that any British soldier would give active help in a Bolshevik rising of this nature. But the fact remains that these Bolshevik agitators really think they have reason to hope for encouragement and even support from British troops, and there must be some grounds, however slight, for this belief. Put in a nutshell, I think we can say that it is caused by an impression that our troops here are " fed up," and that they, together with Labour in England as a whole, are converted practically to Bolshevism. We know the last to be untrue ; but there is undoubtedly a feeling of discontent amongst our men, which is fostered by a pernicious and ignorant Press, and they feel themselves entitled to rather more than the average grouse which is characteristic of the British soldier. This, coupled with exaggerated

APPENDIX 315

articles in the English papers, and also, I am afraid, with the sometimes unwise talk of officers, has led the agitators to believe that our men are really in sympathy with the Bolshevik movement.

Now, what can we do to alter this attitude of our men, which, though it is nothing like so extreme as Bolsheviks here imagine, is yet capable of doing great harm in surroundings such as these ?

Whatever can be done must be done by you officers, who are, or should be, in close touch with your men—and it is in this that I ask your help.

Your first object must be to get hold of their point of view, and I think you will agree with me that you would find them express it something as follows :

" We are fed up with the whole show, and want to get home. Men in France and elsewhere are being demobilized by thousands a day, but we see no demobilization here, and little chance of leave. The War is over, and we don't see what good we are doing here. In any case it's only a rotten political show, in which we don't take any interest, whilst some of us even feel that in fighting the Bolsheviks we are going against our own interests. For don't the Bolsheviks represent Labour ? "

That, I take it, is roughly the way in which the men regard their position out here ; but, if you examine their view closely, you will find that, in reality, they have much less to grouse about than they imagine : and surely if you, as their officers, can persuade them of this, you will have accomplished something well worth doing.

Take the grievance of " no demobilization " first. It is quite true that many thousands in France are being demobilized every day. Popular clamour and an excited Press demanded this ; but are the men thus demobilized finding employment after the expiration of their furlough ? My own information points to hundreds being unable to get employment, simply because the war has so upset the labour market that it is a sheer impossibility to absorb the men at the rate they are being sent back to civilian life. There seems to be clear evidence of this from the fact that munition workers are being given another three months' wages, because it is recognized that it is out of the question for them to find employment as yet in ordinary civil trades.

Again, quite apart from the 900,000 required for the Army of occupation in France and Germany, there are many hundreds of thousands who will be hung up in France and Germany for months to come. In the meantime, men of this force have a very distinct advantage in the matter of pay over those who are thus held up, and over other armies of occupation, and our men should be made to realize this. I will try to put the situation clearly.

In France there are now two classes of men. First, those who have been retained compulsorily, or who have volunteered, for the army of occupation; and there are 900,000 of them. How do our men compare with them as regards pay and prospects of returning to civil life? As regards pay, our men get the full bonus, just as the 900,000 do; but every one of the 900,000 has got to remain in the army till February 1st, 1920: and I can guarantee safely that every man out here will be relieved long before that date. Then take the second class, namely, those who are entitled and wish to be demobilized. These men may be, and certainly hundreds of thousands of them will be, hung up for months and months, owing to transportation and other difficulties, and over them our men score hand over fist. For our men of the same category (owing to representations I made to the War Office) get the full bonus pay from February 1st, whereas those who are held up in France get nothing at all up to May 1st, and only half the bonus pay after that date. Our men do not understand their luck in this respect, and should be made to see it.

As regards the question of leave, as large a proportion has been granted leave from here as from France, and a far greater proportion than from Salonika and other distant theatres of war. The shortage of shipping and the necessary evacuation of sick and wounded have lessened the numbers I hoped to send on leave. But leave has not been stopped, and more men will be sent at the first opportunity.

Now, as to the utility of this force and its object. I wonder if the men, or even you yourselves, realize the useful work we have done here.

[*A short account of our doings followed, showing how we had helped to checkmate Germany.*]

But there is another side to the matter. We could not have done what we did without the support of the loyal Russians out here, who backed and supported us, regardless of the revenge promised by the Bolsheviks. Are we going to leave in the lurch those who stood by us, and helped us in no small degree to win the War? The Britisher loves fair play, and I cannot but think that our men, if the facts were placed before them, would not dream of deserting at the present moment those who sided with us at a critical time, when such desertion would mean certain death to them at the hands of the Bolsheviks. And it is up to you to place these facts before your men.

And what about the conditions out here? You will agree with me that these are not so black as they are painted. Now that the winter is over, the rigours of the climate are comparatively nothing to a healthy man, and there are thousands of pleasure-seekers who would gladly pay high prices for the privilege of a month's ski-ing tour out here, at this time of the year.

The men's accommodation, too, is now as good as anything they could expect in any theatre of war, so far as my experience goes; and their rations are the best ever issued to any army in the world's history. Yet I have visited troops during the dinner-hour, and have heard complaints and grousing about their food. This, I must tell you, gentlemen, is your fault. In my own headquarter mess we live almost entirely on our rations, except on such occasions as we have to entertain distinguished foreigners—and we do ourselves proud. Surely, then, you can make certain that your men are properly fed ? It is your job to see that meals are well cooked and varied ; and it is your job to bring forward at once any case of shortage of rations. The food is here in sufficient quantity and of first-class quality ; and if the men do not get it, you are responsible, and not myself. If you can show that the rations, as issued, do not come up to the mark, I am quite ready to take the necessary action. If, on the other hand, you get the proper ration, and your men are not properly fed, you are the ones who ought to be hanged.

I come now to the question of the feelings of our men towards the Bolshevik movement. We must make allowances for such of them as sympathize with Bolshevism, because they are utterly ignorant of the true state of affairs, and have been led astray by equally ignorant Labour publications. But this is no reason why we should not set them on the right lines.

Their idea is that the Bolshevik leaders out here are on the same footing as the Labour leaders at home who are endeavouring to place Labour on what they—rightly or wrongly—consider a sound footing. That this is an entirely false conception, anyone with the least acquaintance with Bolshevism knows well. But, though we may know this, some of our men may not ; and, as mentors to your men, it is your duty to put them right.

Bolshevism, so far from ensuring true representation of Labour, is the most autocratic form of so-called government the world has ever seen. The Russian labourer may or may not believe that it is necessary to exterminate everyone who is better educated than himself, or who is in possession of more worldly goods. At any rate he must pretend to do so—and there his duties, and his privileges also, end. He is given no voice whatever in the regulation of Labour affairs. He is a nonentity, and obeys blindly his autocratic leaders, partly from hope of gain, but chiefly from fear of death.

In England there are no signs whatever of Bolshevism on these lines, even amongst the most extreme of the Labour leaders. They are out for a definite policy—such, for instance, as the nationalization of mines or railways—because they wish to ensure that the workers get what they consider a fair share of the profits; but this is a very different affair from the anarchy which the Bolshevik régime has imposed on Russia.

I have got here a copy of the *New Statesman* of March 1st. This is a publication holding extreme Labour views, and an extract from it is worth reading to you:

" The most interesting information which has recently come from Russia is contained in an interview given to the *Westminster Gazette* by Mr. H. V. Keeling, a British trade-unionist who left Russia so recently as January 9th. Mr. Keeling speaks without bias against the Bolsheviks, and he offers no judgment on the possibility of their political theories, or anybody else's, being realized under other circumstances. He is content to describe facts as they see them; and his picture is certainly terrible. He says that only a privileged class of Bolsheviks, mainly soldiers, are entitled to get food; that these are used to keep down the starving masses of the population; that supplies are running shorter and shorter; and that Lenin and Trotsky and their colleagues, whatever they may think about the ruin which they have made, ' don't know how to get out of it, or what to do. The slightest sign of weakening, and they are done. So they simply go ahead.' The people do not rise because ' they have been used to tyranny, and have a sort of submissiveness which makes them accept things. I can assure you they are sick to death of it, and that nine-tenths of the people who keep in with the Bolsheviks, and have to pretend to like them, would do anything to get rid of them, if they knew how.'"

Then, again, if you want anything to damn Bolshevism into heaps, you have only got to read the official proclamation dealing with the " nationalization of women." If you have done that, can you imagine any decent Britisher being willing to say that Bolshevism and the upholding of the Labour cause in England are one and the same thing? Again it is up to you to explain this to your men.

When I was doing regimental duty—and it was not so long ago—I was more or less a pal of my senior N.C.O.s, and used to discuss with them all sorts of questions affecting the welfare of my unit. Surely you can maintain sufficiently close touch with your N.C.O.s to ascertain the feeling amongst your men, and if you find they are on the wrong track, get them again on the right one.

In this respect you can help me, and you alone; and it will be a great step in the right direction if you can only make your men realize that, out here, they are the representatives of the British nation, and that, as such, it is up to them to uphold British honour amongst this crowd of mixed nationalities.

I come now to the " unwise talk of officers " to which I referred when trying to work out the causes which led Bolshevik agitators to believe they would get sympathy from our men.

Unfortunately we cannot prevent the English papers printing articles which, from our point of view, are highly undesirable; nor is it possible to prevent the circulation of such articles out here. But, although we cannot do away with the harm our newspapers may do, there is no reason for us to go out of our way to add to it—and that, I fear, is what some of you have been doing, however unwittingly. What I mean is this. In your talk with Russians and Allied officers, and also of course amongst yourselves, you are apt sometimes to put the very darkest interpretation on the strikes, and on the unrest amongst both soldiers and civilians at home. You make it appear to your listeners (who, if they are foreigners, naturally take as gospel every word you say) that England is in a most appalling state, given over to riot and anarchy, and practically Bolshevik. Now, even if this were true, the very worst thing you can do is to noise it abroad in a place like this. I know for a fact that talk of this nature has done enormous harm here, and some of those Russians and foreigners who have heard you speak in this way have felt bound to inform me of the bad impression caused. You see, the Russians look to us far more than to any other nation for support, and not only are they horrified at the bare suspicion of their support crumbling to pieces, but they know well that news of that nature acts as the best tonic in the world to the Bolsheviks. I ask you therefore to be very careful how you discuss home affairs in the presence either of your men or of any foreigner.

To summarize roughly what I have said. We British are the backbone of this expedition, and it will be absolutely fatal to the whole show if we allow the *moral* of our men to deteriorate further. There is danger of this, and we have got to fight against it with all our power. I have explained what harm has been done already by the views which Bolshevik agitators hold about our men, and we must try to put things on such a footing as to prove clearly to these gentry that they are leaning on a broken reed. In all this I need your help. I ask you therefore not to dismiss the matter from your minds as you walk out of this room, but to go back to your jobs with the determination to lend a helping hand. Make a greater effort than formerly to look after the comfort and welfare of your men; discountenance needless grousing; and explain to your men (if you feel it would be a good thing) how they are far from being unfavourably placed as regards pay, chance of returning to civil life, quarters, amusements, etc.

I have given you sufficient to go on, even if you did not know it all before. Above all, I ask that you yourselves should set an example of goodwill and cheerfulness.

SKETCH MAP OF
NORTH RUSSIA
Approximate English miles
50 40 30 20 10 0
50
100
150
RAILWAYS
MAIN TRACKS
NORWAY
Petchenga
Alexandrovsk
Drovanoi
Murmansk
Kola
Rastikent
Tulema River
Loparskaya
Imandra
KOLA PENINSULA
Kandalaksha
Knyaja Guba
FINLAND
L. Pyavozero
Ukhtinskaya
KARELIA
WHITE SEA
Mezen
Kem River
Kem
Soroka
Olimpi
Rugozerskaya
Undozero
L. Undozero
Onda
Onda R.
Sumski Posad
Nadvoitskaya
Nukhla
Onega
Segeja
L. Vigozero
Vojmosalmi
Urosozero
L. Segozero
Tolekina
Karelska Maselga
Maselga
Danilova
Povynetz
Medvyejya Gora
Kapaselga
Tolvoya
SHUNGA PEN
Lijma
Sordavala
Petrozavodsk
LAKE ONEGA
LAKE LADOGA
ARCHANGEL
Pinega
R. Pinega
Bolshiozerki
Seletskoe
Tarasova
R. Onega
R. Dwina
Shenkursk
R. Vaga
From Vologda
Kotlas

Lightning Source UK Ltd.
Milton Keynes UK
UKHW041447030320
359688UK00001B/50

9 781845 748227